a
GLUTTON for
PUNISHMENT

To my favorite
Chinese chef & comrade
in gluttony food
appreciation.

David

ALSO BY JAY JACOBS:

RFK: His Life and Death
A History of Gastronomy
The Color Encyclopedia of World Art
New York à la Carte
Winning the Restaurant Game
Cooking for All It's Worth

a GLUTTON *for* PUNISHMENT

Confessions of a Mercenary Eater

JAY JACOBS

ATLANTIC MONTHLY PRESS · NEW YORK

Published simultaneously in Canada
Printed in the United States of America
First edition

Library of Congress Cataloging-in-Publication Data

Jacobs, Jay.
    A glutton for punishment: confessions of a mercenary eater/Jay Jacobs.—1st ed.
ISBN 0-87113-397-0
    1. Gastronomy.   I. Title.
TX631.J32   1990   641'.01'3—dc20   90-847

The Atlantic Monthly Press
19 Union Square West
New York, NY 10003

First printing

For the various tablemates, from Alison to Zanne, and including Ann, Anne, several Barbaras, Betty, Brenda, Carla, Catherine, Cathleen, Constance, Darcy, Dayan, Diane, Elaine, Eva, Gail, Gena, Gin, Ginny, Gisela, Gloria, Hope, Janet, Janis, Jean, Jessica, Judy, Kathy, Kirstin, Kristi, Lila, Linda, Linn, Lorraine, Maggie, Margaret, Marie, Marilyn, Monique, Nancy, Pamela, Paulette, Regina, Ruby, Sally, Sharon, Sherry, Stephanie, both Susans, Susanna, Suzanne, Sweater, Terrell, Wanda, Wendy, Yvonne, and especially Curtis, who risked their waistlines in a questionable cause.

Acknowledgments

My indebtedness to various friends, acquaintances, and colleagues is tacitly acknowledged in references to them throughout this book. More specifically, I'm grateful to a longtime colleague, Irwin Glusker, with whom the idea that I do this book originated; and to my literary agent, Joe Spieler, who aided and abetted; to John Appleton, who supplied an inspired title; to my editor, Ann Godoff, for her patience and counsel; to Hollis Bright, who does things beyond my comprehension with a word processor; and to the restaurateurs and chefs of New York City, past and present, without whose generous tutelage I'd know a lot less than what little I've learned at their tables and in their kitchens.

For years, however, I thought that gastronomy was an essential part of my life.

Georges Simenon, When I Was Old

Contents

a
GLUTTON _for_
PUNISHMENT

A Few Words
to the
Reader

"Tell me what you eat," wrote Brillat-Savarin in the most celebrated of his aphorisms, "and I will tell you what you are."

I often wonder whether Brillat-Savarin's grand bluff was ever called, and I sometimes imagine him pontificating along these lines: "So, monsieur, you tell me you eat *canard aux olives, céleri rémoulade, chartreuse de perdreau, boeuf braisé, anguille à la bonne femme, moules à la poulette, pâté de cailles, rognons de veau à la Bercy, soupe de poisson, tête de veau farcie,* and Twinkies. But of course! *Vous êtes* a dealer in used coaches, born in Anjou (Saumur to be precise) and married to a former milliner's clerk from Dijon by whom you have two daughters, Yvette, aged twelve, and Simone, ten, and a son, Hippolyte, nineteen. Like myself, you play the violin a little. You are also an avocational student of phrenology, occasionally fish for gudgeon in the Loire on Sundays but seldom catch any, and . . ."

Almost from the day I began to write about food and restaurants, I've believed that Brillat-Savarin's proposition could be inverted with no loss of truth, and perhaps with appreciable gain.

Answered as simply as they're propounded, however, neither the original formulation nor its transposition offers any startling insights. Tell anyone that you eat the dishes enumerated above, and you'll be told you are either French or a gastronomic Francophile. Identify yourself either as French or a gastronomic Francophile, and you'll be told you eat things like the dishes enumerated above. *Et alors?*

Unless they elicit a significant quantity of information, neither "Tell me what you eat" nor "Tell me what you are" opens productive lines of inquiry. At best, simple itemization of one's customary diet may eliminate a number of unlikely possibilities, but it won't yield any significant information. Owning up to a preference for frogs' legs Provençale, Burgundy snails in herb butter, and the truffled livers of force-fed geese, for example, indicates that you are probably not an Aleut, a rug merchant from Dar es Salaam, or a Tibetan yakherd, but it won't produce much in the way of specific information about what you, as an individual, are.

Similarly, the personal data you might jot on a job application will convey no idea of what you eat. The epigrammatic form represents only the germ of an idea; as they stand, both Brillat-Savarin's formulation and its inversion are overly facile propositions that could be applied, with comparable results, to a dozen other human activities besides eating. In Brillat-Savarin's case, I suspect it was on the basis of form, rather than content, that he expected to draw his conclusions. In all likelihood, it wasn't what he might be told was eaten, but the manner of the telling that mattered.

During my years of covering the restaurant beat, I expected my readers to draw their own conclusions about what I ate largely by making them privy, in some detail, to what I was: what sort of background and outlook colored my dining experiences, what manner of man they were dealing with.

We don't recapture gustatory virginity before sitting down to each meal. All our eating experiences are conditioned by what we have (or haven't) eaten from infancy onward and by everything in our lives that has made us what we are. The Nebraska-born food writer who sings the praises of a dish of *risotto nero* hasn't experienced the same sensations as the native Venetian with whom he has shared the dish, which is part of the Italian's cultural and gastronomic patrimony. Nor will a bouillabaisse taste precisely the same and afford precisely the same sort of satisfaction to both a Marseille fisherman and a Parisian diplomat with a *de* appended to his surname.

Eating is one of the two most fundamental human activities and, on any level above mere subsistence, a communion. It's not merely the sharing of food, however, but the sharing of the self, although some food writers seem to think they're exempt from the latter obligation. I don't. In my view, our perceptions of what we eat are so much a function of who we are that a degree of autobiographical indulgence is unavoidable in any conscientious attempt to write meaningfully and evocatively about our eating experiences. (Food criticism isn't art or music or literary criticism. While the intellect and sensibilities may come into play, it is, after all, one's *body* that's absorbing the works under consideration. To pretend otherwise, to adopt the disembodied voice of the nonperson, just won't get the job done properly.) Hence, what follows is in part an account of my life, such as it has been, in which, I hope, some revelation of what I am and have been delineates what and how I have eaten with more immediacy than could mere descriptive evaluation.

Adjectives are the least reliable parts of speech, and the adjectival inventory of the food writer in particular has become worthlessly threadbare with overuse. A "delicious" leg of mutton tastes nothing like a "delicious" octopus salad or a "delicious" apple pie, and the promiscuous use of the adjective adds nothing to (and may detract from) sensations the writer is attempting to convey. The same holds true for such ubiquitous clichés as "creamy" and "buttery" as they are applied mindlessly and indiscriminately to a whole spectrum of altogether dissimilar dishes, any of which may or may not contain cream or butter. If I've refrained from preceding every reference to a loaf with the epithet "crusty" invariably invoked by other food writers (and by myself in years past), it has been in the hope that the crustiness of some of the personalities on these pages will convey the character of the bread they eat more vividly than a knee-jerk adjective possibly can.

Memory is notoriously unreliable, and my own is perhaps more unreliable than most. The experiences recounted here may or may not have occurred precisely as set forth; at this distant remove, it seems to me they did. If an occasional detail has blurred or been aggrandized with the passage of time, neither you nor I will ever know and only I will care. Any dialogue included certainly hasn't been transcribed verbatim, but rather represents an attempt to capture its flavor and essence to the best of my ability. A few names have been changed to protect the innocent or guilty, as the case may be, and a few have been invented as replacements for those long forgotten.

1

My
Daily
Bread

Except in the case of *Homo sapiens,* the vocation of all creatures is eating. Ask any featherless biped what it does for a living, and it will tell you it practices law, fills prescriptions, sells automobiles, plays the piccolo, or does something else unrelated to the ingestion of its food. Ask the same question of a talking moose or goose or mongoose, and you'll be told that your companion eats; that its primary wakeful activity is the procurement and consumption of comestibles.

During countless millennia, man too worked solely at the task of filling his belly. He didn't live by bartering his skills or labor for bread and meat purveyed by middlemen, but went straight to the sources of supply, his methods essentially the same as any other creature's. His working day was spent rending flesh, gathering nuts and berries, sucking plundered eggs, grubbing for larvae, foraging for grains and greens. Later, as he gradually civilized himself, man's occupational status underwent a change so radical that ultimately just a minuscule proportion of his number continued to work at the business of eating. These quaint throwbacks to the Neanderthal epoch survive today as restaurant reviewers and food critics.

The writer who ekes out his daily bread by gorging on truffled foie gras isn't quite what he appears to be. He may communicate intelligibly in a few—a precious few—cases; he usually stands erect in suitable habiliments; and in some cases he has mastered the use of advanced tools. At any social gathering, however, it soon becomes apparent that evolution has passed him by. Try as he may to obscure the anachronistic singularity of his calling, he is by nature more closely akin to the anteater, the sapsucker, or the flycatcher than to the board chairman, the mud wrestler, or the dean of admissions. He may try to palm himself off as a journalist, writer, critic, or reviewer, but he's soon exposed for what he really is: a professional eater, a hired belly whose work, alone among all human vocations, culminates in ignoble defecation.

For reasons best left to qualified ologists of one sort or another, a good many otherwise well-adjusted citizens view the lot of the mercenary eater with undisguised envy. Or so I found to be the case during my decade and a half as *Gourmet* magazine's New York restaurant pundit. My chronic flirtation with poverty and future financial insecurity notwithstanding, I was perceived as fortune's darling. While I nursed my gout, others nursed their jealousy of my supposedly privileged position. More often than I can remember, I was informed that casual acquaintances would gladly kill for my job, and it didn't require the deductive powers of a Sherlock Holmes to establish the identity of the prospective victim.

Those who didn't covet the gig in fact coveted it in fancy. Movers and shakers who outearned me by six figures or more cornered me at cocktail and dinner parties to establish their credentials as my epicurean peers, to confide that they had ferreted out some sushi prodigy or fajita virtuoso I had missed, or to one up me by announcing that some object of my recent praise had gone to pot.

The seriousness of these encounters was altogether alarming. Notables from all walks of life hung on my every word as though my narrowly hedged pronouncements were engraved in stone. Although I had drifted into a highly subjective line of work for which my sole objective qualification was that I had eaten roughly the same number of meals as anyone else my age, people who dined out in big-ticket bastions of haute cuisine fourteen times a week (whereas I could seldom afford to eat *in*) avidly sought my advice and opinions. Women who normally wouldn't have been caught

dead in the company of so nerdly a specimen fought for the privi-
lege of sharing my evenings. Headwaiters trained from birth to
heap contumely on pillars of society groveled when I approached.
In the process of regaling myself and my tablemates with the best
of everything, I was disbursing more pelf each year than most
Americans earned, and our expenditures were limited only by our
appetites. In short, I had it made.

Granted, lionization by a grub-crazed cult of *feinschmeckers,*
caught up since the late 1970s in an unprecedented feeding frenzy,
may not be the most reliable indicator of a hired belly's importance
to society in general. Granted, too, his perspective may get skewed
a bit when he overhears whole paragraphs of his adjective-larded
twaddle quoted verbatim by some twit who couldn't recite half a
line of Shakespeare to save her life. Still, being a widely exposed,
accredited foodie during the period in question was a heady trip.
With a monthly constituency of roughly two million readers, I may
not have had the following of a network anchor, but I wielded my
own share of clout in a world less concerned with developments in
South Africa than with the emergence of radicchio as the salad leaf
of choice.

Although critical journalism of any kind is hardly an exact science,
restaurant reviewing may be the least exact of all genres. Eating is
an activity to which just about everyone brings a roughly equal
body of experience and opinion, along with an inherited set of
prejudices and preferences that even the most cosmopolitan diner
never quite relinquishes. Like Charles Shulz's Linus, we all carry a
security blanket stained by the accidents of our earliest eating experiences. History is replete with the refusals of various cultures to
accept unfamiliar foods in times of extreme hunger, and it's no
coincidence that elderly hospital patients are fed the comfort foods
most ate as small children. Behind the soigné facade of any connoisseur of caviar, truffles, or pedigreed wines huddles a naked infant
blindly groping for the breast, a toddler smearing its face with
mashed potato, a sick child consoling itself with warm milk.

Literally and figuratively, food criticism is journalism in its most visceral form. Given the inexactitude of the procedures involved, it seems ludicrous that most restaurant reviewers attempt to quantify their findings, awarding stars, toques, crossed forks, or whatever as though eating, the most subjective of common human experiences (love and grief possibly excepted), were as measurable as the day's temperature or as amenable to statistical analysis as the GNP.

To an insider, it seems equally ludicrous that the public swallows these ratings whole, disregarding the fact that they are applied elsewhere only by a few featherweight movie reviewers, and never in any other form of criticism. The reviewer of books, art, music, or theater who applied numerical ratings or their equivalents to the output of an Updike, a Rauschenberg, a Bernstein, or an Albee would be hooted out of town, but let a widely circulated restaurant reviewer bestow three stars on some greasepit he mistakes for a temple of gourmandise, and the foodniks will be battering down the establishment's doors before the ink is dry on the morning's paper.

The proposition that a restaurant's performance can be quantified with any accuracy is advanced with particular fervor by the highly regarded Gault Millau guides, which featured the most exquisitely calibrated rating scale in use anywhere before the emergence of the Zagat guides, whose ratings are obtained by averaging the findings of a substantial corps of volunteer reviewers. While the Michelin guides, the originators of the form, award a top grade of three stars ("worth a journey") and a few other publications go as high as four or five, Gault Millau measures its subjects on a scale of zero to twenty. The implication, of course, is that Gault Millau's findings are the authoritative result of sedulous research and a degree of consideration that outfinesses Michelin's rough ballpark evaluations by a meticulous seventeen gradations. The facts of the matter are somewhat less reassuring.

As it happened, I was interviewed by a representative of Gault Millau not long after my *Gourmet* gig came to an abrupt halt. The interviewer, whose name I've forgotten—let's call him Auguste Pétard—received me with characteristic Parisian graciousness at his midtown Manhattan hotel, where he stuffed his patrician face with a hearty breakfast before somewhat grudgingly offering me a cup of tea. As our discussion progressed, I asked M. Pétard how often the Gault Millau undercover agents (a half dozen or so anonymous stringers) visited a given restaurant before assessing it in print. Just once, I was told. Just once? *Mais oui.* Gallic parsimony, it developed, dictated restraints that could hardly be inferred from the Gault-Millau rating scale, with its intimations of exhaustive field research. To visit restaurants with the sort of frequency I was accustomed to, M. Pétard confided, would entail setting a prohibitive sticker price on his product.

Gault Millau's half-assed approach to restaurant evaluation might easily have been inferred from a cursory reading of its contents. Still, my interview with M. Pétard was a bit disillusioning, especially when it became blatantly apparent that the mistitled *The Best of New York* (wherein a bastardized Chinese restaurant is given a rating of five on a scale of one to twenty and described as "the most spectacular restaurant in all of SoHo, and also one of the worst") is not, as it claims to be, "written by Henri Gault and Christian Millau," but *re*written by a putative editor for whose six months of service M. Pétard is reluctant to pay the equivalent of an illegal alien's sweatshop wages.

Depending on the number of tablemates who accompanied me, my own policy had been to eat at least three, and occasionally as many as six or seven, times at any restaurant before shedding ink on its behalf, consuming or tasting, over the course of a week, no fewer than eighteen dishes, and often as many as forty. Conversely, a patent bummer of no redeeming social value—

> *A restaurant so flat-out dismal*
> *That the plat du jour was Pepto-Bismol*

—might be tried just once and written off as an unreviewable loss. (The magazine's tacit understanding with its readership was that coverage was limited to those establishments that merited patronage, all things considered, whatever their enumerated shortcomings might be.)

To the best of my knowledge, the more conscientious—or at least the more ethical (we'll get to *that* later on)—of the town's other reviewers checked out their subjects with comparable frequency, but those journalists could be counted on the toes of a sloth's hind foot. A few publications with marginal impact on the restaurant scene picked up the tab for a meal or two, while a few sleaze rags expected their reviewers to swap favorable prose for cadged meals or paid advertising. Of the supposedly reputable review vehicles, though, only Gault Millau saw fit to palm off a lick and a promise as responsible evaluation, and only in the case of Gault Millau did dupes within and outside the food game take such flimsy material with any seriousness.

As the plot thickens in the later chapters, we'll find that diligent research in itself is no guarantee of a restaurant reviewer's competence or ethicality. Still, without reasonably representative samplings of what a kitchen has to offer, a reviewer, however perceptive and incorruptible, can no more praise or damn a place with any authority than a sportswriter can dismiss a Wade Boggs as a bush leaguer after watching him go hitless on a given evening, or hail as a future Hall of Famer some marginal hanger-on who happens to have a hot bat on a particular night. Unlike a movie, which is presented as a *fait accompli* that presumably reflects its director's intentions in every way, a restaurant can't be judged with any fairness on a single encounter, even if some supergut were to eat through the entire menu at one go.

I've had mediocre individual dishes, and occasional lackluster meals, at great restaurants. Just as Joan Sutherland isn't always in good voice and Shakespeare could stuff an actor's mouth with lines as preposterous as "But, look, the morn in russet mantle clad,

Walks o'er the dew of yon high eastern hill," great chefs are no less fallible and no more immune to the odd culinary debacle. I've also had praiseworthy dishes and decent meals at places that later turned out to be incapable of sustaining what at first blush had seemed creditable standards. The reviewer who bases his supposedly considered opinions on minimal input is merely reporting on the luck of the draw: a dubious methodology, at best, when his readers' time and money, let alone his subjects' survival, are at risk.

As noted earlier, the *Gourmet* ground rules precluded publication of negative reviews. The magazine's reasonable assumption was that a well-heeled, self-indulgent readership was interested only in those restaurants that could be recommended with confidence and that no useful purpose would be served by anatomizing the deficiencies of those that couldn't. This condition required some adjustment on my part. Much of my previous journalistic work had been concerned with the evaluation of films (still called movies in the unaffected parlance of my early days on the beat), books, and art. Like most casual reviewers (as opposed to serious critics), I had found negative assessment a far more tractable genre than its opposite. I could be wickedly sardonic at the expense of any floperoo that came my way, and I pounced on every passing turkey with unseemly glee. Appreciation of uncommon accomplishment, on the other hand, demanded degrees of perspicacity and analytic acumen I had no reason to believe I possessed.

In short, I was a journalistic hit man; my days were made by doing sadistic little numbers on blockbuster Hollywood extravaganzas of no discernible merit, on functionally illiterate authors, on hapless daubers. I reveled in the outraged response of the maligned and their partisans and attained nirvana when a San Juan newspaper dubbed me El Severo after I had savaged the Puerto Rican art establishment, such as it was, *en bloc*. I was the holy terror of benighted creativity by the time I connected with *Gourmet*. I had racked up a sitting-duck body count comparable to the aggregate casualties of the Vietnam War. Then, with my anointment as the magazine's certified *bec fin,* I was inducted into a sorority whose members' heads were planted firmly in the sand and whose daintily extended pinkies pointed the way to Impeccable Taste.

During my tenure with *Gourmet,* I developed a marked tendency toward evasiveness when the conversational icebreaker "What do you do?" was broached. I soon found it to be a question that, answered truthfully, would be followed by three more: "What's your favorite restaurant?"; "How do you stay thin?"; "How does someone break into your racket?" In each case, I didn't have a satisfactory answer—and still don't. To nominate a single restaurant as one's favorite is to reveal an outlook so parochial that the nomination becomes meaningless. I've never given much thought to the second question, assuming that the size of my waistline has been determined by metabolic happenstance; contrary to the prevalent notion, a restaurant writer's food intake isn't necessarily any greater or more frequent than anyone else's. Finally, if I knew how to break into my former dodge today, I'd break back into it with another publication; whatever the rewards of my current journalistic activities may be, they don't include lavishly subsidized dinner dates.

In retrospect, it would seem more accurate to say I oozed, rather than broke, into restaurant writing. My immediate predecessor at *Gourmet,* Donald Aspinwall Allan, was a close friend with whom I had worked at another magazine, *The Reporter,* where he was the managing editor. Don worked for UNICEF after both *The Reporter* and the *Saturday Evening Post* went belly-up in rapid succession. His new job allowed him to moonlight as *Gourmet*'s hired belly until his transfer, early in 1972, to UNICEF's office in Beirut.

By that time, I had eaten fairly extensively around southern Europe, mostly in the cheapest restaurants I could find, and was growing, foraging, and cooking most of my own food on the South Fork of Long Island. I could turn out a creditable French, Spanish, or Italian meal and preside with reasonable authority over a New England clambake, but my acquaintanceship with New York's better restaurants was minimal. I had held down four or five salaried editorial jobs for brief periods and had sporadically enjoyed the business lunches that went with them, but most of my working life—first as an artist, then as a writer—had been spent as a relatively indigent freelancer, and my experience of higher gastronomy not of my own making was rather limited.

As it turned out, *Gourmet*'s sole standard for qualification appeared to be my sexual orientation. Mincing no more than two-thirds of her words during my job interview, the editor, Jane Montant, got right to the point. "Are you married?" she asked. My assurances that I was the divorced father of four sons and committed to another marriage (which, alas, never came off) seemed to settle the issue. I was told to write a sample review of a restaurant of my choosing, did so, and was anointed the magazine's New York *bec fin.*

At that time, the city wasn't yet in the throes of what *New York* magazine a decade or so later would term "restaurant madness." *Nouvelle cuisine* wasn't yet much more than a gleam in anyone's eye, and the future exponents of the so-called new American cuisine were still in grade school. The impact of Hunanese and Szechuanese cookery was just beginning to be felt, and only a handful of Italian restaurants had ventured beyond the bastardized repertory tailored to American expectations and perpetuated for generations by opportunistic Calabrian immigrants and their offspring. The astonishing proliferation of Japanese restaurants (and resultant rise of gastronomic sophistication) hadn't yet begun, and a great many of the German, Czech, Polish, and Hungarian places that had flourished in the Yorkville district of Manhattan had succumbed to a variety of neighborhood changes, including high-rise development, concomitant population shifts, and the generational attrition of a once-entrenched ethnic clientele. (A few years earlier, when that bastion of *Mitteleuropa* was being infiltrated by the first waves of junior executives and airline stews from the corn-fed heartland, I turned up one evening at my favorite fishmonger's to find the proprietor—a fat, slovenly ruffian who somehow always managed to maintain a three-day growth of stubble on his booze-blossomed

responsible journalism, and nothing about me coincided with the magazine's concepts of propriety. I had been inducted into a cadre of food and travel writers made up mostly of females of a certain age whose tripartite and/or hyphenated names contrasted unflatteringly with my own hiccuping moniker, whose articles on exotic venues read like voice-over narrations from 1930s travelogues, and whose eyes were sedulously averted from anything resembling reality. The putative travel writers seldom ventured beyond the verandas and finger sandwiches of the best hotels in the cities they covered. They saw, heard, tasted, felt, and smelled nothing of local life and managed to invest the most abject Third-World nations with the staid presentability of Wimbledon in the days before Gussy Moran and Messieurs Nastase, Connors, and McEnroe.

Aside from the autocratic Jane Montant, the magazine's editors were easily bullied young women who papered the walls of their cubbyhole offices with pictures and posters of pussycats and puppy dogs, panicked at any suggestion of adult discourse between writers and readers, and unfailingly manifested complete opacity when confronted with any sentence more abstruse than a monosyllabic line from a Dick and Jane primer. As a matter of policy they split all splittable infinitives and saw to it that any first- or second-person references were rigorously eschewed in favor of "one" and "the diner." The essential adjective "tasty" (part of the language since at least 1617) was a proscribed vulgarism, although the puerile "crispy" was preferred to the crisper, more onomatopoeic "crisp," and dining rooms, according to one resident stylist, were "festooned" with chairs. Jane Montant's emphatically professed contempt for affected Briticisms notwithstanding, "storey," a Dickensian aberration that appeared without documented precedent in 1841 (in *Barnaby Rudge*), was and remains the magazine's accepted version of "story" as a designation for the floor of a building. The sole male of any ostensible consequence on the editorial side, the art director (since deceased), was a shambling, openly embittered serious painter manqué and chronic malingerer who specialized in illustrational non sequiturs. I had known him at *The*

Reporter years earlier, when he had lost or otherwise disposed of thousands of drawings, including hundreds of my own, that had been banked on speculation and for which the artists were never paid. Typical of the art directors of his generation, he considered the written word to be a mildly annoying intrusion into magazine layout and, during his days at *The Reporter,* hadn't been averse to illustrating articles on the Middle East with sketches of Eskimos, and vice versa.

At *Gourmet,* he was a relatively harmless timeserver who pushed photographs around on pages, filled copy shortfalls with scratch-board spot drawings by Mario Micossi (a self-styled "visual Mozart" whose aesthetic hadn't—and still hasn't—undergone a scintilla of change since the early 1950s), refrained from making waves of any sort, and spent as much time as he could *in absentia.* I never really got to know the only other male concerned with the magazine's content, the house photographer, whose work I admired for its clarity and candor. To its credit, the magazine never doctored the dishes photographed for its pages. All the foods illustrated were uncosmeticized; no adventitious substances enhanced the sheen on pastries, no shaving cream was substituted for schlag under meltingly hot studio lights, and what was shot was usually scarfed down by the staff once the shoot was finished.

The travel photographs, on the other hand, matched the travel writers' roseate prose for calculated evasion and distortion. Chemically and mechanically juiced up far beyond credibility, they were unrelievedly luscious—in my eldest son's blunt assessment, the socially acceptable, coffee-table equivalents of the skin magazines' centerfold. Neither the photographs nor the prose they accompanied had anything to do with journalistic probity or responsibility to the magazine's readers. Both were promotional material pure and simple, and, as the sun sank slowly over romantic somewhere-or-other, subscribers were given no reason to suspect they might encounter any of the inconveniences and hazards inherent in travel—inherent in life, for that matter—anywhere in the world.

In *Gourmet*'s sanguine view, Montezuma's revenge didn't exist in

Mexico, insects were extinct on earth, and ripoff artists no more operated in Paris or New York than purse snatchers did in Rome or on the Costa del Sol. Beggary, traffic, pollution, bollixed transportation schedules, unsafe Third-World aircraft, inadequate plumbing, extortionate money changers, schlock merchandise, primitive sanitation, oppressive politics, and all the rest went unmentioned in a "service" magazine supposedly devoted to the welfare of its readers. In a way, it was self-fulfilling prophecy: readers who confined their adventures abroad to rote retracings of their journalistic cicerones' tepid experiences (and many of them did, as was made clear by the coyly styled letters department, "Sugar and Spice," from which any hint of spice was rigorously excluded) were no more likely to be discommoded on alien turf than in their own living rooms. All they missed was travel in any meaningful sense of the term.

To the best of my knowledge, my own infrequent travel pieces were the only ones the magazine published that even glancingly touched on such embarrassments as poverty, vice, squalor, the texture of ordinary life, political realities, or the odor of anything but flowers and good cooking. In view of some of the innocuous material that was edited out of both those and my restaurant pieces, I'm still baffled by the inclusion, in a report on Bangkok, of a description of an evening spent in the company of a clutch of hookers in a topless bar on Patcong Street and, in an article on Montreal, of a Mountain Street saloon (also topless) called The Sex Machine, where a motorized abstract frieze above the bar eerily replicated the movements and rhythms of copulation.

In a report on Hong Kong, I was permitted to quote a local Chinese garment tycoon, who, after taking an overseas telephone call from Seventh Avenue during dinner, drily remarked, "If only we spoke Yiddish, we'd really have it made." In one of my restaurant pieces, however, a reference to the irrefutable fact that most Chinese eating establishments in New York were dependent on a predominantly Jewish clientele was squelched, as were all other restaurant-related demographics involving Old World ethnicity of any kind.

The policy was carried to its reductio ad absurdum when I turned in a review of the Upper East Side restaurant Czechoslovak Praha, in which I quoted a waiter's facetious response to a request for the check: "Which one, sir? The place is full of Czechs." The exchange was blue-penciled, as were any other suggestions that a restaurant might attract a fair number of customers who shared the proprietor's gastronomic heritage. Curiously, the proscription was never applied to Orientals. In Jane Montant's view, it was perfectly acceptable—indeed, expectable—to note that a sushi bar was frequented by Japanese businessmen or a dim sum parlor by Chinese families, but any intimation that Caucasians of any particular ethnic background might gravitate toward *their* cooking was summarily scrubbed.

Sometime during my seventh or eighth year with *Gourmet,* I made the mistake of referring to a certain Upper East Side restaurant as a haunt of socially prominent Wasps (which it was and remains, and which I mentioned in an altogether nonjudgmental fashion, merely in order to convey some idea of the character of the place). The reference was more or less predictably deleted, and I gave it no further thought until several weeks later, when the executive editor abruptly informed me at lunch one afternoon that Montant had decided to get rid of me.

It had been my practice to visit prospective review subjects as anonymously as possible (about which, more later) and then to set up an interview with a principal once I'd decided a restaurant merited coverage. After several gastronomically rewarding but otherwise lackluster evenings at the Fifty-seventh Street establishment called Le Chantilly, I approached one of the owners, a lizardly type who ostentatiously prowled the dining-room carpet while his partner, a gifted chef, sweated in relative obscurity in the kitchen. I introduced myself and announced my intention of reviewing the place—an announcement that was met with obvious suspicion.

At that time, the consensus among New York restaurateurs was that coverage in *Gourmet* was the ultimate journalistic desideratum; that the magazine's imprimatur would yield sustained patronage by a well-heeled, cosmopolitan readership prepared to indulge itself unstintingly. It was generally conceded that a laudatory critique in *The New York Times* or *New York* magazine generated more short-term response, but response that many of the more prestigious restaurants would have gratefully done without. As the irate owner of one citadel of classical French cookery put it a few days after his place had been awarded three of a possible four stars by the *Times*'s resident hired belly, "Who *needed* that bitch's three goddamn stars! The phone hasn't stopped ringing since her review appeared, and all we're getting is polyester from the outer boroughs and New Jersey. They come in, order the cheapest dishes on the menu, drink Coca-Cola with their meals, drive our regular customers away, and never show up again!"

The then co-owner of Le Chantilly (since deceased) apparently couldn't quite credit the notion that *Gourmet* was prepared to boost his stock without the expectation of some sort of quid pro quo. After considerable equivocation, he consented with some reluctance to an interview the following week.

On the morning of the appointed day, the restaurateur in question telephoned to inform me that the interview was off; neither he nor his partner were inclined to become "involved." I had occasionally encountered obtuseness of this sort on the part of marginal operatives—owners of modest neighborhood ventures who found it hard to believe they could be singled out for attention in a national publication unless reciprocation of some kind (advertising or outright payola) was forthcoming in return. Le Chantilly, however, was a big-ticket, presumably sophisticated enterprise whose management could hardly be unaware of journalistic ethics. (In my naiveté, it hadn't occurred to me that *Gourmet,* its manifold shortcomings notwithstanding, was a paragon of ethicality compared to several highly respected publications whose reviewers regularly traded their encomiums for significant amounts of pelf, sexual accommodation, or open-ended freeloading. Le Chantilly had already received favorable reviews in most of them, and I began to wonder just how its owners had become "involved" with, and ultimately spooked by, the fourth estate.)

Stonewalled by Le Chantilly, my copy deadline imminent, I called *Gourmet*'s executive editor and explained my predicament. It was, of course, theoretically possible to review a restaurant without interviewing a principal, and a number of my colleagues saw no practical need to establish a rapport with a prospective subject. With some fifteen hundred words per restaurant to produce, however, I needed a good deal more than a mere evaluation of a given establishment's menu, atmosphere, and service. As I saw it, a restaurant's history and working philosophy played major roles in its overall functioning. Besides, I was pissed at the co-owner's insulting attitude and in no way inclined to give him the benefit of my ink. "Why don't you do '21'," the executive editor asked me. "It's been about five years since you last reviewed it, and you've been there often enough since. Let's have lunch there today. Unless it turns out to be a total disaster, you can do a review off the top of your head."

Three of us—the executive editor, the food editor, and I—lunched at "21" that afternoon. As was almost invariably the case at "21", the meal had its ups and downs, but nobody was inclined to quibble about any culinary deficiencies; the restaurant, a unique social entity, altogether transcended the frequent shortcomings of its kitchen, and that's what I wrote in my review.

The piece was presumably read and approved by several editors, including Montant, who, in theory anyway, was ultimately responsible for whatever appeared in print. Shortly after the review appeared, I was told I'd had it at *Gourmet*. Why? "Jane said she was at a cocktail party the other night, and somebody told her you really came down hard on '21'." As I was to learn during the course of the next seven or eight years, "somebody said" was irrefutable proof of guilt in Jane Montant's view.

After an interval of several weeks, during which the magazine sought a replacement, I was told that the executive editor had prevailed on Montant to let me stay on, at least provisionally, and that it might clear the air if I took Lady Jane to lunch in the not-too-distant future.

Although I regularly dined, boozed, and partied with several of her underlings, I'd never socialized with Jane Montant, lest any overtures be construed as apple-polishing. She turned out to be a charming tablemate, and we spent a couple of pleasant hours at a French restaurant near the magazine's offices, talking of nothing in particular. Then, as lunch was winding down, I broached the subject of my near dismissal. Two months after deciding I had to be got rid of, the woman obviously couldn't remember why. "Well, you know that's all over with," she said.

"I'm glad of that," I replied, "but I'd really like to know why it ever began."

An expression of utter confusion crossed her face. Then she blurted, "I was told you didn't like Wasps."

An expression of utter confusion must have crossed my face. When I was able to speak, I said the reason I'd been given had to do with my review of "21". "Oh, yes" was her reply. "You never mentioned the rice pudding in that review."

What really began to bother me after two or three years of writing for the magazine was an increasing tendency on Jane's part to suggest candidates for review. Despite long exposure to the finest restaurants on at least two continents, the restaurants she recommended almost invariably specialized in altogether pallid, unadventurous cooking. Because it was tacitly understood that my reviews were limited to restaurants that could honestly be recommended, Jane's "suggestions," which became thinly disguised demands as time went by, amounted to what I perceived as thought control.

For the most part, I dealt with Jane's decrees by ignoring them. The places she suggested would be dutifully investigated and, if they were found wanting (as was usually the case), they'd get no ink. Of the dozens of establishments she insisted I cover during my years with the magazine, just three were reviewed. All three were borderline ventures given the benefit of the doubt and perhaps damned with faint praise. In each case, I received an inordinate volume of complaints from readers.

It was commonly assumed that there was a direct correlation between paid advertising and editorial coverage at *Gourmet*. The assumption was spelled out in so many words by Nora Ephron in an *Esquire* piece in which it was amply demonstrated that stones *can* be thrown by people who live in glass houses. The fact is that, at least during my tenure, there was no connection between the two whatsoever. An overwhelming majority of longtime advertisers in the magazine never were reviewed, and a roughly equal proportion of reviewed restaurants never bought advertising space. From time to time, I'd be asked by an advertising-space salesperson to check out a regular or prospective advertiser's establishment. Unless the place was known to me as an irredeemable bummer, I'd give it a whirl. It was a fairly safe assumption that any restaurant aggressively pursuing editorial coverage was hurting for good reason, but there were occasional exceptions. The advertising department understandably wasn't overjoyed about the minuscule proportion of its recommendations that received coverage, but to that department's credit its somewhat wistful requests never took the form of demands, and no undue pressure was brought to bear on me by anyone save Jane Montant, the editor in chief and supposed guardian of the magazine's integrity.

Flouting Jane's directives, I relied on her notoriously uncertain memory. What I failed to take into account was that while she might easily forget the specific circumstances that generated a particular affront, her grudges not only survived her faulty recall but became their own self-stoked justification. As a longtime editor and writer for various publications, I viewed my loyalties, in descending order of importance, as to my readers, my publication of the moment, and any editor to whom I reported. Jane Montant's priorities obviously reversed that order, and she evidently didn't share my conviction that the buck stopped at the desk of the top editor, who was accountable for whatever appeared in print under his or her stewardship. It was apparent almost from the outset that Jane and I were on a fatal collision course, despite our momentary truces and the odd evening of good fellowship.

2

Plight

du

Jour

Most American food writers attribute their putative expertise to their early exposure to the definitive cookery of a parent or mentor—usually a mother or household domestic who specialized in regional or some sort of ethnic fare. I had no such exposure. My father and mother fancied themselves an epicure and a cook, respectively. Both were mistaken. My old man inhaled Russian caviar, Cuban cigars, old cognac, and ripely odoriferous French and Italian cheeses on the rare occasions when he was solvent, but his tastes were formed solely by the market value of his choices, and if potatoes had been priced at twenty dollars an ounce, he'd have scoffed down the spuds just as ostentatiously. A dedicated philanderer, he spent as little time as possible in the bosom of his family (thereby sparing himself my mother's cooking) before cutting out for good when I was in my late teens, and my memory of him is largely olfactory. A self-styled inventor among other things, he spent his infrequent sessions at home in the kitchen, where he cooked up noisome batches of chemicals and reeking paraffin mixtures in his bootless attempts to perfect a fire-retardant paint and a hard-boiled egg with an infinite shelf life. His scheme for the latter was to stock vending machines with the immortal hen fruit and install the machines in gin mills across the nation, with a fair proportion of which he was intimately familiar.

My mother, a freelance fashion illustrator, sometime photographers' model, and erstwhile companion of assorted bohemians in her native Greenwich Village, could boil water without noticeably diminishing its flavor, but that was about the extent of her culinary skills. During my early tadpolehood, she specialized in what might be termed audiovisual cuisine. The first meals I can remember with any clarity took the form of storybook landscapes, with castles of mashed potato, forests of spinach, stepping-stone paths of sliced carrot, and gardens of topiary broccoli, all overcooked to a uniform grayness (her style was sculptural, rather than painterly), with a voice-over narration by the author. Every meal was a novella, rich in incident but short on flavor.

Gastronomically, life took a turn for the better during my tenth and eleventh years, which were spent in the Pocono Mountains of eastern Pennsylvania. Having deposited his family on a farm there one summer, my father decided to prolong our visit indefinitely while he conducted a dalliance in New York with a young woman who, it was rumored, was a redhead, a communist, and the mother of his bastard son. (I never was able to determine which of the charges most incensed my mother, but I suspect it was the first. She herself remained raven-haired, and proud of it, until her death in her early seventies.)

The owners of the farm rented a few rooms to summer guests, who were fed, family-style, three times a day. It was at the communal table that I tasted, actually tasted, food for the first time. Honest-to-God, dirt-scratching chickens were killed every Sunday for dinner, and great heaping platters of flapjacks were served every morning with home-cured ham or bacon, eggs fresh from the hen-house, butter churned an hour earlier, and foaming milk still udder-warm and redolent of cow. Sweet corn was picked while the pot boiled, and tomatoes were sliced and eaten while they still smelled of sun and vine. Behind the barn was a vast thicket of raspberries, and I'd devour handfuls of fruit on the spot, like a young bear, lacerated by thorns and bitten mercilessly by the mosquitoes that swarmed there. I gathered cool peppery watercress from the shallows of the creek and was paid a dime a bushel for the elderberries

I picked, which I assumed were named for the female elders who made wine from them.

On the farm, I got my first lessons not only in how real foods smelled and tasted, but in the genesis and nurture and the often brutal realities of their production and preparation for the kitchen. I'd been told from infancy that hens laid eggs, cows gave milk, and bacon came from pigs. As a city kid, however, I'd seen less evidence in support of these fables than in support of the Tooth Fairy or Santa Claus. My knowledge of most of the foods I'd eaten was made up of abstractions so confusing that, in an attempt to find out something about egg production at age six or seven, I had asked, "How many chickens [meaning to say eggs] get laid in a week?" It wasn't until the onset of puberty that I learned what my parents had found so hilarious about a simple slip of the tongue.

During that summer, I learned to milk the cows, gather the eggs, feed the stock, and skin whatever eels I caught, after nailing them by their heads to the barn door. I witnessed the beheadings of the Sunday chickens and wondered for some years thereafter whether Marie Antoinette had flapped around in a bloody circle when the blade fell on her neck. I became intimate with chicken shit, cow flop, and slop buckets and learned respect for their usefulness in the food cycle.

Between chores and play, I'd hang around the kitchen, where the women of the farm spent the better part of their daylight hours putting up the next winter's provisions as the summer wore on. Happily immersed in the sweet steamy fug that built up as hundreds of pounds of fruit were converted to jams and jellies, I was given the job of slipping peaches from skins loosened by a brief bath in boiling water. I lugged case after case of quart Mason jars from a storeroom to the kitchen, where they were sterilized and filled with stewed tomatoes, beans, corn, and various pickle relishes, later to be arrayed in gleaming rows in the dark cellar pantry. As summer waned, cabbage was shredded, salted, and weighted in earthenware crocks for a long winter's supply of sauerkraut, and tubers were stored in the root cellar. From time to time, when the sweet sultry air of the kitchen began to cloy, I'd wander off to the icehouse, toss a couple of burlap sacks over a frozen block, and drowse in a cooler season, inhaling the clean aromas of earth, lake water, and wet sawdust.

Summer's end changed the tempo and texture of life on the farm. The other boarders were gone (including a kid my age named Billy Steeper, who had never tired of reminding me that a wooded hill on the property was steep but he was Steeper), and the kitchen increasingly became the focus of activity as the days grew shorter and cooler. I was enrolled in a one-room schoolhouse some two miles through woods and fields from the farm and adjacent to a general store that stocked a maddeningly comprehensive assortment of penny candies. My school days began with light chores and the usual hearty breakfast. Then I'd be handed my lunch box (invariably packed, like everyone else's, with a ripely fartable egg sandwich) and sent off to dawdle through terrain exploding with pheasant and partridge.

Lessons began after allegiance to the flag was pledged and the morning's hymn—"The Old Rugged Cross," "Rock of Ages," or the like—was sung by the entire student body, whereupon sliding partitions were closed, separating grades two through five, and the hours until midday recess ticked interminably by.

Recess impelled a mad rush to the general store, where forty-odd kids would jostle for position at the candy counter, each clutching a penny or two and stooping before the bowfront glass in agonies of indecision. There were licorice ropes in red and black and nonpareils and jawbreakers; gummy red Indian-head coins and the inch-high chocolate figurines then universally known as "nigger babies" and Hershey's Kisses in bright foil sprouting tissue umbilical cords; rock candy (both crystalline and amber) and peanut brittle and sour balls; marzipan bananas that tasted disconcertingly like castor oil and colored sugar dots stuck on yard-long strips of paper and crinkly foil cups with peanut butter fillings; sugary green peppermint leaves and cayenne-charged red devils and candy corn and a near-infinitude of other delights. Decisions were taken and changed as many as a dozen times by each kid before the irrevocable choice was made; finally, in a poignant ritual altogether new to me, each child would return to the schoolyard and solemnly present what had been chosen to another.

Much later, it seemed obvious that the recess exchange of penny candies was an acting-out in microcosm of the prevailing ethos of the region during the Depression. The sharing of food by people who had little else to share amounted to a way of life in the Poconos, as it probably did in much of rural America at the time. Farmers who could afford a few rounds of shot would parcel out their bounty of game to the entire community, and people who were seldom able to put butcher's meat on the table would regularly feast in season on squirrel, rabbit, venison, bear, partridge, quail, and pheasant. When the women of the area gathered in a farmhouse parlor for the weekly quilting bee, they'd bring covered dishes along, and marvelous cakes and pies and homemade candy. My own contributions were windfall hickory nuts and black walnuts, gathered on the way home from school and cracked open with a hammer on an iron stove lid.

The gastronomic high point of the season was Halloween, when everyone in the region turned up at dusk in Stroudsburg, the nearest town of any size, where trestle tables laden with food ran end to end along the length of the main drag and communal gluttony continued long past everyone's normal bedtime. As I remember the scene, it was straight out of Pieter Brueghel the Elder's Peasant Wedding, with the addition of half-naked young bucks, painted up as Indian braves, who pounded huge war clubs against the macadam, setting off the light explosive charges loaded in the club heads.

We left the farm toward the end of the year, with several months' board unpaid, and relocated to the smaller of Stroudsburg's two hotels. It was a momentarily wrenching break for me to be cut off from an extended family (with whose only daughter, eight years my senior, I thought I had fallen eternally in love) and what had seemed an idyllic existence. Life in town soon took on an allure of its own, however, although the food didn't measure up to the other compensatory pleasures. Breakfast was provided by the hotel, but otherwise my mother exercised her meager culinary talents on a hot plate in our rooms. Our meals seemed pathetically inadequate after months of sumptuous feeding on the farm; indeed, they were pretty awful. My mother was the only cook I've ever known who regularly resorted to canned potatoes. An occasional piece of donated game and the odd few slices of baloney excepted, the only meat I can recall eating during our stay in Stroudsburg was the hotel's breakfast bacon, most of my share of which was snaffled up by Skinny Brand, an impoverished farm kid who went miles out of his way to join me in the dining room on his way to school.

Having defaulted on our hotel rent (as he had on our farm board) for months on end, my father was reluctantly compelled to resume some semblance of familial responsibility. Temporarily forsaking his red-haired mistress and their rumored child, he turned up in Stroudsburg one weekend, packed us into the car, and drove us to New York, where he had rented an apartment on the extreme Upper West Side, somewhere on the outskirts of Newfoundland. Perhaps because I detested the neighborhood, my memories of life there are rather spotty.

My best friends and only social dining companions of that period were Johnny Bloomer and Mario Gangi. Johnny, an Irish janitor's son, subsisted exclusively on potatoes, eating them three times a day, boiled, at home, and roasting them over street bonfires between meals. The roasted spuds, known as mickeys, were filched in wholesale lots from the neighborhood greengrocers, who unwittingly abetted the thieves by providing them with fuel in the form of discarded fruit crates. The roasting of mickeys did not require the culinary genius of an Escoffier. The potatoes were simply tossed into the fire and left there until thickly encrusted with charcoal. Mickey connoisseurs were readily recognizable by their blackened lips and teeth, their blistered fingers, and their smoky aroma.

Thanks to the flavorlessness of my mother's cooking, the taste memory of those mickeys is one of the very few I can summon up from that time of my life. In retrospect, their charred sapor seems as delectable as the hot paving tar kids chewed in rural Pennsylvania.

Mario Gangi was an uncommonly handsome kid with huge liquid brown eyes and wavy black hair. These features looked even better on his sister, who also had breasts that left me sick with desire. Mario and I occasionally played ball after school. One afternoon, when he had neglected to bring his glove, we went to get it at his family's apartment. His mother, an immigrant from Naples, insisted that we have something to eat before we left. Classically, she exhorted us to *"Mangia, mangia"* as she served up heaping plates of *pollo alla cacciatore.* It was the most savory food I'd ever put in my mouth, and it introduced me to a culinary genre with which I've since conducted a passionate love affair.

The wholesome, hearty food of the Poconos had been a revelation of sorts, with its straightforward, uncomplicated flavors of earth and air and sunshine and rainwater, but Signora Gangi's dish, a commonplace in the Italian repertory, invested eating with dimensions I'd never suspected. Judiciously applied quantities of gently sautéed garlic, unknown to the Pennsylvania Dutch, lent subtle pungency to the orchestration, as did olive oil, oregano, rosemary, mushrooms, tomatoes, and onions. The dish resonated with a vibrancy I could no more have imagined than I could a previously unknown color. It contrasted textures and aromas I'd never before experienced; it was the mucilaginous product of elderly, flavorsome flesh, gently braised on the bone until it fell away at the touch of a fork, releasing clouds of seductive perfume. Decades and thousands of meals after the fact, it remains the most affecting dish I've ever experienced and the one I try to replicate when in dire need of elemental maternal comfort. Mario Gangi lived in a roach-infested cold-water tenement flat. I envied his startling good looks, his beautiful sister's disturbing presence, and his mama's chicken cacciatore more than I ever have envied anyone else's more generally coveted blessings. If some parsimonious fairy godmother offered me just one of the usual three wishes, I guess I'd go for the chicken.

On the infrequent Sundays when he was in evidence and relatively flush, my father would take us to a restaurant—usually a cellar dive in Chinatown or a family-style Hungarian place, presided over by matronly women in paprika-dusted aprons, on the parlor floor of an Upper West Side brownstone. My kid brother Ted and I much preferred the excursions to Chinatown, where, it was rumored, all manner of depravity went on behind kitchen doors. Not only were "wily" cooks said to pee in unsuspecting customers' egg drop soup, but to do unspeakable things with joss sticks (whatever *they* were), smoke opium, wage tong wars, and sell hapless occidental visitors to the ladies' room into white slavery (whatever *that* was). As Sinologists who never missed an episode of the comic strip "Terry and the Pirates," my brother and I knew these things to be indisputably true. If any corroboration of Chinese otherness were needed, it was abundantly provided along the community's narrow thoroughfares: in those days, many Chinese men still wore pigtails and middle-aged women still tottered along Mott and Pell and Doyers streets on bound feet.

As has been the case with just about every transplanted ethnic cuisine in America except the French, Chinese food in this country underwent an initial stage of bastardization. Following in the tracks of the first wave of immigrant Italian restaurateurs, the first Chinese expatriates had emigrated from a narrowly circumscribed region (Canton, whereas the Italians had come mostly from Calabria and Sicily) as outdoor laborers. Having established a precarious foothold in the land of opportunity and their own ethnic enclaves, both cultures set up a few mom-and-pop (pop-only in the case of the virtually womenless Chinese) feeding outlets, adapting the dishes they normally ate at home to their notions of what would sell to Americans in general, preferably with optimal profitability for the sellers. Hence, the early Italian establishments specialized in spurious dishes like the spaghetti and meatballs mentioned earlier, in which the minimal acceptable amounts of animal protein were padded with inordinately large quantities of cheap starch. The Chinese followed suit with dishes like chow mein, lo mein, and chop suey (some were debased versions of traditional preparations; others were created to meet a perceived demand). Although the Italians from the historically meat-poor south were never overly generous in catering to supposed carnivorous American tastes, the Chinese bulked up astonishingly small quantities of flesh, hacked into minute scraps that cooked quickly and economically, with immoderate amounts of cheap fodder and rice. Both cuisines depended on savory sauces to overcome the blandness of the bulking agents, and it was then axiomatic that everyone was hungry again half an hour after putting away a copious Chinese meal. Most Italian restaurant buffs, on the other hand, waddled from their tables stuffed to the eyes with carbohydrates mired in dyspeptically acidic red sauces, convinced that they'd never be hungry again.

Slight as my father's claims to epicureanism may have been, he knew enough to avoid the restaurants that catered to non-Chinese; he usually took us to scruffy places where we were the only Occidentals in sight. Aside from the frightful state of their sanitation, the chief drawbacks of his haunts were that nobody in them spoke English, the menus were hung like laundry on wires strung along the walls, and even had my nearsightedness not prevented me from making out the characters scrawled on sheets of foolscap, there was no way I could have made sense of them. Our meals were ordered by jabbing fingers in the general direction of anything that was being eaten with apparent gusto anywhere in the house, and I never learned the names of any of the dishes we were served or was able to reorder a particular favorite unless someone else happened to be eating it when the waiter turned up.

It was those Chinatown excursions that inspired my earliest attempts at cookery, I suppose in self-defense. Most were ill-conceived exercises in what might be termed culinary chinoiserie, hacked-up mélanges of whatever meats (usually leftover Spam or baloney) and veggies came to hand. The results *looked* reasonably Chinese, but my ignorance of sauces, herbs, and spices left them tasting nearly as bland as my mother's exercises in merciless over-cooking. Their only saving grace was that they were cooked quickly and therefore retained some of their natural flavor. Somehow, I had gathered that the stir-fry was the principal Chinese cooking tech-nique, but I had no idea what the proper lubricating agent might be. Settling for what was available—margarine—even I realized that it failed to produce the expected flavor and finish. Nor did my liberal use of Worcestershire sauce, which *looked* and therefore should have *tasted* like soy sauce, add any verisimilitude to my Cantonese creations. (The Worcestershire was kept on hand by my father, one of whose defenses against my mother's cooking was an occasional indulgence in tartar steak. The dish, which he prepared and consumed as he did his other favored delicacies, in solitary splendor, was regarded by the rest of the family as another of his perverse affectations, especially by my mother, whose idea of edible meat was meat cooked beyond recognition.)

I was thirteen the summer my father decided to take us on an extended "vacation" tour of the country. Actually, the decision was forced on him. He was then a traveling salesman for a vending-machine manufacturer, and his extended territory was the Deep South, the Midwest, and the Rocky Mountain states. As usual, he had neglected to pay our rent for the better part of a year, and he solved the problem by ducking it. In the parlance of the day, he "shot the moon": packed us up and cleared us out in the dead of night, while the landlord slept the sleep of the just. We were loaded into the car and headed south. With the home office footing the bills for his mileage, hotel rooms, and business entertainment, the old man was prepared to tolerate more intimacy with his family than was his wont. Our sleeping accommodations (four to a room) wouldn't show up on his expense account and, by entertaining prospective clients a tad less lavishly than was his custom, he could feed his family with the company none the wiser.

My memories of that summer are chiefly gustatory. I was exposed to regional foods and ways of eating altogether new to me and developed an insatiable passion for the barbecued pig of the Carolinas in the process. With all due respect to Calvin Trillin, the great apostle of Kansas City barbecue, I also developed a settled conviction that although his home town's steaks were incomparable in those days (not that my experience had provided me with anything to compare them with), the city's best barbecue didn't come close to run-of-the-mill examples of the genre in the Carolinas.

Passionate claims by various regional chauvinists notwithstanding, the pig, not the steer or any other quadruped, is the supreme vehicle for barbecue. Moreover, its meat must be at least partially smoked and the sauce must contain the clearly discernible tang of vinegar. For optimal enjoyment, barbecue also should be unmanageably sloppy, as it is at its best in the Carolinas. These convictions were the first of any consequence I formed, and I'm still impressed, on the threshold of my dotage, by my immediate grasp of immutable truths. Latecomer though I may have been to the appreciation of such crude but honest fare as the livers of force-fed geese, the roe of Caspian sturgeon, the raw flesh of the *tora fugu,* and the hauntingly pungent white Piedmont truffle, I never cease to be amazed by my precocious recognition of the absolute superiority of Carolina barbecued pig among civilization's more complex and subtle beneficences.

Not all my southern eating experiences were equally rewarding. In Tennessee, we stopped for lunch one afternoon at a typical Dixie restaurant of the Depression era, a fair number of which had relocated and were operated up north. Run by a couple of genteel maiden ladies of a certain age and reduced circumstances, it occupied what once had been the ballroom of a splendid antebellum plantation house (by then sans plantation and somewhat decayed). The dining room was deserted when we arrived and looked as though it had been empty at least since Appomattox. Other than the maiden ladies, ourselves, a wraithlike ancient who may have sired the ladies sometime after being mustered out of the Army of the

Confederacy, and a Stepn Fetchit–type waiter, there was no one in sight. Lunch, we were informed by one of the ladies, would consist of hayum, spoonbraid, black-ahd peas, collard greeyuns, and pah (type of pah unspecified and, as it would turn out, unidentifiable by sight or taste).

The hayum, we were further informed, was not V'ginyuh hayum or anything resembling it, but Tenn'see hayum, which, we were to understand, was the *ne plus ultra* among the known universe's hayums. Given the paucity of paying customers, it was understandable that the single available entrée would be a cured meat with a lengthy shelf life, and I looked forward with immoderate appetency to my portion of the vaunted Tennessee ham. It arrived in a state of total petrification, impenetrable by fork, impervious to knife. In utter frustration, I picked it up and licked it. It tasted of nothing but salt.

My father had an Armenian client in Denver. As we approached the city, we were told we'd been invited to Sunday dinner *chez* the Armenian. In those days, the proper noun "Armenian" was invariably preceded by the adjective "starving" as naturally, it seemed to me, as "dervish" was preceded by "whirling," "southpaw" by "gangling," or "Oriental" by either "wily" or "inscrutable." Our prospects of being adequately fed at the Armenian's did not seem encouraging.

The starving Armenian in question turned out to be an immense man who looked as though he hadn't missed a meal in his life. In my particular frame of reference, he was a middle-aged ringer for Ernie "the Schnozz" Lombardi, who might have been the greatest hitter in the history of baseball had he any more mobility than the Rock of Gibraltar. (Notoriously slow of foot, the Schnozz was routinely thrown out at first base after rattling a drive off the left-field wall, and he regularly stretched booming triples into hairs-breadth singles.)

Our host lived in a large, comfortable, well-appointed house on the outskirts of town. A man of planetary girth, he ruled his household like a pasha. At first, I took his various female relatives to be members of his harem, but closer inspection divested the relationship of its intriguing exoticism. A dozen or so of the younger women turned out to be his daughters, who lived under his roof along with his many sisters and cousins, all apparently bereft of whatever men, other than the paterfamilias, who may once have figured in their lives. The sole occupation of all these women seemed to be to rush relays of food from the kitchen (where other, unseen women prepared it) to the dining room. Soaked with sweat, they bore a seemingly endless procession of outsized brass salvers to the table, each heaped with mountains of lamb, rice, okra, eggplant, chickpeas, and all manner of things I couldn't identify, in a near infinitude of combinations and permutations. The meal commenced promptly at noon and continued until early evening, as our host exhorted us to keep pace with his cetacean intake. Stuffed bug-eyed after a mere ten or twelve courses, with at least as many to come, I'd never seen as much cooked food in one place in my life, never eaten as much, and never expected to eat as much again, assuming I survived the afternoon. As it would later turn out, dinner with the starving Armenians merely foretokened a number of even more outrageous exercises in open-ended gluttony.

During my mid-teens, I held down a number of tenuously food-related jobs while my attendance at school became increasingly spotty. None of the jobs lasted very long or gave me any reason to believe I might some day become professionally involved with food and eating on a long-term basis. We then were living (with the old man again *in absentia*) in a beachfront community on Long Island, where I worked successively as a tricycle-mounted peddler of Good Humor ice cream, a grocer's delivery boy, a boardwalk soda jerk, a burger cook–carhop at a roadside pit stop, and a supermarket stock clerk.

I distinguished myself in none of those capacities. Before being summarily divested of my Good Humorousness, I had allowed my stock to undergo a succession of catastrophic meltdowns as supplies of dry ice evaporated while I goofed off in the town's sandlot

outfields. As a still-virginal, excruciatingly horny errand boy preoccupied with my inability to capitalize on the frustrations of the
underserviced wartime hausfraus who received me in flagrant dis-
habille, I constantly misdelivered cartons of comestibles and was
soon sacked. My most memorable moment on the boardwalk came
when I was inadvertently locked inside a walk-in coldbox and
damned near froze to death before my absence was noticed an hour
or so later. The burger joint's owner, a Greek named Theofanides
whose advertised "all beef" patties were composed of pork and
veal trimmings in roughly equal measure, irately canned me when,
after leaving me in charge of his ramshackle establishment during
what he said would be a morning-long absence, he turned up earlier
than expected, found the place unattended, and, after a search of
the neighborhood, found me playing in a pickup ballgame. I was
dismissed from the supermarket when the manager found me absently fondling a couple of cantaloupes while gazing, catatonic with
desire, at a remarkably pneumatic checkout clerk, a recent bride
whose husband was eating mud and dodging shrapnel somewhere
in Europe.

I was in uniform myself not long thereafter, having memorized at
close range a vision-test chart I couldn't otherwise have read with
the aid of the Mount Palomar telescope. Assigned to what was then
the army air corps, I found GI food to be a marked improvement
on what I'd eaten throughout most of my life. Even the generally
despised creamed chipped beef on toast—"shit on a shingle" in the
demure parlance of the mess hall—was a good deal more toothsome than my mother's Sunday Spam roasts, and there was no
resemblance between GI calf's liver, which I found eminently palatable despite its service from a steam table, and the desiccated,
impenetrable substance served at home. If military chow was somewhat deficient in green vegetables and seafoods, what I didn't know
didn't hurt me. Green was a color I long since had forgotten to
associate with anything edible, and a periodic ordeal of my childhood had been my mother's shrimp dinners, for which egregiously

overripe (hence affordable) crustaceans were boiled mercilessly in an unavailing attempt to expunge their pervasive malodorousness, until they were texturally and palatally indistinguishable from balsa wood. On relaxed Sunday mornings, when attendance at the mess hall was discretionary, all the eggs you cared to eat would be cooked to order, two at a time in any style you liked, with accuracy I've seldom encountered since, even in the finest restaurants. As the saying of the time went, I had found a home in the army.

My teens were ended by the time I boarded a troopship bound, as it would turn out, for Bombay via Hobart, Tasmania. I still hadn't got laid and, because the previous several months had been spent trying to rectify that educational shortcoming while absent without leave, neither had I quite mastered the intricacies of my ostensible military specialty. On paper, I was a qualified aircraft radio operator; in fact, I'd have had a hard time tuning in to a Jack Benny broadcast on anyone's parlor Philco. My nights in uniform had been spent ineffectually grappling—on front-porch gliders, under backyard blankets, in tavern booths, and in parked cars—with a succession of otherwise complaisant but ultimately impenetrable small-town girls who enunciated their refusals to go "all the way" in the nasal twang of the Midwest or molasses-thick southern drawls. My days had been spent dozing through training courses, drained by the futile exertions of the previous nights.

The trip across the Pacific and up the Indian Ocean took more than a month, with the ship changing course every few hundred yards to maintain the rickrack pattern thought to be the most effective means of evading Japanese torpedoes. The *General Billy Mitchell* was a waterborne sardine can with bunks stacked five or six deep between decks. After weeks of windless equatorial heat, it stank like a field latrine, a condition in no way ameliorated by a mass outbreak of food poisoning about halfway across the Pacific. (As noted earlier, the color green didn't signify edibility to me. Hence, I abstained from breakfast one morning when the plat du jour took the form of reconstituted powdered eggs and Vienna sausages richly patinated with what appeared to be verdigris. A thousand-odd

other guys didn't, with predictable consequences. I spent as little time as possible belowdecks, with the pervasive reek of puke,
thereafter.)

Most of my waking hours at sea were spent leaning on a topside
rail amidships, gazing at an albatross that with no perceptible movement maintained an unvarying position relative to my own. Seemingly as inert as marble, the creature was simply, effortlessly *there,*
floating at eye level, its starboard wingtip just beyond my reach, its
white-on-white chiaroscuro delineated with telescopic clarity
against an indigo ground occasionally highlighted by a diamond
glitter of flying fish. That bird was the most mesmerizing living
thing I've ever seen, motionless in its unbroken motion. It was
there for a week or ten days, and then it was gone one morning
when I awoke to find that we had steamed into Hobart harbor by
the light of the Southern Cross.

After a couple of days in port, during which collective dreams of
thick steaks ashore were replaced by the drab reality of mutton pies,
the ship proceeded to Bombay.

Like my memories of my father, my memories of Bombay are
largely olfactory. From some distance offshore, the aromas of burning cow dung and burning hemp were pungently detectable, along
with a spiced medley of cooking odors, tar, crude tobacco, rotting
vegetation, and human sweat. Within the city itself, these smells
were intensified and augmented by myriad others, contrasting
sharply with the bland asepsis of Hobart. We were allowed only a
few hours on the town before embarking by train for Assam, time
I spent wandering the streets, accosted at every step by self-maimed
beggars and their deliberately blinded infant children.

If I actually ate anything in Bombay, I don't remember it, but I
seem to have absorbed a comprehensive sampling of the city's
cooking by osmosis. Wherever I turned, women were preparing
meager family meals over small fires of dried dung, and any pass-
erby could "taste" the whole spectrum of Indian cookery in the
normal course of respiration. Not until decades later, when subsi-

dized travel turned out to be one of a hired belly's more desirable perks, did I realize that the particular character and texture of my subsequent experiences abroad had been shaped and defined by a few hours of roaming at random around Bombay. To this day, my first order of business in an unfamiliar town is to dog down its more obscure streets and alleys, following my nose along whatever digressive paths an intriguing odor may lead it, mingling with the street people, haunting the street markets, eating street food.

The trip from Bombay to Assam on a narrow-gauge railroad took upward of a week and in no way advanced my gastronomic education. Except for the fruit hawked by vendors who clustered beneath the windows whenever the train stopped to refuel and take on water, we subsisted on C and K rations. Our powdered coffee, brewed in mess cups held beneath the open petcock of the locomotive's boiler, was thick with rust.

Our destination turned out to be an air base in tea country, not far from the foothills of the Himalayas. We had missed our last chance to see action of sorts by just a day; a lone Japanese plane had dropped a single bomb, somewhat wide of the runway, the previous afternoon, with no casualties. The one real threat to our physical well-being, we were informed by previous arrivals, might be posed by the region's single restaurant, which could be reached only by way of a narrow forest trail that snaked through Naga territory. The Naga were then one of the last two headhunting cultures on earth. In an uneasy arrangement negotiated through British good offices, they had agreed to leave unmolested any American GIs rash enough to patronize the restaurant, on the condition that we didn't stray as much as an inch from the aforementioned trail. Ingestion of the restaurant's fare, however, was undertaken solely at the customer's risk.

By the time payday finally arrived, a number of the guys, myself included, could hardly wait to sample whatever epicurean delights the restaurant had to offer. It turned out to be the most singular eating place I've ever experienced. It was run by a pair of Chinese who spoke no English or any of the Indian languages or dialects.

Located in a mud hut with a leaky thatched roof, it stood (or, more accurately, slouched) in the center of a forlorn little clearing, where a few scrawny, disconsolate chickens scratched dirt beneath a tattered banana tree. Its name, conferred on it by a red-lettered sign salvaged from a British rubbish dump and proudly displayed above the doorway, was WATER CLOSET. Geckos scuttled over its walls, preyed upon by snakes that nested in the thatch. Patrons stacked their carbines in corners of the dining room and usually ordered both the available dishes: banana fritters for openers and fried chicken for the main course. The fritters were molten goo within a concrete crust; the chicken, juiceless flesh within an equally impenetrable batter. As the sole alternative to mess-hall chow, the place did a land-office business.

It was on the way to the Water Closet for the third or fourth time that I had my first and only close encounter with a Naga tribesman. Another *bec fin,* a Kentuckian named Warren "Doc" Sights, and I were threading our way along the trail, with Doc some five yards in the lead, when this vicious-looking little creep materialized beside the path, naked as a snake, eyes smoldering like hot coals, spear at the ready. We were armed but under orders to do nothing to provoke the indigenes. Besides, our carbines weren't loaded. "Just keep walking as though the fucker doesn't exist," I muttered. Doc just kept walking, and so did I, until we were well out of range. For years afterward, though, I could feel that spear lodged between my shoulder blades, its shaft quivering as I pitched onto my face. As we discovered some weeks later, the Naga's reputation for savagery wasn't exaggerated. A guy from another outfit, a notorious scapegrace, got brawling drunk one night and strayed onto Naga turf in search of a woman. He was found belly-up in a shallow stream some days later, minus his head and genitals.

The Water Closet cuisine had begun to pall somewhat, as had our unit's largely functionless role in the war, when we were finally assigned to what would be our post for the duration: a good-sized air base at Kharagpur in Bengal, some seventy miles west of Calcutta, and within easy distance of a number of smaller cities. For most of the men, keeping the installation in good working order was not particularly burdensome. Indian civilians did all the drudge work, including our housekeeping, and many of us were assigned personal bearers. Our workdays were split into three shifts, leaving plenty of free time for everyone, and a good deal of that time was spent in search of civilian food. Most of the restaurants we patronized in the towns around Kharagpur were run by opportunistic Indians who catered as closely as they could to GI tastes, and the menu of choice was steak, eggs, and sliced tomatoes. The cow, of course, was sacred and its flesh taboo. Our steaks derived from water buffalo and were tasty enough, but tough as nails. There was little inclination on the part of most of us to sample native foods, but a few of us occasionally tried authentic Indian restaurants. Most of the genuine Indian food I ordered bore a disconcerting resemblance to the contents of diapers, or so it seemed to me at the time. Although I later overcame my initial aversion to Indian cookery to some extent and, I think, was able to assess it on its own terms, my reviews of Indian restaurants were always somewhat lacking in spontaneous enthusiasm. Of the various cuisines I was required to evaluate as a hired belly, the transplanted cuisine of the subcontinent was always the most problematic.

When the war came to an end, activity at the airstrip dwindled to almost nothing. I had been in charge of the flight operations office at Kharagpur, occasionally filling in at the control tower. It had been a cushy, more or less autonomous job, but I jumped at the chance to accompany the unit's now-uncensored mail to Calcutta twice a week. The job, which provided me with a generous per diem allowance, was a snap: another guy, Eddie Suhoski, and I merely had to strap on .45-caliber automatics, board a railroad car reserved for our use, and supervise its unloading at the military post office in Calcutta. The work was finished by lunchtime and, with money in our pockets, we were free to enjoy the pleasures of the city until we caught the last train home late in the evening.

By general agreement, the best restaurant in Calcutta during the

British Raj was Firpo's. It was certainly the grandest restaurant in which I'd ever set foot, the previous claimants to that distinction having been Jack Dempsey's (where the champ himself had sat down briefly at our table, taken a hand I didn't wash for a week thereafter in his bricklike paw, and autographed an eight-by-ten glossy of himself for me) and the restaurant of The Gunter hotel in San Antonio, where I had eaten the first filet mignon of my life in the company, among others, of a luscious blonde who wore a trench coat throughout dinner and, for dessert, opened it briefly to provide her tablemates with a glimpse of an otherwise naked body.

As I remember it, Firpo's was located on Chowringhee Road. It was opulent even by the standards of today's world-class citadels of haute cuisine and seemed even more so in the dung-pungent context of leprous, festering, pullulating Calcutta. Turbaned bearers in immaculate gold-braided white tunics prowled barefoot over deep-piled broadloom beneath improbably lofty ceilings adrip with crystal chandeliers. Commodious tables, isolated from one another like Micronesian islands, were flawlessly appointed. The clientele was made up predominantly of senior Brit officers—the primogeniture-victimized remittance men who formed the backbone of the Empire—and the atmosphere was that of the poshest of old-boy clubs.

"Holy shit!" Suhoski and I chorused as we entered the restaurant for the first time. A thick-featured Polish kid from the Pennsylvania coal country, Suhoski was the only guy in our outfit who spent more time discussing food than sex. He had devoted our first train ride to Calcutta to rhapsodic descriptions of his mother's blood-thickened duck soup, stuffed cabbage, and homemade kielbasa, but his restaurant experience was even scantier than mine. Both of us were awestruck by the splendor of Firpo's, which, as he put it, looked "like a church."

We were led to a table and both ordered Scotch, which, because of its wartime scarcity at home and the prohibition against anything more potent than beer in enlisted men's service clubs, neither of us had ever tasted during our brief period of alcoholic eligibility. When we also ordered steaks, our resplendently uniformed waiter suggested that perhaps the sahibs might first care to sample a few of the restaurant's *excellent* chilled prawns, a suggestion to which we acceded, having no idea whether prawns were animal, vegetable, or mineral. Peering across the room at the approaching server a few minutes later, Suhoski growled, "Goddamn waiter didn't tell us they got shrimp."

The goddamn waiter padded up from behind me, bearing an elaborately chased silver platter a yard wide and heaped with enough fat pink decapod crustaceans for a large wedding reception. He tonged a pound or so onto each of our plates, barely denting the mountain of prawns, and padded off. Five minutes later, he returned with a freshly replenished platter. Would the sahibs care for more prawns? Damned right they would. Once again outsized portions were transferred to our plates, and once again the waiter retreated, reappearing with another fully loaded platter as soon as we'd snaffled the goodies. "More prawns, sahibs?" Suhoski and I eyed the prawns, eyed each other, and eyed the prawns again. "What does each plateful of these things cost?" Suhoski asked. There was, we were informed, no additional charge for any subsequent helpings served once the dish was ordered; one simply paid the price stipulated on the menu and ate as much as one liked. "Well shit," Suhoski said, "just leave the platter on the table, then, and save yourself all that walking."

Some three hours, eight or nine shared pounds of prawns, and two thick steaks apiece later, we had gluttonized ourselves comatose. Unable to rise from our seats, we stared at each other glassy-eyed over hugely distended bellies, trying somehow to will our digestive systems into action. At last, after another hour of torpor, Suhoski emitted a thunderous belch and heaved himself to his feet. Groaning with gut-ache, I struggled up, and we waddled out of the restaurant.

The same lunch, identical in all its particulars, became as regular a feature of our trips to Calcutta as did postprandial sex—alfresco or in the shelter of a taxicab—with the city's contingent of Chinese whores. We abruptly lost our appetites for further gorging at the restaurant, however, when after a typically disgraceful pig-out, we staggered from the table to the revolving door, which was jammed by what I took to be a bundle of dirty rags. On closer inspection, the impediment turned out to be the body of some poor wretch who had starved to death, apparently with his nose pressed to the glass while watching us stuff ourselves.

I never again returned to Firpo's. Or perhaps I did, decades later and thousands of times, when fifteen years of my days and nights were spent consuming rarefied delicacies while Ethiopia starved, much of the rest of the Third World went hungry, and some elderly Americans subsisted on cat food.

Returned to civilian life and earning a precarious living as a freelance magazine and newspaper illustrator, I wasn't eating with any great regularity. When I *did* eat, it was mostly in the cheapest Greenwich Village restaurants. In keeping with its original function (as one unit in a brownstone brothel), my first independently occupied apartment lacked a kitchen. The single meal I cooked during my residency there consisted of a steak broiled in the fireplace. I had read somewhere that President Eisenhower's technique for broiling steaks was to pitch them directly into a blazing fire and dust them off with a whisk broom when they were done to his taste. I followed the presidential recipe, with disastrous results. Ike, I concluded, either didn't know beans about beef or didn't use busted-up fruit crates and his landlady's bordello-baroque furniture for firewood.

I ate mostly in Italian restaurants. Although they seem almost uniformly awful in retrospect, I had no complaints at the time. The grub was plentiful and cost almost nothing, and I neither knew nor cared that the main dish of choice, spaghetti with meatballs, was unheard of in its putative land of origin. For a couple of years, I lived almost exclusively on waterlogged carbohydrates, which were invariably mired in a tar-textured sauce so overcooked that its resultant sourness had to be masked with a heavy admixture of sugar. During what were still the gastronomic dark ages in America, it didn't much matter in which Italian restaurant you took your chances. With the rarest of exceptions, they were interchangeably awful, but my coevals and I loved them. We drank the sour, headache-inducing swill that passed for Chianti and took the emptied *fiasci* home and stuck candles in them. We romanced our dinner dates over frayed red-checked napery, exchanging garlicky kisses at shadowed corner tables, and marveled at our own worldliness when we reluctantly passed up the biscuit tortoni in favor of a piece of underripe fruit and a hunk of rat cheese.

My first inkling of the broader possibilities of Italian cookery materialized when, for some forgotten reason, I turned up for dinner one night at a place called Fellin's on Thompson Street, south of Washington Square Park. One of the few Italian restaurants in the neighborhood actually patronized by Italians and not operated by Neapolitans or Sicilians, it was owned by a family from Genoa who had Anglicized the name Fellini a couple of decades before the film director made it fashionable. There was a boccie pitch to one side of the rear dining room, and the house specialty was spaghetti with "green sauce." I ordered spaghetti with green sauce and was astonished by its flavor, texture, and fragrance, not to mention its bizarre color. It was like nothing I'd ever tasted, and I couldn't get enough of it during the next couple of years. It wasn't until a decade later, when I visited Genoa for the first time, that I realized I had been eating what may have been the first pesto served in the United States. (By the mid-1970s, pesto had become such a commonplace in the so-called northern Italian restaurants that it appeared on a *New York Times* list of once "in" but by then infra-dig edibles. When I tasted it for the first time in the early 1950s, I underwent an epiphanic experience.)

Unlike the Italian, Chinese, and most other ethnic restaurateurs of my salad days, the French in New York were trained professionals. Neither they nor their workers had emigrated in significant numbers from impoverished areas, as had the Cantonese, the southern Italians, and others who had drifted into the restaurant game as a way out of the unskilled labor force. They went through no interlude in this country as grunt workers who laid track, dug ditches, or carried hods. They came here for the express purpose of operating restaurants, and they brought skills acquired during long years of apprenticeship in the kitchens of Paris and the Côte d'Azur or the dining rooms of the French ocean liners. They also brought a devout belief that they were God's own anointed arbiters of good eating, charged with the responsibility of keeping the planet's preeminent cuisine as virginally pure as make-do foreign ingredients permitted, brooking no concessions to American tastes or ignorance.

The French have an honest but somewhat misguided sense of transcendent superiority in every sphere of human activity, which has little basis in actual accomplishment and is perhaps best exemplified by the Western world's veneration of French haute cuisine, which has been accurately characterized as a creation of madmen for the delectation of fools. By mere happenstance, my introduction to French cookery was accomplished through the inadvertent agency of a barroom bimbo picked up in a scuzzy Eighth Avenue gin mill, and I was thereby spared a baptism of fire in one of the city's more celebrated bastions of Gallic epicureanism.

She was a brass-blond anatomical wonderment whose nearly prehensile proboscis I found easy to overlook while staring pop-eyed at a sweaterful of what appeared to be torpedoes in midlaunch. I've described the encounter and its aftermath in an earlier book, when my memories of both were a bit fresher. This is what I had to say:

> After a brief conversation (which, as I remember it, had to do neither with Shelley nor Schopenhauer), the lady let it be known that she'd had enough of slumming for one evening. If I craved more of her company, she added, I could escort her to a higher-class joint around the corner. I followed her to a little French bistro on Fifty-first Street, disbursed half my severance pay for the privilege of looking on while she marinated herself in Chivas Regal, and then was abruptly informed that she had urgent business elsewhere but would meet me at the same restaurant the next night.

Needless to say, my inamorata didn't show, and, without the distractions of the previous evening, I was able to have a leisurely look at my surroundings. I liked what I saw. So much so that I remained in more or less permanent residence for the next half-dozen years.

The bistro in question was, and is, called Tout Va Bien. It was one of a score or more of similar places then operative within a few square blocks sandwiched between the theater district and the Hudson River piers. Its clientele was made up in large part of theatergoers, actors, stagehands, and French sailors ashore. For the convenience of the sailors, a contingent of French and Algerian whores made an office of sorts of the bar, as did a colleague of theirs from Pottstown, Pennsylvania, who neither spoke their language nor, presumably, had perfected any other oral accomplishments imputed to them. A few French middleweight boxers, notably including Marcel Cerdan but mostly outgunned pacifists, came in to lick their wounds after battering their opponents' fists with their faces at Madison Square Garden (then just around the corner on Eighth Avenue), and Vivien Leigh occupied a corner table at least once during the later, more distressed years of her stardom. Other ingredients of a thoroughly eclectic mix included ranking members of the French diplomatic community; a number of import-export nabobs who macerated their doxies in champagne at discreetly arcaded tables for two; a postman from New Jersey; an Irish pharmacist from the Bronx; a self-styled philologist from Andorra; and a hack architect from the French Pyrenees who looked and spoke like a clone of Salvador Dalí.

Like the Italian restaurants of Greenwich Village and Little Italy, the French bistros of the West Forties and Fifties were more or less interchangeable. Most were operated by transplanted Bretons, many of whom were related by blood or marriage. A few, including Tout Va Bien, were owned by earthier, more easygoing southerners, but all the menus were virtually identical, and there was little to choose between, say, the onion soup at Café Brittany and at Du

Midi; the coq au vin at Le Berry and at A la Fourchette; the frog's legs at Pierre au Tunnel and at Café des Sports. Wherever you went, you could depend on the kitchen to produce a good cheap meal.

Most New Yorkers of my generation and modest means were introduced to French cookery at Café Brittany, a rather staid establishment on Ninth Avenue, but I preferred the more raffish Tout Va Bien, where a lot more French was spoken and where I was babied outrageously by the resident hookers, the matronly waitresses, the older regulars, and, especially, the *patronne,* Irès, whose last name I never learned.

Then in my early twenties, I looked a good deal younger and apparently aroused Irès's long-dormant maternal instincts. She was a stocky, putty-complexioned, spectacularly bawdy, and unstintingly openhanded Marseillaise whom I adored from the moment I met her. Reputed to have been a great beauty in her day, she was then in her rip-roaring sixties and hardly conformed to the stereotype of the aging Frenchwoman concerned only with the state of her soul and finances. Most nights, she would lock the door once the last diners had cleared out, feed the jukebox with enough nickels to keep Edith Piaf in full cry until daybreak, announce that all further bar service was on the house, and cook up a huge pot of spaghetti for the regulars. On occasion, she'd impulsively decide to move the party to another venue and would parade a ragtag assemblage of seamen, strumpets, waiters, horse players, pool hustlers, and favored squares to some competitor's place, where she'd pick up everyone's tab.

By then, I was trying to teach myself to write while living precariously as a commercial illustrator and occasional furniture mover. Although I avoided facing the reality of the situation, most of my eating was dependent on Irès's solicitude. In rare moments of relative solvency, when I'd sold a few drawings, I'd take a dinner date to "my" restaurant and impress the hell out of her with my command of menu French, my dexterity with escargot clamps, and my general savoir-faire. On those occasions, we'd shoot what I fancied to be the works: hors d'oeuvres *variés,* onion soup, boeuf bourguig-nonne (or bouillabaisse on Fridays), a salad (from which the usual overdose of garlic was discreetly omitted if Irès suspected I had any prospect of bedding my tablemate), *crème caramel,* and coffee. As did all the other bistros in the neighborhood, Tout Va Bien main-tained a perfunctory wine list consulted only by a few middle-aged men with impressionable coevals of their daughters in tow. Like most other customers, I regaled my companions with the house plonk, grown in Algeria, labeled in Bordeaux, ordered by the glass, and not much better than the alleged Chianti served downtown.

When I was shy the price of a full dinner, I'd nurse a beer all night, order a plate of hors d'oeuvres (professing a lack of appetite for anything more), and have a substantial meal for less than a dollar. On nights when even that was beyond my means, I'd nurse a beer or glass of wine for hours, until Irès either treated the house to one of her spaghetti suppers or sent me back to the kitchen to rustle up a meal of my own devising once the chef had called it a night.

I was allowed into the chef's domain on condition that I never disclose my forays to him, and the sense of trespass heightened the thrill of poking around in the first fully professional kitchen I'd ever seen, ransacking cupboards and pantries in search of a reheatable pot of soup or the makings of an omelet, a salad, or a thick sandwich of country-style pâté. My first whiff of the walk-in coldbox sent me Prousting back through delicious hours of solitude in the old ice-house on the Pennsylvania farm, and my first experience of the distinctive aroma of a restaurant kitchen shut down for the night seemed as heady as the faint traces of perfume left to linger in a room deserted by a beautiful woman.

In perhaps the most poignant line he ever wrote, Dylan Thomas had one of the drowned sailors in *Under Milk Wood* cry, "What's the smell of parsley?" It was on the muted, commingled odors of cut parsley and trimmed radishes, of iced fish and stewed tripe, of chilled charcuterie and cold cooked beets, and of the ice-muffled bouquet of *blanquette de veau,* waiting through the night to shape and declare itself as it was reheated the next day—it was on these and uncountable other olfactory sensations, momentarily reduced to faded suggestions of what they'd been a few hours earlier and would be again when the chef went back to work, that I fed most satisfyingly at Tout Va Bien.

My affectionate relationship with French bourgeois cookery, begun under Irès's casual tutelage and reinforced by a long stay in rural Provence, has been a long, comfortable marriage, although *la bonne femme* was somewhat neglected for a while, during an infatuation with haute cuisine that was destined not to last. Irès is long gone, buried in her native Marseille, but I still return to Tout Va Bien on occasion, to comfort myself with the dishes I learned to love there. The calf's head vinaigrette, the tripe à la mode de Caen, the boeuf bourguignonne, and all the other predictable standbys of a changeless menu are precisely as they were, as they should and always will be wherever *tout va bien.*

During the mid-1950s, I shared an apartment with a friend, Sumner Williams, whose younger sister I would marry a year or two later. Although the pad was equipped with a small kitchen, I seldom cooked or ate there. For that matter, I seldom ate anywhere during that period. Sumner was between jobs, I had hit a prolonged dry spell during which none of my stuff sold, and we were both flat broke. Aside from a couple of folding cots, a glass-topped table, and four rickety straight chairs, all scrounged from friends, our two rooms were bare. Ironically, we were the proud possessors of a dozen magnificent heirloom dinner plates heavily bordered with fourteen-karat gold—a gift from the parents of Sumner's new fiancée, who apparently mistook their prospective son-in-law for a man of substance who maintained their same standard of living.

Donated with the best of intentions, the opulent china mocked us cruelly. With one exception, we were never able to serve a proper meal on it, and we usually served nothing at all. In *Down and Out in Paris and London,* George Orwell had observed that plenty of garlic, even when eaten with little else, creates an illusion of having eaten substantially. During our leanest weeks, I'd put Orwell's theory to the test every second or third day by frying a dime's worth of salami with a nickel's worth of garlic and dividing the pungent mess with my roommate. It had to be the poorest food ever served on plates of that quality.

I don't remember where the money came from, but when an elderly spinster cousin of Sumner's wrote to say she was coming to New York from Minnesota, with a young boy in tow, we managed to cobble up a relatively festive meal for the visitors—the single respectable meal cooked in situ and served on our splendacious dinnerware during our occupancy of the apartment. It may have saved our lives several months after the fact.

Cousin Anne, as the old lady insisted I call her, was a retired truant officer, but she in no way resembled any of the truant officers of my considerable acquaintance. Although she looked like a Norman Rockwell grandma, her fluttery skittishness in the presence of males betrayed lifelong virginity. Her traveling companion was a bright, handsome, well-mannered kid of eight or nine, a boy with whose parents Cousin Anne was friendly and of whom she'd made a sort of surrogate grandchild. Their mutual adoration was clearly evident, and the old lady explained that the boy had been given the choice of inheriting a small sum of money at her death or taking a week's trip to Washington, D.C., with her, with a sightseeing stopover in New York. Understandably, he had opted for the excursion.

Our dinner consisted of shrimp cocktail, thick lamb chops broiled in the oven, baked potatoes, sautéed spinach, a tossed salad, a presentable Bordeaux, and ice cream. It was the first decent meal I'd eaten in months, which may account for my lasting impression, some twelve thousand meals later, that I've never tasted better food.

Cousin Anne returned to St. Paul a few weeks before Christmas and sent us an effusive bread-and-butter note, promising to express her gratitude for our hospitality in more tangible form in the very near future. A flurry of letters followed over the next couple of weeks, during which time Sumner and I reverted to our diet of sporadic fifteen-cent salami dinners washed down with tap water. In Sumner's case, severe malnutrition eventually contributed to what would have been diagnosed as walking pneumonia had he been strong enough to walk. Half his size, I was marginally better sustained by our infrequent, pathetically inadequate "meals" but was beginning to look like a Buchenwald inmate. Mostly, we just lay on our cots, too weak to do anything else, ignoring the doorbell, which was rung with increasing frequency by the landlord and various other creditors. Each afternoon, I'd drag myself off my cot and totter downstairs to the mailbox, hoping against hope to find a check from some art director. Each trip would produce only more angry creditors' notices—and another letter from Cousin Anne.

The letters—in some cases followed within hours by a special-delivery postscript covering particulars inadvertently omitted from the regular installments—had to do with a plum pudding Cousin Anne proposed to send us. The product of an heirloom recipe, it would, she assured us, provide a fitting culmination to our Christmas dinner, which, on the basis of what she'd seen of our culinary efforts, would doubtless progress from oysters through roast goose to a selection of desserts, with all appropriate soups, salads, stuffings, veggies, garnishes, relishes, breadstuffs, and wines along the way. Our sole contribution to *her* contribution was to be a hard sauce, detailed instructions for the preparation of which would be forthcoming in subsequent letters.

I've never cooked a hard sauce, a substance that makes my teeth ache, in my life. As I understand it, however, it's nothing more than confectioner's sugar, water, butter, and booze. Cousin Anne's recipe for hard sauce was as voluminous and convoluted a document as the Warren Commission's report on the John F. Kennedy assassination. With her memory apparently failing, she tested and retested traditional family procedures, making minuscule corrective adjustments from batch to batch of the stuff and relaying her findings to us in exhaustive detail. While we starved and thirsted and hallucinated on our miserable pallets, she exhorted us to use nothing inferior to the *finest cognac that money could buy,* precisely so many milligrams of sugar, only the finest tub butter, the most pristine bottled water, and so on, ad infinitum.

The doorbell rang two or three days before Christmas. "Ignore it," Sumner whispered. The racking cough produced by this minimal exertion precluded any chance that our presence would go undetected. "Postman," came from the other side of the door. "Package." I opened the door, half-convinced I'd be confronted by another irate bill collector, and was handed a parcel. I clawed through several layers of wrapping and ripped open an elaborately decorated tin. "Sweet Jesus!" I shrieked. "Food!" I slapped a skillet onto the stove, turned the heat up high, and literally bounced Cousin Anne's painstakingly crafted plum pudding off the surface of the pan. I broke the thing in two, tossed half to Sumner, and we wolfed the suety hunks down in seconds.

Sumner married a few months later. His sister Gwynne and I married a year or so after that and spent the following and few subsequent summers on the Maine coast, where my widowed mother-in-law maintained a large house on extensive waterfront property. There, for the first time since my childhood interlude on the Pennsylvania farm, I was able to forage for my own food and was again exposed to a simple, bounteous regional American style of cookery.

The village of Friendship then had a year-round population of about 250, made up almost exclusively of descendants of original Down East settlers and Acadian émigrés who shared half a dozen surnames and either fished lobsters or built boats. (The Lash Boatyard on Hatchet Cove, at the foot of the Williams property, produced the Friendship sloop, a beamy, notably seaworthy work boat that enjoyed a measure of cult status among sailing buffs.) Inbreeding was so prevalent that it came as no surprise when, a year after the community's prettiest (indeed, only pretty) young woman had been knocked up and abandoned by a certain Wayne Simmons, I learned that she was the happily married mother of an infant son and that her husband was none other than Wayne Simmons. When I told her I was glad that the father of her child had seen the light and accepted his parental obligations, she said, "Oh no, that bastard's long gone. This one's *another* Wayne Simmons."

The most prosperous of the hundred or so local lobstermen was Stillman Havener, who was said to earn a then princely thirty thousand dollars a year and to tithe to the Advent church. Even wearing work clothes and handling the nauseatingly rank fish carcasses with which he baited his pots, there was a fastidiousness about Stillman more suggestive of a small-town banker than a hereditary lobsterman—until you glanced at his hands, which had been converted by a lifetime's immersion in seawater to a pair of fat knuckleless starfish. A thick-waisted man in his early middle age, he went to work an hour before sunup as city executives go to their offices, freshly shaved, correctly groomed, steel-rimmed glasses polished.

Stillman provided the Williamses with their lobsters, charging them the forty-five or fifty cents a pound he normally received from the local shipper in those days. At this remove, it hardly seems possible that we gorged nightly on a brace of the crustaceans apiece for a dollar or less per head. Nor, in view of my present susceptibility to gout (an occupational hazard, as I was to discover, of reviewing restaurants), does it seem possible that I normally consumed upward of 150 pounds of *Homarus americanus,* drenched in clarified butter, during the course of an extended summer.

I thought I had seen live lobsters before I accompanied Stillman for the first time on a ten-hour round of his traps. I was mistaken. The lethargic creatures that bumble aimlessly in aerated holding tanks or lie torpid on beds of ice bear as much resemblance to a lobster fresh from its natural habitat as a patient on a life-support system bears to an Olympic sprinter exploding from the starting blocks. After a couple of hours of captivity, the eastern blue crab (*Callinectes sapidus*) remains as feisty as it was the moment it was taken, but the American lobster, which lacks the blue crab's staying power, is the most spectacularly animated of the two by far during its first few seconds of contact with man and an alien environment. Of course, the lobster has the short-term advantage of its flexible articulated tail, while the crab's rigid exoskeleton limits its movements to its legs and chelae. Hence, however high the crab's dudgeon may be, the restraints imposed by its own seamless carapace leave it stewing more or less literally in its own juices, whereas the lobster expresses its rage magnificently before punching itself out early in the first round.

Stillman brought his boat dead on the first of his two hundred deep-water pots in pitch darkness, a few minutes before the glimmering of first light disclosed fog so thick that our bow was invisible from amidships. He poured steaming coffee from a thermos and passed cups to Gwynne, me, and his crewman, Irving Lash, a fattish kid in his mid-teens. Downing the scalding liquid in two gulps, Stillman got to work, winching the trap to the surface, then hauling it by hand out of the water and onto his gunwale work counter. The maneuver can be roughly equated to leaning across a waist-high brick wall to snatch a two hundred-pound barbell from the ground. Ballasted with slabs of rock and thoroughly sodden, its lift impeded by several cubic yards of seawater, a yard-long slatted crate isn't to be hefted by a man with back problems, and repeating the operation every five minutes or so over a ten-hour stretch is as strenuous as any work I know of.

The commotion created by the single lobster extracted from the first pot astonished me. Held behind its eyes, the critter bucked and jackknifed furiously, clattering like a pair of castanets as it flagellated its plated belly and eight bicycling legs with its armored tail, snapping its crusher claw murderously, hooking the smaller of its pincers in vicious rapid-fire swipes. With what seemed to me one hand too few for the job, Stillman pegged the chelae with the traditional wooden wedges (they were then universally in use and weren't to be replaced for some years, first by plastic pegs and later by theoretically more humane rubber bands). He tossed the lobster into a bin as the Lash boy cleared the trap of various creatures that had strayed into it (crabs, sculpin, starfish, and the like), rebaited it, and sent it over the side. The boy snapped the largest of the paired claws from each crab, dropped the claw into a tin box, and sent the dismembered interloper skimming through the fog and into the sea, where in due time, if the temporarily handicapped crustacean eluded its predators, its missing limb would regenerate spontaneously. ("You mean it'll grow back? You're pulling my leg!") "He'll have a couple hundred of those claws by quitting time," Stillman explained. "His suppah tonight'll be some sweet." As is the case among the watermen of the East End of Long Island— descendants of seventeenth-century settlers from New England— "some" usually precedes an adjective rather than a noun among coastal Down Easters, who will say a day is "some foggy" or baked sardines are "some good" but will seldom say "That was some fog" or "Those were some sardines."

"Want to peg a while?" Stillman asked, a dozen-odd pots later.

"Sure," I replied, forgetting his scarred hands and convinced I'd mastered the technique, at least theoretically, after an hour's obser- vation. The next lobster was handed to me as it came clattering from the pot. I extracted a wedge from the peg box with my free hand, made a tentative pass at the juncture of the crusher claw and the first knuckle, and felt an excruciating pain at the base of my thumb, which the lobster seemed to be enjoying immensely. I flailed my arm in a wild overhand arc and brought the critter down against the countertop. Its grip tightened. I slammed it against the winch, a panicky stratagem that merely whetted the beast's destruc- tive appetite. Taking the Lord's name in vain and shrieking profani- ties I didn't even hear, I smashed my tormentor against anything hard within reach. Each blow reinforced its determination to divest me of my thumb.

By the time a grinning Stillman pried the thing off me, I was weeping with pain. "Nothin' but a little chicken lobstah," he said. "No more'n a pound, but it sure made you sing some pretty. Wasn't language I've heard in church, but it was some educa- tional." With timing too diabolical to be mere coincidence, Still- man's son's boat loomed out of the thinning fog, fifty yards or so to starboard. "How you doin', Wayne?" Stillman called. Wayne held up a monster specimen about the size of an adolescent beagle. "This is the kind I'm gettin'," he called back before dropping the colossus into the water.

Although it's common practice elsewhere around the country for restaurants to sell crustaceans weighing as much as ten pounds as "Maine lobsters," such claims are spurious. Strictly enforced Maine law prohibits the taking of lobsters measuring more than five inches from the base of the eyestalks to the juncture of carapace and tail. As a result, Maine lobsters seldom exceed about two and a half pounds. As Wayne Havener dropped his twenty-five-pounder over the side, I offered up thanks for a law that tempers justice with mercy. I could have lost an arm trying to peg something *that* size.

Eventually, learning the hard way, I got the hang of handling and disarming live lobsters. Somewhat less painfully, I learned to eat them with optimal efficiency. Gwynne, whose estival diet since childhood had consisted largely of seafoods, could fieldstrip a lobster faster than she could crack and eat a boiled egg, extracting every last obscure morsel—all the sweetest buried treasures neglected by ostentatiously macho steakhouse diners who loudly order six-pounders only to let four pounds go to waste. Following her example, I soon became almost as adept at dismantlement as she and was thereby later spared the professional indignity of ever having to don a ridiculous bib or otherwise embarrass myself in public confrontation with decapod crustaceans.

During that first summer in Friendship, I became altogether compulsive about the digging of soft clams, gathering of mussels, and picking of wild blueberries. I learned which seaweeds were edible, which clumps of succulent shore greens were tastiest, and how to construct and conduct a proper Down East clambake. I also learned—sickeningly—that sand sharks are viviparous: as a five-foot-long female died at my hands in the bottom of a dory, thrashing in her own blood, a perfect little replica slid from her body, orphaned at birth.

The abundance of wild foods, all free for the taking, obsessed me. When the tide was out, acres and acres of fat mussels made a vast cobblestoned piazza of Hatchet Cove, and bushels could be picked up in minutes. Curiously—inexplicably to me—I had the mussel beds all to myself. Today, farmed Maine mussels sell briskly all over the country for upward of a dollar a pound. Back then, mussels literally couldn't be given away anywhere but in urban Italian or Portuguese neighborhoods (where they sold for a dime a pound) and a few French restaurants. The attitude of those who had easiest access to them, the natives of coastal Maine, was summed up for me one morning when, as I was filling a second bushel basket, a fat bay constable parked his patrol car up on the cove road and came clumping down across the beach. It had never occurred to me that a permit might be required for the taking of all this bounty, although I had suspected there must be *something* illicit about an activity in which I was the sole participant. Squinting suspiciously at my harvest, the constable said, "You a marine biologist or somethin'?" Informed that I was somethin', I guessed, but not a marine biologist, he said, "What in hell you think you're gonna do with all them things?" I said I was planning to eat them, but, of course, if there was a law against . . . "You're gonna *eat* that garbage?" The man stared at me aghast, then shrugged his most eloquent crazy-summah-people shrug, clumped back to his car, and burned rubber.

The free availability of so much good food imposed an obligation to use it intelligently and imaginatively. For the first time in my life, I began to take a serious interest in cooking, for which I seemed to have some aptitude. We had marvelous seafood dinners every night, felicitously topped off with the lemon soufflés at which Gwynne excelled or by the lemon meringue pies for which a couple of elderly women were locally renowned.

I had eaten blueberry pancakes for the first time in a Cambridge, Massachusetts, students' hangout where they were a vaunted specialty of the house and had gagged on them. Thick as mattresses and blotched with the seepage of unseasonal frozen berries, they had seemed to me about as poor as food can get, their local popularity

notwithstanding, and I had written off the whole subject of the
blueberry pancake as a culinary aberration that only Harvard kids
could mistake for acceptable fare. Or so it seemed before my first
encounter with the wild low-bush blueberries that in August
frosted the sun-numbed fields around Friendship with a shimmering haze. Picking a quart of the buckshot-size fruit was maddeningly
slow work but eminently worth the next morning's stiff back. With
berries so small, so firm, and so gloriously sweet, I decided to
reinvestigate the possibilities of the blueberry pancake. I had
learned to cook a passable crêpe at Tout Va Bien, and the crêpe
seemed to me a far more suitable vehicle than the bloated American
flapjack for the containment of the minuscule berries. Beginner's
luck produced an absolute wonderment—a crisp golden disk spangled with clearly delineated dark polka dots. We ate stacks and
stacks of those blueberry pancakes as long as the season lasted each
summer.

An inexhaustible supply of sweet lobster garbage, the remains of
our nightly dinners, produced rich bisques and chowder bases. An
equally inexhaustible supply of freshly dug soft clams resulted in
huge heaps of the critters, either steamed or in the form of belly
sautés, or deep-fried or chowderized. We had crab and lobster
salads and mayonnaise-slathered lobster rolls and spaghetti sauced
with periwinkles and the other marginal beach trash I gathered, and
we ate pollock reeled aboard Stillman's boat between trap liftings.

All this was a decade and a half before food and cookery became
national preoccupations. Someone gave us a copy of James Beard's
The Fireside Cookbook after our return from my first summer in
Maine. It was the first cookbook I'd ever owned, and I'd never
heard of its author (although I was vaguely familiar with the work
of its illustrators, Alice and Martin Provenson). I had no way of
knowing that some three decades later, in the last year of Beard's
life, I'd be writing a two-part biographical profile of the man who
by that time had been firmly established as the supreme guru of
modern American cooking. The cookbook I received, a perennial

best-seller from which Beard never realized a dime in royalties (he was paid a flat fee), hardly measured up to the standards of the myriad cookbooks it engendered, but a couple of generations of professional foodies, my own included, cut their culinary teeth on it.

I don't remember making any practical use of the Beard book, or of *L'Art culinaire français,* a massive tome written in a language I could read with just marginally better comprehension than I could read Tagalog or Serbo-Croatian. I had picked up the French cookbook on impulse in a secondhand bookstore, dazzled by color photographs of dishes that looked more like Tournament of Roses Parade floats than anything that could actually be cooked and eaten. Like the Gideon Bible I had stolen from some hotel room years earlier and opened only when stumped for an answer to a Double-Crostic puzzle definition, the books filled me with a sense of virtue merely by occupying space on my shelves. But it was from the Hudson River, and not any culinary literature, that I began to get some inkling of the passions that cooking and eating could inspire.

I had come into possession of a magnificent old eighteen-foot canoe a couple of years before marrying Gwynne, and until the birth of our first child I had taken a two-week excursion on the Hudson in it each September. Built in Canada for some fur trapper's use, it was a flat-bottomed, ribless, eggshell-thin bentwood craft that could carry half a ton of cargo but be portaged when empty by one man. As I was to discover later, in Maine, it was seaworthy enough for open-water use. The first year I had it, my brother, a friend of ours, and I loaded it with camping gear just after Labor Day (when, after a summer of power-boat congestion, traffic on the river dwindled to a few trains of tugboat-towed barges and an occasional tanker or freighter), and set off from upper Manhattan for Troy, New York, some 150 miles to the north, on an early evening upriver tide. Unwittingly, we had embarked on a gastronomic odyssey.

We had barely cleared the New York City limits when someone on a dock at Sneden's Landing, on the river's west bank, hailed us.

A hurricane was coming, he hollered, and we'd better get our asses off the water. It was pitch dark by then, and we were sweeping the riverbank with a flashlight, looking for a landing and finding only unbroken ramparts of jagged rock, when the storm caught us on its way north, where (as we learned the next morning) it was to blow the steeple off Boston's Old North Church. By sheer luck, we ran aground on the only patch of open beach within miles and got our tent more or less pitched on a grassy slope. As we soon discovered, we might as well not have bothered: with rainwater cascading madly down the incline, the canvas kept us no warmer or drier than it would have on the riverbed, and our bedrolls were drenched through before we crawled into them.

That the rain let up toward the end of the most miserable night of my life made no difference; the three of us were soaked, quite literally, to the skin and shuddering uncontrollably, our teeth chattering like castanets. Our changes of clothing were as sodden as what we were wearing, and there was no way of starting a fire. By an act of will of which neither Ted nor I was capable, our friend Skip struggled out of his bedroll and stuck his head out of the tent. "There's a house up on the hill," he said. "Let's see if they'll give us something hot to drink." Wanting only to die where I lay, I told him to fuck his house on the hill, his hot drink, and himself. He returned a few minutes later to announce that he'd wangled invitations to a hot bath and breakfast.

The house up the hill turned out to be just a tad less palatial than Versailles. We were admitted through a service entrance by a uniformed Irish maid, who led us to a marble-sheathed bagnio I recognized from a painting by Ingres; all it lacked was a mob of naked odalisques. We were handed Turkish towels the size of horse blankets and instructed to deposit our muddy habiliments outside the door, through which the maid disappeared. We stripped and eased ourselves into a steaming sunken pool commodious enough to house a pod of whales. I estimated the hot-water bill for our soak to be somewhat more than I earned in a month but supposed it little mattered to the chatelaine (an elderly lady in frail health, the maid had informed us, who refused to allow her identity to be disclosed to a trio of hobos such as we); the fixtures, I noticed, were gold plated.

"Are yez decent?" the maid called after an hour or so. We received her in Roman splendor, seated on marble benches and swathed in our borrowed togas, as she wheeled in a breakfast-laden trolley. "Yer clothes are in the dryer now and will be ready when yez finish eating. The missus wants yez out of here soon's yez're dressed." The breakfast was the most sumptuous I'd ever seen: crystal goblets of fresh-squeezed juice, all manner of oven-hot breads, butter in heavily embossed silver crocks, a selection of five or six fruit preserves, a dozen eggs for the three of us, kippers and rashers and rashers of bacon, pots of both tea and coffee. It was the first of a whole string of exceptional meals that I was to have on the river during the next three years.

Lavish as her hospitality was, the missus made damned good and sure we were out of there as soon as we'd eaten and dressed: a state trooper showed up at the door as I scrawled a to-whom-it-may-concern thank-you note. "Okay, let's go," he said. Then, "Hey! You guys didn't pass Sneden's Landing in a canoe last night, just before the storm hit? Christ, am I glad to see you. We were getting ready to drag the river for your bodies."

The sky cleared as we made our way down the slope to our waterlogged camp. I've never seen a sky so hauntingly, eerily lovely before or since. By some atmospheric alchemy, it wasn't blue but an otherworldly luminous, altogether surreal pea-green. It fore-tokened twenty-four hours of sheer visual enchantment. We spread our gear to dry in the sun and rode an upriver tide late that after-noon (the Hudson is tidal for some distance). On a hunch, I insisted that we make for a narrow tributary on the east bank, marked Wappingers Creek on the Coast and Geodetic Survey chart we carried, even though we had no chance of reaching it in daylight.

We were crossing Haverstraw Bay, the river's widest point, when we found ourselves in the midst of a vast oil slick. It was about an hour before dusk. Environmentally destructive as it may have been (to the planet's grievous cost, almost nobody gave a damn about the ecology in those days), I found the spill aesthetically gorgeous. Shimmering hypnotically, as though some cosmic peacock had dragged its tail across several square miles of water, the slick eddied and pinwheeled and coruscated around us in endpaper swirls of lapis lazuli, lavender, and myriad iridescent, metallic hues I can't put names to. From a canoe on a broad expanse of dead-calm evening water, depth perception has no reliability: you don't know whether you're sunk into, riding on, or floating somewhere above the surface. We lost ourselves in a hallucinatory haze of Persian carpeting. Safely out of sight in the stern, I wept quietly at the beauty of it, as I wouldn't again until years later, when I was similarly overcome in Granada, at the Alhambra.

The star-clotted sky was pierced now and then by the remnants of the annual Perseid shower as we paddled silently along the east bank, turned into the mouth of Wappingers Creek, slid under an old railroad trestle, and found ourselves suspended in deep space. Or so it seemed. The inky water was dead calm; looking up or down, we saw the same thousands of stars spangling the same blackness. In effect, we floated free amidst the galaxies, light years from spaceship earth.

By starlight, the waterway looked more like a Louisiana swamp than a Dutchess County creek a short commute by rail or car from midtown Manhattan. There was no clearly defined bank, just a reciprocal infiltration by water and woods with knobby tangles of exposed roots gleaming wetly. "We've got the paddles," someone muttered, "but we're up the creek. There's no place to beach the boat." Continuing upstream, we spotted a lighted window, made for it, found a small dock, and, again, a house on a hill. Ted went up to ask whether we might sack out on the dock. He didn't return for nearly an hour. Finally: "We're okay. The man of the house speaks Spanish and was starved for conversation." Ted had recently learned the language from his mistress of the moment, an Englishwoman who had spent most of her life in Argentina. "He wants us to stay over for dinner with his family tomorrow."

What had been interstellar space by night became a Japanese painting at first light. Thick, raggedly torn mist shrouded the scene, alternately disclosing and obscuring foreground details. A ghostly disk rode low behind the scrim. Sun? Moon? There was no way of knowing in the white, disorienting numbness. Two yards off our starboard bow a small gap materialized in the smothering opacity. An egret posed within it, the only visible object other than the pale disk riding to port.

Señor Mestre was a small, wiry Cuban aristocrat who had been raised in a palace in Havana and whose family had fled to this country when Fulgencio Batista came to power. An elegant, fiftyish dandy and a man of obvious cultivation, he worked as a self-employed house painter around Wappingers Falls (the nearest town). In addition to his wife, a plain, heavy-bodied local woman with legs like courthouse pillars, his household consisted of his father-in-law, who had built their house with his own now arthritically crippled hands some sixty years earlier; Mrs. Mestre's daughter by a previous marriage; *her* husband, a full-blooded Mohawk; and the couple's infant child.

They were an intensely loving family whose affection was expressed most eloquently through the sharing of food, which they laid in in carload lots, cooked magnificently, and ate joyously. They bought their bananas by the stalk, their seafoods by the bushel, their beef by the side, their staples by the hundredweight. They grew their own figs and pears and apples and peaches. They bought their chickens and ducks a dozen at a time from one local farmer, who also supplied their suckling pigs; their butter, cream, and eggs came from another. They subsisted (to understate the matter egregiously) in large part on seafoods but, because Señor Mestre was phobic about finfish bones, were forced to make to do with lobsters, crabs, oysters, and the odd dollop of caviar. Their table conversation was confined almost entirely to rhapsodic discussions of what was being eaten, what had been eaten on past occasions, and what would be eaten in the future. Señor Mestre was the first person I'd

ever met who regarded eating as an art form and a subject worthy
of philosophical discourse.

The several meals I shared with the Mestre family during my trips
up the Hudson have long since merged in my memory. We may
have had oysters and infant pig and Cuban rice and beans and a
selection of Mrs. Mestre's pies on that first evening, or perhaps it
was a different, equally festive menu. What I remember more
clearly is the box lunch packed for us the next morning, when we
regretfully declined an invitation to stay on for the midday meal:
a first course of classically garnished smoked salmon, then split
lobsters slathered in homemade mayonnaise liberally lashed with
the beasts' coral. There was also a salad of adolescent greens (and
a bottle of excellent vinaigrette), two or three fine cheeses, and a
selection of superb ripened fruits from the Mestre orchard.

Farther up the river that night, a tug nosed laterally toward the
east bank, its crew curious about our mast-mounted kerosene lantern. We were hailed from the darkness and asked whether we
needed help. To make up for the extra morning spent at the Mes-
tres', I asked if we could bum a tow through the night. We were
tossed a line, tied it to a cleat, and were told to haul up close and
come aboard. The captain, a transplanted Swede, received us on his
bridge. "I suppose it's been nothing but franks and beans for you
boys on the river," he said. We did our best to look sheepish while
savoring our first three river meals in retrospect. "Well, boys," the
captain said, "at least tonight, you'll eat something better." We
were served one of the best versions of boeuf bourguignonne I've
ever tasted.

On that and subsequent trips on the river, we availed ourselves
of every opportunity to wangle a tow—not because we were in any
hurry to get anywhere in particular or too lazy to pull our own
weight, but because of the caliber of riverine eating. The bargemen
and tug cooks who worked the Hudson were as discriminating
about their gourmandise as any occupational group I know, food
professionals included. The bargemen in particular were superla-

tive cooks and sophisticated eaters. They were paid well and had no work to do from port to port. The money they spent in the towns along the way was spent on the finest culinary raw materials they could find, and much of their time on the water was spent in their galleys. Big, burly, and exuberantly profane, they were exquisitely fastidious housekeepers, secure enough in their masculinity to take pride in their mastery of what generally were considered feminine skills. They hung starched gingham half-curtains in their cabin windows, grew petunias and pansies and geraniums in windowsill planters, laundered and ironed their linens compulsively, and shopped for their food with the scrupulousness of marketing Parisian housewives. A few, including one notorious bigamist, kept their women aboard, but the overwhelming majority traveled alone, and the small feminine touches they added to their working lives seemed poignantly compensatory. Our towage requests were never refused, and, to a man, the bargees we met insisted on sharing their meals with us.

It was the bigamist, a fat, tattooed, stubble-jowled ruffian whose two wives were no more comely than he, who confided that he'd taken canoeists aboard once before: a honeymooning couple who "bedded down on deck and screwed like a couple of fucking eels all fucking night long." The performance was closely witnessed, according to the narrator, and so excited his spouses that he "was fucking fucked out" by his double-barreled emulation.

It was another guy, whose unloaded barge rode too high out of the water to allow us to come aboard, who lowered a bucketful of consolingly hot Irish stew, seductively redolent of herbs and chockablock with outsize hunks of beef, on a line to the canoe. And it was an enormous Melvillean black from the Cape Verde Islands—six-foot-eight if he stood an inch—who picked us up at Troy, the northernmost port before the river gives way to navigable locks. Laughing thunderously at the thought of our little pea pod carrying us that far, he insisted that we accompany him all the way back downriver and share his exuberant ragouts of *pili-pili-*spiced kid, his *foutous,* and *caldeiradas,* and curries. His repertory was part Portuguese, part pan-African. He had spent most of his life at sea and most of his time ashore learning to eat and cook the specialties of every port he hit. He cooked marvelously and joyously, chanting tribal songs in a rolling basso profundo as he stirred his pots, and he ate hugely, expecting his guests to follow suit. A third his size, I did my damnedest to match his intake. He would look crestfallen and miserable when I left a third or fourth helping of some dish unfinished, and I was saddened by my inability to do full justice, by his gargantuan standards, to his culinary efforts. He'd brighten once the table was cleared, however, and promise that the next meal would be more to my taste.

3

A
Feeder in
France

If you've ever driven through southern Provence, taking the most direct route from Arles to Marseille, you've passed unaware through St.-Hippolyte. Arles, the major Gallic outpost of the early Roman Empire and the nearest city of any size, lies some nine miles to the west, and the nearest village, Raphèle, is obscure enough to have long ago adopted the coattail designation Raphèle-les-Arles to facilitate mail delivery from other parts of France. St.-Hippolyte itself, a couple of miles east of Raphèle, is a mere flyspeck on the most detailed maps of the region, a fork in the road whose dozen or so inhabitants incorporate into *their* mail address the locator *"par Raphèle-les-Arles."* According to Juliette Treillard, the place is properly called Croix-St.-Hippolyte after its single distinguishing feature: a rusted wrought-iron roadside cross, half-hidden by foliage, unnoticed by passing motorists (except the few who stop to pee beside its pedestal), and in truth not worth noticing.

Such as it is, St.-Hippolyte, with its half-dozen small buildings hunkered down against the southward sweep of the mistral, straddles route nationale 113, which divides the fragrant hay-rich plain of La Petite Crau from the rock-strewn barrens of La Grande Crau. The little Crau is unmistakably van Gogh country, just as the environs of Aix-en-Provence, some thirty-five miles to the southeast, unmistakably belong to Cézanne. (The transition between the two is startlingly abrupt, and, on their respective turfs, both painters turn out to be surprisingly naturalistic.)

Le Diable Vert, a superb restaurant, is within reasonable walking distance of St.-Hippolyte, and L'Oustau de Baumanière, a world-famous one, is a fifteen-minute drive away. At the time of which I write, however, neither establishment was any better known to lifelong residents of St.-Hippolyte than was the dark side of the moon.

During the year and a half we spent there, the population of St.-Hippolyte totaled fewer than twenty-five, including the three of us, our cat Jeoffry, and the half-dozen goats kept by our landlady Juliette Treillard and her sister Marie-Antoinette, both maiden ladies of a certain age. (More accurately, of an *un*certain age: they looked to be sixtyish but appearances can be deceiving on the Crau, where women work hard and weather fast.) Although the demoiselles Treillard made what they considered adequate meals of a shared brace of small mackerel or a thin slice apiece of cold ham, thereby contributing nothing of statistical significance to the community's general penchant for unrestrained gluttony, the per capita food intake was staggering, and our immediate neighbor, Pierre du Bellon, was the hamlet's undisputed champion gourmand, his whip-lean physique notwithstanding.

Du Bellon subjected us to a rude awakening on our first morning in residence by firing off both barrels of a shotgun right underneath our bedroom window: BLAM! and BLAM! again. After scrambling through the two upstairs rooms and satisfying myself that none of us had been murdered in our beds, I threw open the shutters to see what the hell was going on. My first glimpse of du Bellon was of a reedlike figure with gingery receding hair, gun cradled in the crook of one arm as he extended the other toward a diminutive grounded ruffle of bloody feathers. Dangling from a large plane tree in our communal front yard, a caged Judas bird frantically tried to explain away its betrayal of the victim.

M. and Mme. Pierre du Bellon, as it soon transpired, were prosperous forgers of Spanish antiques and, respectively, a Norman transplanted to the Midi for reasons of health and a Swiss-Corsican blonde who would have been some punkins on the Champs-Elysées, let alone a rutted quagmire in rural Provence. Du Bellon, an indefatigable hunter and insatiable eater of larks, thrushes, warblers, buntings, and the other songbirds collectively known as *petits oiseaux* or ortolans, didn't often bag anything in his own dooryard, having long since annihilated the edible avian population of St.-Hippolyte and the proximate fields. He owned what was then reputed to be the only home freezer in the region, which he stocked with birds he shot one at a time over an area of a hundred-odd square miles. (Artillery in hand, he'd leap into his car at the merest rumor of a chirp having emanated from a cypress or fig tree ten miles distant.) Periodically, when he had accumulated quarry he deemed sufficient to a proper tuck-in, he'd sit down for an evening of open-ended gourmandise, while Mme. du Bellon served the spit-roasted delicacies in relays of four. He would bag just one more bird at St.-Hippolyte, and—thanks to Jeoffry the cat, who happened to be standing nearby and gazing aloft open-mouthed as it fell—wouldn't get to eat it. Until that moment, he had found *très amusant* the idea of an American family bringing a Persian cat to that part of the world. *At* that moment, the cat might well have been blown to kingdom come had du Bellon not expended the last of his ammunition.

Du Bellon was routinely affable during our first discouragingly bleak winter in sunny Provence; his daughter Marie-France, a woman of an interesting age (going on seven), became our three-year-old Roger's inseparable inamorata, and the prospective in-laws necessarily established an entente cordiale. With the onset of warmer weather, however, his cordiality toward his expatriate neighbors increased apace as Roger and I began to return from our explorations of the neighborhood's irrigation ditches bearing dozens of dozens of fennel-fattened snails. Although free for the taking, the gastropods cost me dear: I'd come home with a face swollen to pumpkin convexity by the monster mosquitoes that populated the ditches, while Roger invaded their haunts with impunity.

"I can eat more escargots than you can," du Bellon announced one morning, slapping me across my swollen face with a nonexistent glove. "The hell you can," I replied. Ground rules were set forth: I would supply the escargots; Gwynne would do the initial preparatory work; du Bellon's wife would stuff and broil the buggers and serve them two dozen at a time; du Bellon and I would eat them in unison until one of us cried *oncle*. Informed that his arrangement wasn't altogether fair to the ladies, du Bellon grudgingly allowed Gwynne to participate as a contestant but explained that *his* wife would necessarily be *hors de combat*. "She can't cook *and* eat," he reasoned. "Anyway, she's not too fond of snails."

According to *Larousse Gastronomique*, "To avoid the risk of poisoning, snails must be deprived of food for some time before they are eaten, for they may have fed on plants harmless to themselves but poisonous to humans. Furthermore, it is advisable only to eat operculated snails, that is to say snails which have sealed themselves into their shells to hibernate." In my own reasonably extensive experience, snails will retreat behind their opercula as soon as they're convinced that nothing is to be gained by continued public exposure. With several hundred operculated snails on hand, I borrowed a couple of ancient burlap sacks from Juliette Treillard, filled them with operculated escargots, and hung them in an upstairs closet. The idea was to deprive them of nutrients until any potentially toxic substances had been expunged from their digestive systems. As a final step in the process, Gwynne would immerse the snails in heavily acidulated water, which impels the critters to barf up whatever residual matter may remain in their innards.

Somewhere in her writings, if memory serves, M. F. K. Fisher describes an experience of her own that ours duplicated in every particular. In short, operculated snails are merely playing possum: if a single captive snail among the multitudes finds a way out of its predicament, every last one of its fellows will follow suit. (This, as I would learn some time later, is a talent snails share with lobsters. I once lost three dozen specimens of *Homarus americanus* when one of their number found an escape hatch in a storm-damaged lobster pot and led a freedom march from riverine imprisonment on the Maine coast to open water somewhere this side of Cherbourg. For a couple of summers thereafter, any local lobsterman I ran into made a point of informing me that "something real peculiah" had happened to him that very morning; that he had "pulled up a lobstah" whose claws were already pegged. By the end of the second summah the process of genetic mutation set in motion by the first escapee had engendered something like four hundred pre-pegged lobstahs.)

To get back to the snails, the sacks I borrowed from Juliette were so threadbare that the captives' weight apparently split the burlap within minutes of their incarceration. An ill-fitting closet door in no way impeded their travel plans.

Now, when the poet Theodore Roethke wrote "Snail, snail, glister me forward," he may have been in a bigger hurry to get home than he realized. As a speedster, the snail has been given bad press throughout history. In English, the term "snail's pace" goes back at least to the fifteenth century, and English writers have been denigrating the snail's footwork since, with John Heywood, Will Shakespeare, Fanny Burney, George Borrow, and others using the gastropod mollusk as a metaphor for sluggish locomotion. (The word "sluggish" itself is of course an aspersion on the snail's close kinsfellow, the common garden slug, which moves at about the same rate of speed and is simply a snail without a roof over its head.)

According to statistics randomly gathered by *Playboy* magazine, which usually concerns itself with racier matters, a snail's pace is 0.00758 mph. Unfortunately, *Playboy* neglected to specify which of the twenty-four-thousand-odd species of terrestrial snails it had clocked, or whether the figure represents the average speed of snails in general. Whatever it represents, 0.00758 mph works out to a little better than ten feet per hour. My own impression, based on altogether unscientific observation, is that a Provençal escargot of the *petits gris* variety can cover a good deal more ground than that, but even ten feet amounts to a significant distance in a very small two-bedroom house.

In any event, my own escargots glistered themselves forward

with astonishing alacrity, leaving mucoid contrails to mark their passage over floors, walls, ceilings, and freestanding objects. Within hours, every pocket of every garment in the house had become an operculated snail's sleeping bag. Snails invaded the wine cellar, gluing themselves to bottles and demijohns; the chimney, where they inadvertently converted themselves to smoked delicacies we didn't have the perspicacity to market commercially; the garden, where they fattened on day lilies and vine leaves; the beams, the pantry, and our infant son Mathieu's cradle. They attached themselves to the undersides of furniture, the top of the mantel, the insoles of boots. Attempts to corral the critters were something like trying to empty the Mediterranean with a bailing bucket. For every escargotcha, a dozen or more free spirits turned up where they shouldn't have been.

The evening of the showdown was approaching apace, and the inhabitants of St.-Hippolyte, naturally predisposed in favor of experienced local talent, took a dim view of my prospects, or so I was informed by Juliette Treillard. Juliette! Juliette of the shrewd, hooded liquid-brown eyes and long, probing bill-like nose: a nose perpetually adrip during the winter with a single crystalline droplet at its end; a nose beside which she would lay a bony forefinger in moments of reflection, slowly drawing one felt-slippered foot up from the wet earth and into her voluminous skirts like some great shawled stork.

Juliette was the owner, the historian, and the social arbiter of St.-Hippolyte, its grande dame and the most delightfully dotty woman I've known in a lifetime of consorting with mixed nuts. She and Marie-Antoinette maintained and lived above a murky monochromatic general store stocked for the most part with defunct ballpoint pens and empty cardboard cartons; the latter, piled higgledy-piggledly from floor to ceiling, periodically avalanched all over the premises, burying groceries, yard goods, cats, and cashbox with Pompeiian finality. With Marie-Antoinette's gentle acquiescence, Juliette leased St.-Hippolyte's meadow spring and fall to itinerant shepherds, and to hay balers during the summer. She rented the community's smithy and a few dwellings to an astonishing assortment of oddballs, kept her goats in a dilapidated barn, and, I devoutly believe, played the piano under water by the light of the full moon.

On a morning after one of Juliette's midnight recitals (which rendered Chopin and Debussy as *glong, glong, glong*), I entered her store, with Roger in tow, to pick up a few staples. Juliette was gutting some mackerel purchased a half-hour earlier from the fishmonger who visited St.-Hippolyte twice weekly. Today, Roger is no Adonis. At that time, though, he might have fluttered down from the frescoed ceiling of some rococo Bavarian chapel. With his full mop of spun-gold curls and saucer eyes of cornflower blue, he'd had a devastating effect on older women of Mediterranean derivation even before he got to the south of France. Riding my shoulders back in New York's Little Italy during the street festival of San Gennaro, he'd been mobbed by Neapolitan-born matrons who, apparently identifying him with the Christ child of countless chromolithographs, insisted on laying adoring hands on him. Perhaps as a result of the experience, he would spook when fussed over in foreign languages, and he remained adamant, after two weeks in France, in his refusal to learn so much as a single word of French. (He was quick, however, to mock the accent. "Ees eet expahn-seeve?" he had asked of a toy cash register seen in an Arles Christmas display and sorely coveted.)

Roger's first encounters with Juliette Treillard had been brief and violent. *"Oh, il est tellement mignon!"* she would exclaim as he joined us in the dooryard, whereupon he would kick viciously at her single accessible shin. Picking herself up from the ground, the poor woman would lay a forefinger alongside her nose and again retract half her landing gear. *"Soyez sage, mon p'tit ange,"* she would coo, again to be unceremoniously dumped on her derriere. Then, with Juliette in full retreat, the little angel would be marched back into the house and given what-for.

The language barrier was soon broken through the agency of Marie-France du Bellon. Like her mother, Marie-France was a honey-haired looker. Normally, she would have passed our house only while running each day's single errand to and from the Treillard store, where she picked up such staples as milk, flour, soap, and *vin ordinaire*. Once aware of Roger's presence, though, she had begun to make individual trips for each of the needed items, parading endlessly past our yard with her pert nose in the air and with a brown eye cocked slyly in the direction of the *petit étranger*. Roger had observed her comings and goings with feigned indifference for four or five days before breaking down. At last, he had sidled up to me and, blushing scarlet, mumbled, "How do you ask someone to play with you in French?" I told him, and after whispering the talismanic phrase to himself a few times, he had raced across the yard, yelling, "Hey! My name's Roger. *Voulez-vous jouer avec moi?*" We seldom saw him between meals thereafter, and within two weeks he was speaking French like a native, rolling his *ars* exaggeratedly in the Provençal style.

Once he had mastered the language, Roger found Juliette's effusions much more to his liking. On the rare occasions when Marie-France was unavailable, he'd seek out the old spinster's company, clamber onto her lap, and revel in her embrace. On the morning in question, he launched himself at her as soon as we entered the store, but she shrank back, crying, "Not now, little angel, I'm covered with mess from these fish." Deprived of physical contact, Roger stood as close beside her as he could, while Juliette went on with the job at hand, of which she was making a royal bollix. After an uncharacteristically perfunctory recital of the usual pleasantries, she laid a finger beside her nose, fixed me with the sort of gaze ordinarily reserved for family scapegraces and terminally ill loved ones, and got down to business.

Du Bellon, she informed me, was a renowned eater from a race of renowned eaters. Although she admired me for rising to his challenge, discretion in this case would have been the far better part of valor. There was simply no way that I, an American through no fault of my own, with no tradition of grand gourmandise to sustain me, could possibly defeat a man of M. du Bellon's vast experience, innate savoir-faire, and heroic appetite. If the truth be told, I had been taken monumentally unfair advantage of by an unprincipled opportunist who had everything to gain and nothing to lose. Reflect, I was told: when had M. du Bellon ever challenged anyone to an ortolan-eating contest, an agon that would entail the sacrifice of any of his hoarded birds to any belly but his own? M. du Bellon, Juliette concluded, had merely devised a ploy whereby he could enjoy the limitless fruits of my labors at no cost to himself. Worse, he would add insult to injury by subjecting me to a humiliating trouncing that generations of St.-Hippolytans yet unborn would evoke and cackle over as long as Frenchmen felt the need to assert their God-given superiority to callow outlanders.

As she'd warmed to her subject, Juliette had forgotten her fish and absently fondled Roger's curls, smearing them thoroughly with blood and guts. I took the kid back to the house, stood him beneath the kitchen pump, and sluiced him clean. On reflection, Juliette's homily seemed predicated on some false suppositions. After all, I decided, *she* had no way of knowing that as a ten-year-old I'd eaten eighteen pancakes at breakfast one morning and nine years later had put away seven mountainous helpings of fried oysters in an air force mess hall.

What I'd overlooked, however, was that both feats had been accomplished spontaneously, whereas a couple of challenge situations had damned near hospitalized me. The first of these debacles had been set in motion by my innocent assertion, while I was still in my teens, that "I could eat these things all night." "These things" were ordinary commercial potato chips. The setting was a raffish tavern in Carthage, Missouri, where I was maladroitly attempting to romance an Ozark mountain girl over a few late-evening beers.

I should have known better when my inamorata bet me I couldn't finish two family-size sacks of chips in ten minutes. As an occasional ingester of glass and razor blades (talents she would display after a pleasant sufficiency of 3.2 brew), Kate had made herself privy to certain masticatory arcana of which I was altogether ignorant. (Another of her wee-hour specialties was traversing a lengthy railroad trestle in the seminude while hanging by her hands from its underside, a hundred feet or so above a boulder-strewn gulley.) Hell, I reasoned, two large sacks of chips don't add up to a pound of provender. How could I lose? "What do you bet?" I demanded. "You do it, and you can feel my tits," she replied. I don't remember what I'd have forfeited had I failed. Perhaps just the chance to fondle the flesh.

The upshot of the story is that I felt Kate's tits that night. I also felt as though a troupe of Cossacks had performed a saber dance in my mouth and rubbed the contents of a salt mine into my myriad wounds. What I'd failed to take into account was that potato chips snaffled up in inordinate quantity and inordinate haste have the same effect on human tissue as so many improperly masticated razor blades or drinking glasses. Exquisite as it might have been in other circumstances, the first real feel I'd ever copped didn't seem worth a week of painful convalescence.

The second of my great alimentary disasters had occurred a few months after the potato chip incident, in a scruffy café in the Mexican quarter of San Antonio, where a couple of other GIs and I were lacing our tacos with progressively more potent doses of Tabasco sauce. With steam hissing out of my ears, I affected a tolerance for the stuff that enabled me, or so I claimed, to chug down a six-ounce bottleful of the stuff in one gulp. Pelf was tabled ("One'll getcha two you can't"), and a fresh bottle was ordered and uncapped. Once again, I damned near died in the process of collecting on a bet. The last thing I remember seeing (in a john mirror before submerging my head in a sinkful of cold water) was a pumpkin-sized anthropomorphic tomato, its lips puffed like pillows, its eyes starting out of their sockets. As I passed out, the available options seemed death by strangulation or drowning, but one of my companions fished my head from the sink and flushed enough beer through my system to extinguish the inferno.

On the day of the confrontation with du Bellon, I made a serious tactical blunder. On the theory that the hungrier I was, the more I'd be able to eat, I skipped breakfast and dinner. As a reader of

A. J. Liebling, I should have known better. It was Liebling's tested contention that serious quantitative eating entails constant conditioning; that an empty stomach is no arena for gastronomic heroics; and that the best warm-up for sustained gluttony is a respectably ample meal. Liebling's idea of a respectably ample meal was perhaps best articulated in his sorrowful analysis of Marcel Proust's effete approach to the responsibilities of his craft:

> The Proust *madeleine* phenomenon is now as firmly established in folklore as Newton's apple or Watt's steam engine. The man ate a tea biscuit, the taste evoked memories, he wrote a book. . . . In the light of what Proust wrote with so mild a stimulus, it is the world's loss that he did not have a heartier appetite. On a dozen Gardiner's Island oysters, a bowl of clam chowder, a peck of steamers, some bay scallops, three sautéed soft-shelled crabs, a few ears of fresh-picked corn, a thin swordfish steak of generous area, a pair of lobsters, and a Long Island duck, he might have written a masterpiece.

Pierre du Bellon was no such malignerer as his more celebrated countryman. When I ran into him at the café in Raphèle, a bit past noon on the day of our scheduled match, he was sipping a preprandial pastis and holding forth on his two favorite subjects: what he had eaten at his last meal and what he'd be eating at his next. Kissing his bunched fingertips at appropriate intervals, he described the previous evening's repast and his impending lunch in meticulous detail, larding an extended inventory with *formidables, délicieuxes, magnifiques, superlatifs,* etc. He savored one meal as enthusiastically in anticipation as he did the other in retrospect. Even as he spoke, he informed his listeners, Mme. du Bellon was preparing a light midday collation that would begin with half a dozen of his precious ortolans and progress through *soupe de poisson,* a *friture* of whitebait, a brace of *rougets à la provençale,* assorted vegetables, a tossed salad, a small round of grapeseed-encrusted goat cheese, and *crème renversée.* In a transparent attempt to psyche me out, he refrained from any mention of the impending snail duel, tacitly dismissing it as a mere bagatelle.

The city of Arles has its own recipe for snails, but most Arlesians prefer the standard Burgundian treatment to their own *escargots à l'arlésienne.* Although a gentleman in all other respects, du Bellon, as the challenger, had violated the traditional code of honor by choosing the weapons: *escargots à la bourguignonne,* which are infinitely richer and more filling than the butterless local preparation. In themselves, snails pose no greater a challenge to anyone's capacity than so many small boiled shrimp or steamer clams. To eat *escargots à la bourguignonne,* however, is necessarily to eat far more bread than, and about as much butter as, snail meat. The sauce, of course, is the essence of the dish, and the only way the sauce can be eaten is with quantities of bread. Hence, to eat snails with anything like proper self-respect, the eater who takes them on en masse is obliged to ingest both inordinate amounts of bread and enough butter to bring his arterial traffic to a standstill.

Somehow, I'd neglected to take these factors into consideration when the gauntlet was flung down, and the magnitude of the task at hand didn't dawn on me until I arrived *chez* du Bellon, to find what appeared to be a small village bakery's daily output stacked like cordwood on the dining-room table. Wine was arrayed in proportionate abundance, and du Bellon sat beaming across this vista like a cat at a tethered mouse.

By the fourth and fifth round of a dozen snails apiece, a flushed Mme. du Bellon had worked herself into an uncharacteristic muck-sweat racing to and from the kitchen, where she was assisted by Gwynne, who had dropped out of the contest early on. I was beginning to bloat like a dead Tanganyikan elephant in midsummer, but du Bellon jauntily moiled bits of bread around in his snail butter, scarfing them down with obvious relish as he held forth on a variety of subjects with quintessential Gallic urbanity, while I gagged, glassy-eyed, in my effort to keep pace. By dozen seven, several liters of wine-swollen bread and gut-lurching cholesterol overload, accentuated by massive overdoses of garlic, had me reeling along what's called Queer Street in pugilistic parlance. By round nine, never wanting to see food in any form again, I was ready to throw in the towel when Mme. du Bellon announced that the contest would be forthwith terminated and adjudged a draw so that the roast might not be overdone.

The termination of the snail duel enabled me to save a modicum of face, but I knew in my heart—or, more literally, had a gut feeling—that I couldn't have gone another round. Du Bellon, who dug into the roast like a ravening hyena, was magnanimous about the contest's inconclusive result. During the rest of our stay at St.-Hippolyte, he would introduce me to his café cronies as the *formidable* American gourmand who had matched him snail for snail in an epic eating marathon, upping our combined consumption by a couple of dozen each time the tale was told. As the year wore on, he treated me as a gastronomic peer, recounting his daily experiences at table in graphic detail and even inviting accounts of my own. He would not discover the utter fraudulence of my credentials until the following Christmas, when my ignorance of local custom produced a great deal of shredded human flesh and the regionally infamous *dindon noir et geometrique,* which will be dealt with in the next chapter.

Our first Christmas in Provence had not been auspicious. We had arrived in Arles in mid-December expecting cloudless skies, only to find them crowded, day after day and horizon to horizon, with what appeared to be dirty brown sheep, not a blue-eyed one in the lot. (Except during the first flush of their lambhood, I was later to find the actual sheep of the Midi as depressingly symbolic of deprivation as their cloudy likenesses. Shut-ins during much of the winter, the younger animals could be heard squalling all night long, in the voices of orphaned human babies. Turned out to pasture as the days grew warmer and the meadows carpeted themselves in wildflowers, each flock seemed to be made up of lost nieces and nephews, their communal plight expressed through the monotonous, forlorn clanking of their bellwether's hardware: *oncle, tante, oncle, tante.* . . . Their invariable good humor notwithstanding, the sheep-dogs that escorted the odd defector back to the fold were as pur-poseful as so many SS guards. The bellwethers were castrati, and the sex-starved, pungently odoriferous shepherds might as well have been gelded themselves. One of the latter, who tended a flock at St.-Hippolyte in season, whiled away his long lonely days in the field by whittling intricate little olivewood boxes from which anatomically precise little olivewood penises would spring erect when the lids were opened.)

Given the absence of the vaunted Provençal sunlight and the palpable presence of an insidious, apparently perpetual dankness, the city of Arles was about as festive as it could be when we got there in the waning days of 1960. The streets of the old quarter were festooned with the usual holiday paraphernalia, the shop win-dows were crammed with beribboned merchandise, and the baker-ies displayed all manner of elaborate Yuletide goodies. It was the *boucheries* though, that aroused my appetency. Their windows were tapestried with furred and feathered small game and with domestic ducks, geese, and turkeys in full plumage (an ominous foreboding, though I didn't recognize it at the time, of the next year's Christ-mas). The overflow, in the form of wild boar, was laid out, facade to curb, on the narrow sidewalks, and I salivated like Pavlov's dogs in anticipation of a Gallic Christmas dinner of unrestrained mag-nificence, wherever and under whatever circumstances it might take place. As it turned out, we had our first Christmas dinner in France at a superb country villa, but I'm getting ahead of my story.

We had come by train after an overnight stay in Paris, having crossed from New York to Cherbourg on the then-obsolescent *Queen Mary.* Our progress had been an unbroken succession of sitcom contretemps, beginning with an irreversible vehicular breakdown at the point of origin, where we abandoned an ancient Buick in the middle of an uptown side street and fled to the pier in a taxi, thereby creating traffic blockage that, as we learned much later, wasn't cleared for months thereafter.

The transatlantic crossing would have been uneventful enough had our third-class dining steward not seen fit to assign us to a table occupied by, among others, a one-eyed Bulgarian who informed the assembled company, in heavily accented English, that he was returning from Pennsylvania to spend his sunset years in his homeland. The conversational ice having thus been broken (after a couple of days of awkward silence), Roger chimed in, popping the question he'd itched to ask from the moment he began his tactless surveillance of the old man's vacant left socket. To the kid's puzzlement and the stupefaction of several veddy proper Brits, the Bulgarian announced with manifest pride that he had "lose mine eye in vulva." Roger's further, relentless grilling elicited the information that the vulva in question was Vulva: "First Vulva. Great Vulva—1914 to 1918."

Today, when blue-haired grandmothers from Keokuk routinely tour the Seychelles and Galápagos islands, and bitch about hotel accommodations in Xian, 1960 seems a remote era of innocence abroad. I had spent time in Asia, as Gwynne had in Greece, but neither of us had been to France before. Our first days there were made up of the stock situations on which many travel reminiscences of the period were based. Fortified with two weeks of sporadic attendance at Berlitz some years earlier, I sauntered into a *tabac* in search of some matches upon our arrival at the Gare St.-Lazare and urbanely asked for "a book of lamps." Meanwhile, one element of our luggage, a wicker basket containing Jeoffry the cat, who had extricated two or three of his legs from the carrier, was making its way across the station floor while another of our possessions was getting itself officially lost, in plain view of its owners, behind a counter presided over by the most priggish petty *fonctionnaire* that a nation noted for his ilk had ever produced.

Enter a lanky, loose-jointed station roustabout whom I immediately dubbed Fernandel, after a horse-faced French comic actor of the period. Seeing strangers in distress, Fernandel put himself at their disposal. In jig time, he retrieved the peripatetic basket from a bemused crowd at the other end of the floor and recovered the "lost" piece of baggage, a hippopotamus-size duffel bag to which nobody in his right mind would have laid false claim. He marched us out of the station with Roger astride his shoulders and our considerable impedimenta under his arms. He booked us into a cheap hotel in the notorious rue de Budapest, a place whose regular clientele consisted of couples who had not been formally introduced. Tipped roughly half the nest egg on which we had planned to spend a year or two abroad and asked to recommend an eating place that met his own exacting standards (he *was* French, ergo a connoisseur), he directed us to his own favorite haunt, a modest establishment, as he described it, but an excellent one.

Steeped as we were in the writings of Georges Simenon and, more particularly, A. J. Liebling, Gwynne and I could hardly wait to try Fernandel's restaurant. We had eaten vicariously with Inspector Maigret in scores of places such as Fernandel described and had never experienced anything less than gustatory bliss. In his "Memoirs of a Feeder in France," which had run in *The New Yorker* some months earlier, Liebling had described just such places with a missionary fervor that was largely responsible for our expatriation. Fernandel's recommendation turned out to be an egregious little cafeteria where the plat du jour, *canard à l'orange,* was a very dead duck embalmed with a substance indistinguishable from breakfast marmalade.

Having spent the better part of our first night in France on a little balcony, watching the working girls of the rue de Budapest as they and their Jeans popped in and out of doorways like so many characters in a Feydeau farce, we took an early morning train to Arles and arrived that evening in a dismal, soaking rainstorm. I went off in search of a room and found the Hotel Terminus et van Gogh a hundred yards or so from the station, on the site once occupied by the eponymous painter's yellow house. Dumping a sodden duffel bag and twenty-five very wet pounds of the English language (in the form of an unabridged Funk and Wagnalls dictionary) on the lobby floor, I informed a startled proprietor that my pregnant husband *("ma mari enceinte"),* the waiter *("le garçon"),* and the cat *("le chat"*) were keeping dry at the station while I booked a room for the four of us.

Half an hour later, the previous evening's stringy candied duck, and the honor of French cooking, was redeemed by a celestial fish soup at the first restaurant we found after slogging across a muddy place Lamartine and through the porte de la Cavalerie. The place attracted us because it looked warm and smelled good. The glass that enclosed the *terrasse* during the winter was misted over with steam, but it didn't prevent the heady Italianate aromas of garlic, oil, and tomatoes from escaping into the street. Along with a smaller café called La Cigale, directly across the way, the Bar des Amis was to become one of our steady hangouts in town for the next year and a half.

Except during the tourist season, the Bar des Amis was best described by its name. It was patronized mostly by regulars: men who played belote and billiards together, came in from the country-side to discuss farm machinery on market days, and teamed up to play pétanque on the place Lamartine on Sunday mornings, while their wives went to mass at the Church of St.-Trophime. Inspector Maigret would have basked happily at the café, bellying up against the bar, munching a sandwich, and washing it down with a beer while absorbing the local small talk. Liebling, a more purposeful eater, would probably have dismissed the food as coarse by Parisian standards, and he would have been eminently correct. As the novelty of actually eating on French soil began to wear off, I realized that I'd had meals as good or better in more than one nondescript bistro on the West Side of Manhattan. Still, the food was tasty and wholesome, and the price was right: if memory serves, the equivalent of a dollar and a quarter for a four-course tuck-in, service and a liter of *vin ordinaire* included.

It was at the Bar des Amis that we met two of the six Americans then resident in and around Arles. They were Frank Graham, Jr., and his wife Ada. Frank, a second-generation sportswriter and now a distinguished authority on wildlife conservation, had been a member of the Brooklyn Dodgers organization until the club's departure for El Dorado. He and Ada were enjoying a sabbatical of sorts in a rented farmhouse at Pont-de-Crau, just outside the Arles city limits. It was through them that we were invited to our first Christmas Eve dinner in France.

As noted earlier, the *réveillon* was held at a country villa, a rambling stone house carved into a hillside a mile or so from the spectral ruins of Les Baux-de-Provence and a long tee shot from the vaunted restaurant L'Oustau de Baumanière. Our host was a rubber-faced drifter from Brooklyn named Mickey something, who lived there, in the absence of the owners, with a tough-talking Parisian gamine stamped from the Edith Piaf mold. Mickey made a marginal living as a part-time high school English teacher in Arles, but, we were told, he really intended to splurge on the dinner.

Something told me as soon as we arrived *chez* Mickey that the dinner I had envisioned right down to the last sumptuous detail might not materialize in every particular. Not only was Mickey himself nowhere in evidence, but just one of the villa's many rooms was in use, and it was as cold as an igloo. A couple of candles guttered on a mantelpiece. The only other light emanated feebly from the hearth, where an altogether inadequate fire was being malnourished by the last sticks of an antique chair that had been broken up for fuel. An hour or so after our arrival, the Piaf type, who sat huddled in blankets on the floor, announced that Mickey was "picking up a few things in Arles" and would be along *tout de suite.* I wondered how he intended to roast a wild boar—or even an ortolan—over a fire the size of a pilot light.

Half an hour later, with everyone's teeth chattering, Frank and I were discussing Floyd Patterson's chances of regaining the heavyweight championship when the Piaf type, a devout believer in the absolute superiority of all things French, broke in to inform us that Pierre Langlois, a journeyman middleweight of the day, "would knock the shit out of Patterson" if only the American had the guts to get in the ring with him. (Back in New York, Pierre Langlois had once come perilously close to visiting that very same indignity upon me, when I cast mild aspersions on his manhood at

Tout Va Bien an hour after *his* clock had been cleaned just around the corner at the old Madison Square Garden. I was a mere bantamweight, however, and he was restrained by a couple of peacekeepers.)

As the evening wore on, I stepped outdoors on the off chance that the air there might be a degree or two warmer than in the house. We all were absolutely famished by then. As I stood in the dooryard under a suddenly cleared sky ablaze with stars, I could hear sounds of revelry from the three-star restaurant halfway across the valley and could see the lights of Les Baux beyond it, where one of France's legendary *réveillons* is held each Christmas Eve. A pair of headlights materialized to the south. Five minutes later, a dilapidated *deux-cheveaux* Renault pulled into the driveway and Mickey emerged, bearing a couple of paper parcels. Our Christmas Eve dinner consisted of gelid take-home *choucroute garnie* and a *bûche de Noël* just a little colder than it had been in the *patisserie* refrigerator.

As they would demonstrate over and over again during our stay in the Midi, the Provençaux can hardly be held to account for American notions of Gallic parsimony. They were generous to a fault, and our Arlesian *hotelier* was no exception. During the week or so after Christmas, he drove us all over the region in search of a car and a place to live, eventually leading us to a secondhand *quatre-cheveaux* Renault and the house at St.-Hippolyte.

Our second child missed being born in Italy by less than a day. Long past term, Gwynne was growing increasingly cabin-feverish as the weeks dragged on. When the weather cleared at last, on a glorious Sunday in February, she suggested a short drive to the village of St.-Martin-de-Crau, about three miles to the east. When we got there, she said there was no reason not to push on to Salon, another fifteen miles down the road. And so it went: with Gwynne in fine fettle, we broke southward at Salon and continued to Marseille, where we stopped for lunch beside the Vieux Port.

The restaurant we chose at random, the Buena Vista, boasted three great distinctions: its interior, its barmaid, and its bouillabaisse. The interior had to be the most preposterous piece of restaurant design ever perpetrated. Some utterly maladroit plasterer had fashioned a ceiling of colossal cows' udders in a benighted effort to represent stalactites. Festooned with fishnet and sea wrack and bathed in the ghastly glow of blue neon light, the clusters hung menacingly low over the tables, like so many swords of Damocles. Roger's morbid interest in his Bulgarian shipmate's disability was nothing compared with the rapture inspired by his first glimpse of the barmaid. She was *the* ugliest human I've ever seen. Cross-eyed and astonishingly prognathous, with a huge nose that broke downward from a horizontal thrust like a split-finger fastball, she made Leonardo da Vinci's sketches of grotesques look like studies of Ideal Beauty. Outvoted two to one, Roger was dragged outside, to a table on the sidewalk, with his head screwed on backward. The bouillabaisse was, and remains, the best I've ever eaten.

Purists insist that bouillabaisse must be consumed within sight of the Mediterranean. More precisely, some hold, its glories are best appreciated within spitting distance of the Vieux Port at Marseille, where early versions of the dish first made their way from ancient Phoenicia. After itemizing such essential ingredients as rascasse, chapon, St. Pierre, conger eel, anglerfish, and the like, the 1965 edition of *Larousse Gastronomique* goes on to say, "no mussels or other mollusks should be added, as is the wont of many Paris restaurants." Had the authors of *Larousse Gastronomique* been aware of the existence of my old New York haunt, Tout Va Bien, where the best bouillabaisse then obtainable in the United States was served on Fridays, they might have added, "and is the wont in New York."

The bouillabaisse at Buena Vista contained neither mussels nor other such mollusks. Nor did it contain spiny lobster (a traditionally acceptable component) or true lobster, the claw-equipped crustacean *Homarus americanus,* which sometimes turns up in overpriced bouillabaisse in Paris and points west. The bouillabaisse at Buena Vista was made up mostly of small bony trash fish, cooked *à la minute* from a standing start, and it was sublime. An old Provençal maxim holds that fish born in water are destined to die in oil, and that's how fish died at Buena Vista, and at other restaurants beside the Vieux Port, where they alternate with fishmonger's stalls.

The afternoon remained splendid and Gwynne remained sanguine about her delicate condition. Little by little, we progressed eastward until we reached Ventimiglia, at the head of the Italian Riviera, just across the border from Menton.

We returned from Ventimiglia in mid-afternoon of the next day, and Gwynne went into labor about two o'clock the following morning, in the midst of a torrential rainstorm. We bundled Roger into the car, dropped him off at the Grahams' at Pont-de-Crau, and got to the Hotel Dieu in Arles (the hospital where van Gogh turned up after amputating his ear on Christmas Eve, 1888, perhaps to avoid eating cold *choucroute* in the shadow of Les Baux) at the height of the deluge. Thoroughly soaked, we were met at the gate, just as Gwynne's water broke, by an equally soaked concierge, who informed us that visiting hours were over.

Seated just outside the delivery room, I could hear the midwives exhorting Gwynne to *"Poussez! Poussez!"*

"Je pousse, goddamnit," she replied. There was a sharp smack of flesh against flesh, then a cry exactly like those I'd heard a few minutes earlier, when we left Roger with the Grahams, whose house adjoined a barnful of lambs.

"Un fils," a midwife announced.

We named him Mathieu.

4

Mathieu's birth was hailed as a historic event at St.-Hippolyte. It had been sixteen years since the community had last produced a child, and it was highly unlikely that any others would be produced there in the foreseeable future, if ever. Most of the few residents were long past their procreative years and, for one reason or another, those who weren't would either have and raise children elsewhere or not at all. The peasant tradition had petered out in that part of the country, and the young hightailed it for the cities at the earliest opportunity. The only nubile female in residence, sixteen-year-old Colette Orgeas, had already made it known that she had no intention of sticking around St.-Hippolyte a day longer than she had to. The sole bachelor of marriageable age, Michel Dijol, missed qualifying as the village idiot only because St.-Hippolyte missed qualifying as a village. To the best of my knowledge, his vocabulary consisted in its entirety of two words—*"le journal"*—which he grunted once a day, when he shambled, drooling, into our kitchen to pick up the newspaper we saved for his parents.

Mathieu may have been conceived in Les Etats-Unis and delivered in Arles, but these were mere technicalities as viewed by the women of St.-Hippolyte, who welcomed him as starvelings welcome bread, joyously proclaiming him a native St.-Hippolytan.

For Mme. Orgeas, who lived across the road, it wasn't a case of love at first sight, but sight unseen. Like the barrels fashioned by her husband, a cooper and wheelwright, Henriette Orgeas was built for optimal capacity, but not even a vessel of her immense girth could contain her emotional responses to the goodness of life as she perceived it. Her eyes brimmed perpetually with tears of joy and love: love for her gruff, feisty little keg of a husband, her wispy little snip of a daughter, and her pompous little fart of a son, a self-styled *inventeur* and *métallurgiste* who graced the family with his presence on his Sundays off from his job at a junkyard in Arles; love for her neighbors, their pets, their livestock, and the odd songbird that escaped du Bellon's gunnery; love for the dawning and dusk of each of her labor-filled days.

It was Mme. Orgeas who waited up for my return from the hospital and hurried through the rain and muck for confirmation of her proprietary rights. *"Un fils!"* she exclaimed, as though one of two possibilities had miraculously turned out to be the single acceptable outcome among myriad alternatives. She pronounced the child, on whom she hadn't yet laid eyes, the most beautiful ever born, the most sweet-natured and least troublesome, *absolument le plus adorable* in all France. Regrettably, I was to understand, she could not herself nurse her little darling, but she would of course prepare a garden for him and cook, puree, and personally feed him his infant *légumes* as soon as he was weaned.

I suspect it was Mme. Orgeas who left a basket of fruits and vegetables for us to find outside our kitchen door on our first morning in St.-Hippolyte and every morning thereafter, but she and everyone else denied any knowledge of the matter throughout our stay on the Crau. As putatively rich Americans, we had been warned by more experienced sojourners in France, who had seen little more of the country than the gaudier tourist traps of Paris, that we'd be skinned alive in all transactions with the French. (The tendency to extrapolate wildly from limited empirical evidence was hardly confined to our narrow circle of friends and acquaintances; somewhere in Henry Miller, I had read that one never sees children in France— an understandable enough conclusion given Miller's wonted haunts and companionship, but in no way a reflection of reality.) In our often frustrating experience, it was nearly impossible to pay, let alone overpay, for goods or services rendered anywhere on the Crau. Moreover, it was just as difficult to spring for a round of drinks or reciprocate a kindness of any sort.

To be sure, one was expected to pay on the spot for a meal, a postage stamp, or one's market purchases, but it was virtually impossible to complete any but the simplest business transactions in that part of Provence. Juliette Treillard, for example, insisted that we (and everyone else) maintain a running tab at her store, an arrangement that resulted in the waste of one afternoon a month as she rummaged through her collection of hundreds of defunct ballpoint pens in search of her single functioning *stylo,* then hunted up the thirty-odd scraps of paper, squirreled away in as many cartons and drawers, on which our accounts were recorded. The better part of a year was to go by while I dunned the hospital for presentation of our bill ("Patience, monsieur, you will be permitted to pay in due time"), and to ask, say, a mechanic how much he was owed for car repairs was to be invited to the nearest café for a companionable aperitif and to be informed that tomorrow would be time enough to concern oneself with the grubby details of quotidian life. Invariably, the mechanic (or woodcutter, bottled-gas dealer, or whoever) would insist on paying for the drinks, and just as invariably the whole rigmarole would be replayed the next day, the day after that, and so on, for weeks on end. In some cases, it didn't even require indebtedness on our part to prompt displays of generosity by the most casual acquaintances. The behavior of M. Bashir was paradigmatic.

Monsieur Bashir, a Christianized Algerian Arab, was the most courtly and exquisitely punctilious gentleman I've ever known. He sold peanuts on the streets of Arles. Slender and delicately constructed, he had the mournful mien of an elderly basset hound. No matter what the season, he wore a gray denim smock that covered him from neck to ankles, buttoned down its entire length. His every movement was considered, his every action ceremonious. He was a heavy smoker (or, rather, a would-be heavy smoker), and each time he lighted one of his beloved Gitanes he would make something like an ecclesiastic ritual of the act.

He would extract the blue box from one pocket of his distinctive garment and a long ebony holder from another. Then he'd remove a Gitane from the box, redeposit box in pocket, tamp the cigarette thoughtfully against the back of a slender brown hand, and solemnly insert it into the holder. Undoing three or four buttons, he'd then extract a matchbook from an inside pocket and regard its contents as though making distinctions discernible only to himself before selecting the appropriate match. After lighting his Gitane and letting the match fall to the ground, he would return the matchbook to the designated inside pocket, rebutton his smock, and take a tentative puff, as though to judge the quality of that particular cigarette before committing himself wholeheartedly to its enjoyment.

Unfailingly, a prospective customer would approach him at this juncture. Just as unfailingly, the customer would be female, and, according to M. Bashir's code of chivalry, a gentleman did not smoke in the streets in the presence of a lady. The Gitane would be ceremoniously extracted from its holder and discarded. The holder would be returned to the appropriate pocket, and the transaction, which involved roughly the price of the cigarette, would be effected. Once the customer had taken her leave, M. Bashir would again rummage through his pockets, repeat the entire ritual, and take his first judgmental puff—whereupon another woman customer would accost him. On a busy afternoon, after a corrida had been held in the old Roman arena and the sidewalk cafés were full, M. Bashir could run through two packs of Gitanes without smoking the equivalent of a single cigarette.

I'd often run into M. Bashir on market days as he started off his morning rounds on the rue de la Cavalerie. Each time I did, we'd nip into one of the cafés together for a pastis and some small talk, but I'd never be permitted to buy the drinks. As tactfully as I could in the circumstances, I'd suggest that, as a relatively solvent American on what appeared to be an extended vacation, it might be incumbent on me to underwrite the refreshments at least occasionally. The old man, whose daily income couldn't have exceeded the drinks' cost by much, would have none of it. He was the gentlest, most soft-spoken creature on the planet, but if my hand moved toward my pocket, he would stay it with his own and threaten to become *"fâché"* if I didn't desist forthwith, implying that his wrath would be terrible to behold.

Eventually, I was forced to avoid M. Bashir. Much as I enjoyed his company, I didn't much fancy driving him to the poorhouse; he not only refused to allow me to buy our drinks but refused as well to accept payment for Roger's considerable peanut consumption, and nearly a year went by before we were able to repay his generosity, even in token form. The opportunity arose one afternoon when Gwynne, the children, and I were lunching at La Cigale.

La Cigale had been operated *in absentia* during most of our stay in the Midi. Then, with the struggle for Algerian independence entering its final phase, the owner, a *pied noir* from Marseille, returned from North Africa, where she had reportedly run a string of highly lucrative whorehouses. Madame Pujol certainly looked the part, with her brassy beehive hairdo, garish facial paint, and multiple chains of heavy gold coins that cascaded down into the ravine of her startling décolletage. Childless herself, she mothered Mathieu extravagantly in her fashion. On the afternoon in question, she had ensconced him in an improvised bassinet: a carrot basket, borrowed from the greengrocer next door and lined with tasseled Algerian cushions.

Mathieu had just been weaned from Mme. Orgeas's pureed veggies. Propped up in sultanic splendor, he was greedily destroying a substantial portion of couscous, altogether unfazed by a hellishly caustic *harissa* sauce, while Madame Pujol cautioned him to go easy on the *merquez* sausage *"parce qu'il est un aphrodisiaque."* Perhaps to change the subject, I remarked that I hadn't seen M. Bashir in some time. *Ah, non,* poor M. Bashir was ill; he was laid up at the Hotel Dieu *avec la pneumonie.*

When Gwynne and I turned up at the hospital, we found a sadly depleted M. Bashir propped up weakly on his pillows but puffing away suicidally on a Gitane, which he of course unscrewed from its holder and discarded at Gwynne's approach. Idiotic as the offering may have been, I was glad we had brought a couple of cartons of cigarettes, along with a basket of fruit, some biscuits, and tins of pâté and *confiture.* "You should not have done this," the old man croaked. As he drifted into sleep, he whispered *"Je suis très, très fâché."*

We ate well in the Midi, but the regional fare hardly met expectations whetted by A. J. Liebling's fervent espousal of the Parisian cookery of his early years in France. Nor did it meet the preposterous expectations set up a couple of years earlier by my acquisition of a secondhand copy of *L'Art culinaire français.* Authorship of the book was credited by its publisher, Flammarion, to *"nos grands maîtres de la cuisine,"* but there may have been more significance in a flyleaf inscription that wished the original recipient a *"Joyeux Noël"* in 1957, *"avec toute ma sympathie."* The tome was a backbreaking thousand-odd pages thick and generously larded with color plates of presumably edible rococo and byzantine ornamentation, any subject of which would have taken a fairly accomplished home cook, working with tweezers and magnifying glass, a month to replicate, and none of which in any way resembled food as I'd known it at home or would find it in Provence. A rather perfunctory section devoted to mixed drinks had little to do with booze as I'd known it either. As late as 1950, according to the grand masters of French cuisine, a proper "martini cocktail" still required a couple of dashes of bitters and a spoonful of sugar syrup. According to the same grand masters, a potable aperitif could actually be concocted of cognac, bitters, Worcestershire sauce, tarragon, vinegar, celery salt, and three shucked oysters ("Serve with a spoon").

Years later, I would realize that Flammarion had enlisted a squad of raving maniacs for its distended cookbook, and I may have been the damnedest fool ever to expect their grandiloquent creations to coincide remotely with culinary reality.

Almost two decades would go by before I'd finally realize that the simple Italianate grub of the Midi, with its heady redolence of fresh mountain herbs and its straightforward reliance on tomatoes, olive oil, and garlic, was the sanest, most wholesome form of cookery in France. At the time, however, it seemed disappointingly plain, and we soon tired of eating out regularly around Arles, having concluded that we could do as well at home. On the advice of Pierre du Bellon, the supreme arbiter of such matters, we shopped for our meats at Trescent's *boucherie* in Raphèle. M. Trescent was not only a master butcher (with a couple of missing fingers to prove it) but a superb *charcutier* whose fresh sausages were tastier and juicier than great sex. (The trope is borrowed from a friend, Terrell Vermont, a former international marathoner who applied it to her sport during the course of a lecture she was giving in Dallas, whereupon a member of the audience bawled, "Lady, either I don't know how to run or you don't know how to screw.") Although a good deal more robust, florid, and demonstrative, M. Trescent was as gentle and sweet tempered as M. Bashir. Nonetheless, God alone knows what irreparable psychological damage his well-intentioned endearments may have inflicted on Roger.

I visited his shop for the first time a week or so after we settled in at St.-Hippolyte. I was the first, and quite likely the last, American customer he ever had. On the basis of our initial transaction and subsequent dealings, I'm reasonably certain he still considers all Americans a trifle peculiar, at the very least. "I'd like a nice *bifteck,* M. Trescent," I announced, after the obligatory five-minute exchange of pleasantries. "The best you have."

Ah, *bien sûr,* I was assured, whereupon the butcher thwacked a whole filet down on his cutting block. *"Comme ça?"* he asked, positioning his knife a quarter of an inch from the butt end of the meat.

"Ah, non, monsieur. Thicker."

Raising an eyebrow ever so slightly, M. Trescent edged his knife a sixteenth of an inch upcountry. *"Comme ça?"*

Well, not precisely. What was wanted was a really thick *tranche,* if monsieur would be good enough to cut one.

The colloquy was repeated several times, more or less verbatim, as the butcher reluctantly moved his knife along in increments about the thickness of the blade. *"Comme ça? . . . Comme ça? . . . Comme ça?"*

Suddenly, the man brightened in the light of revealed truth. "Ah, *oui,* but of course! Monsieur desires a bifteck in le style *américain.* Such beefsteaks I have seen consumed by *les cowboys* and *les gangsters* in motion pictures, and I now realize precisely how Monsieur wishes his beefsteak to be cut."

M. Trescent's knife moved another millimeter or so. *"Comme ça!"* he exclaimed with confident finality.

Ah, non, pas exactement. If monsieur would be kind enough to indulge the depraved proclivities of a ravening American carnivore, what was really wanted was an appreciable hunk of meat, something of a thickness that can't be run through by the light thrust of a fork.

But, with all due respect, if monsieur desired a roast, why didn't monsieur specify a roast?

But a roast wasn't what was wanted; a steak was what was wanted.

"A steak, monsieur?"

"Oui, monsieur, a steak."

The butcher finally cut the beef according to specification but couldn't help averting his eyes as he lopped off the *gros bifteck américain.*

I was preparing to grill the thing for lunch an hour later, when du Bellon showed up at the kitchen door. He had stopped *chez* Trescent for some kidneys, had been filled in on the prodigious appetite of his next-door neighbor, and had to see the evidence with his own eyes. Somewhat diffidently, the evidence was produced. *"For-mi-da-ble,"* he murmured, as though viewing the Grand Canyon or some natural New World wonderment of similar magnitude. He regarded me with manifest respect, and I refrained from informing him that two adults and a healthy child would be sharing what amounted to perhaps a pound of meat.

Until he made the acquaintance of, and began spending his waking hours with, Marie-France du Bellon, Roger accompanied me on my subsequent trips to the butcher's, where M. Trescent would treat him to slices of salami and fondly refer to him as "my little chicken." The endearment always was proffered in plain view of his other little chickens, laid out naked, wrung-necked, and lolly headed in his display case. It wasn't long after Roger's first visit to the *boucherie* that he began asking, "What's *morv?*"

"*Morv?*"

"Oui, *morv*—when a chicken doesn't move anymore."

Something cold in hobnailed jackboots trod on my heart. At three and a half, Roger was absorbing the facts of life apace; it wasn't long after his first intimation of morvality that he raced into the house from the yard, shouting, "Come see! There's a big dog and a little dog stuck together outside." And it wasn't long thereafter, I suspect, before he may have attempted a similar adhesive bond with Marie-France.

Although the discoverer wasn't named, I like to think it was Pierre du Bellon who figured in a story that appeared in the regional newspaper *Le Méridional,* which one morning reported the finding, on the Mediterranean coast, of the largest mussel documented within living memory: a monster measuring some eighteen inches from bow to stern. Headlined prominently on the front page, the article was several paragraphs long and went into exquisite detail about the weight, coloration, state of health, and speculative age of the critter. Its physiology was discussed exhaustively in the course of an extended treatise on its personal habits and those of mollusca in general, as was the history and economic importance of edible bivalves in the region, from biblical times onward. Naively assuming that, like Einstein's brain or a verifiable specimen of the yeti, the record-shattering mussel would have been turned over to some accredited scientific institution for further study, I was stunned to read the last line of the piece: "It was reported to be delectable."

Du Bellon may have talked a better game than anyone else in the vicinity, but he eventually turned out to be just one of a good many world-class eaters on the Crau. After just a few weeks at St.-Hippolyte, I had begun to realize that the locals took their comestibles with the utmost seriousness. I'd been severely chastised by Juliette Treillard one afternoon when I returned from the *boulangerie* and casually tossed a loaf of bread onto our kitchen table, where it landed belly-up. Deeply shocked by what she considered an act of sacrilege comparable to inverting the crucifix she had hung over our bed, the old woman lectured me at some length on the prospects for my immortal soul were my errant ways not mended forthwith. Although I then had and still have a lot less religion than Jeoffry the cat (of whose eponym the eighteenth-century poet Christopher Smart wrote, "For he is the servant of the Living God, duly and daily serving Him"), I've never again treated bread with anything less than reverence. Just how seriously our neighbors took their food didn't dawn on me, however, until Mme. Orgeas invited us to Sunday dinner.

At that time and probably still, the people of the Midi (and of France in general) seldom entertained at home: aside from the snail-eating contest at the du Bellons' and the *réveillon chez* Mickey-from-Brooklyn and his Parisian consort, all our eating had been confined to a few modest bistros in and around Arles and to our own digs. Hence, our invitation to the Orgeases' was nothing less than the social event of the decade in St.-Hippolyte.

Having by then borne two children, Gwynne remained a lissome young woman with (as du Bellon observed more than once, with more than a hint of appetency) remarkably shapely legs. Volumetrically, however, she seemed poor stuff by the standards of Mme. Orgeas, who regarded her two nearest female neighbors, Gwynne and the equally svelte Mme. du Bellon, as a couple of dangerously emaciated unfortunates in drastic need of proper nutrition. Raised in France, Mme. du Bellon had no one but herself to blame for her pitiable state, but *une américaine* born and raised in gastronomic ignorance might still be educable. Mme. Orgeas apparently proposed to redress two and a half decades of deprivation in the course of a single sustained meal. Her Sunday dinner turned out to be the most stupefying eating orgy I've ever experienced, with the possible exception of Sunday dinner with the "starving" Armenians of Denver.

Even before the first course was served, it was obvious that M. Orgeas had every intention of taking my measure. (We were of about equal height, or lack thereof, but he outweighed me by roughly half again in pure gristle.) He poured himself a large tumbler of *vin du pays,* broke off half a loaf of bread, and clearly expected me to follow suit. I did, whereupon he drained his glass in a gulp and stuffed his face with bread while pouring himself a refill. I knew I was engaged in another *mano a mano,* like it or not, and scrupulously kept pace with him. We put away a liter of wine and two loaves apiece before the hors d'oeuvre hit the table. Or, more precisely, before the hors d'oeuvre hit the floor.

Mme. Orgeas was still busy in the kitchen (which was a step above the dining room and divided from it by an imaginary line). She was heaping up a yard-wide platter with a mountainous assortment of salamis, sausages, head cheeses, galantines, pâtés, terrines, and sliced hams of one sort or another—a veritable compendium of M. Trescent's talents. Having arranged the meats to her satisfaction, she heaved the tray up from her work counter with some effort, turned toward the dining room staggering under its weight, and lost both her footing and the cold cuts, the latter of which surged surflike across the terra-cotta floor, leaving the assembled company ankle deep in charcuterie.

According to one of the enduring legends of French gourmandise, Napoleon's archchancellor Jean-Jacques-Régis Cambacérès, purportedly the most exacting epicure of his day after Talleyrand, once staged a meticulously orchestrated mock accident wherein an immense Caspian sturgeon was allowed to flop ignominiously onto his dining-room floor, in full view of fifty or so distinguished guests. As the story goes, the host coolly commanded the servers to bring in the *other* sturgeon. Not to be outdone by the aristocratic Cambacérès, M. Orgeas surveyed the disaster with apparent detachment, shrugged beneath his greasy coveralls, and instructed his daughter to clean up and dispose of the mess while his wife loaded a fresh platter with a second array of meats.

After seven of us—the *famille* Orgeas, Gwynne, Roger, and I—had demolished enough cold meat to sustain a *gendarmerie* for a week, I had begun to hope the main course would be a modest effort, to be followed by a perfunctory salad, a light dessert, and coffee. The *first* of the main courses was chicken; more accurately, chickens—one per customer, spit-roasted in the fireplace and garnished with an anthology of seasonal vegetables. It was as toothsome a bird as anyone could hope to taste, but, as the bread and wine continued to circulate around the table on a challenge basis, it was one more bird than I needed at the moment.

Somehow, I managed to pick the carcass clean, force down a salmis of the innards, and surreptitiously loosen my belt a few notches under the host's evaluative gaze. Then, as I sat back in expectation of a gentle diminuendo while struggling to stifle overt signs of acute flatulence, the *rosbif* was borne to the table. At that stage of my culinary education, I was more or less ignorant of the butcher's art. What M. Orgeas attacked with his carving knife looked to me—and still seems in retrospect—to be nothing less than a whole steer divested of horns, hooves, tail, and testicles (which last would turn up later in a side dish). The thing was a half-scale Rock of Gibraltar, and my piece of the rock was just about the most monumental slab of meat I've ever seen on a plate.

Mme. Orgeas had retreated to her kitchen as each course was served out around the table. Once again, she busied herself there as I grappled dispiritedly with my beef and her husband carved himself a second bloody helping. A few minutes later, she reappeared, bearing another of her outsize cooking vessels: a steaming earthenware casserole filled almost to the brim with a ragout of meatballs redolent of mountain herbs.

My recollection of what followed is decidedly sketchy. After some three and a half liters of wine, four enormous courses of food, several incidental dishes, and upward of a kilo of bread, I found myself drifting periodically into delirium. I remember a second casserole, crammed with baby artichokes, and I seem to remember Roger inviting Colette Orgeas to *"danser le Twist avec moi"* as a radio was turned on. (I'd never heard of the Twist until a week or so earlier, when the *International Herald-Tribune* had run a datelined story from New York on a new dance at something called the Peppermint Lounge. How Roger could have heard of it, let alone mastered it, I have no idea, but I'm reasonably certain he and Colette took a few turns on the floor at some point between the artichokes and dessert.) I remember excruciating gut pain, a fatuous dissertation on metallurgy by Orgeas *fils,* and the certain conviction that I was destined to take a place of my own in the endless progression of courses, after being force-fed like a Strasbourg goose. I remember a savanna of tossed salad, an archipelago of floating islands, a Stonehenge of cheeses. Through a Niagara of my own sweat, I watched Orgeas *père,* in triplicate, dissolve and solidify and dissolve again as he munched his bread, swilled his wine, and helped himself to seconds and thirds of everything.

Hallucinating wildly, I witnessed the dismemberment and service *au jus* of Floyd Patterson by Pierre Langlois while M. Bashir, Patterson's cornerman, intoned, *"Je suis très, très fâché, très, très fâché."* Across the table, M. Trescent, the butcher, moved a broadsword over a whale-sized filet of beef, halting the weapon at one-foot intervals to shout, "COMME ÇA? COMME ÇA? COMME ÇA?"

Somehow, it was over. We had followed Orgeas out into his stave-cluttered front yard, where he poured *marc* while his son continued to hold forth on his metallurgical lucubrations. I excused myself on some pretext or other, waddled across the road to our house, and dragged myself upstairs to bed, where I fell on my back, helpless as a tortoise on its carapace, pants at half-mast to relieve the pressure on my middle. An alarmingly distended belly dominated my view of the room, much as Cézanne's Montagne Ste. Victoire dominated the landscape around Aix-en-Provence, and it felt like a couple of sandbags were weighing down my spine. A few years earlier, *Life* magazine had featured as its Picture of the Week a photograph of a very small dog that had eaten a very large ham.

Presumably the ham had not been swallowed whole, but, to judge by the dog's appearance, the ingested matter had reconstituted itself internally, filling its tumid container to the skin, like hot air in a balloon. I sympathized with the dog as I lay groaning and farting on our straw-filled mattress, where I remained immobile until the next morning, wondering and not much caring whether I'd survive the night.

It wasn't easy to hide oneself around St.-Hippolyte (except, of course, from the world at large), but I did the best I could for the next day or two, mortified by my gastronomic trouncing *chez* Orgeas. Inevitably, however, my tormentor and I crossed paths. Like Pierre du Bellon, he was a man who accepted victory graciously. "You eat very well," he said, with no apparent sarcasm.

Gradually and mostly by osmosis, I learned a bit about cooking and eating on the Crau, committing a good many gaffes along the way. I'm not sure whether Mme. Sasso, who lived in an antiseptically tidy house a hundred yards north of the highway, technically resided in St.-Hippolyte, or whether she, like all our other neighbors, was a tenant of the Treillard sisters. In any event, she played a major role in the life of the community. A widow of long standing who sixty-odd years earlier had emigrated from Calabria as a teenage bride, she was an elfin creature who stood about four-foot-six and resembled nothing so much as a makeshift hand puppet fashioned from a bit of rag, with a clove-studded crab apple for a head. Her sharp tongue and homemade black wine, a syrupy aperitif, were locally renowned, as was her gift for finding useful things beside the road on her daily walk to and from Raphèle, an excursion she would complete rain or shine, laden with baskets of wild mushrooms, bundles of mistral-downed kindling, and various *objets trouvés* casually discarded by passing motorists but of great usefulness to herself. An outrageous flirt, she became convinced that I had what she termed "the lucky hand" after I ran into her at the café one morning as she was about to buy her weekly lottery ticket. "You pick one for me," she commanded. I did, and it paid off marginally more than its purchase price.

After several weeks of covert surveillance of Mme. Sasso's mushrooming expeditions, when I was reasonably certain I'd pinpointed her prime hunting grounds, I loaded a large basket into the car, made several stops along the way to Raphèle, and returned home with a magnificent-looking trove of fleshy specimens. In utter ignorance of their various growing seasons, I tentatively identified some as *girolles,* others as *cèpes,* and still others as *galmottes, craterelles,* and so on, optimistically assigning whichever names I'd heard or read to whichever mushrooms they seemed to fit.

My mycological expertise left Gwynne notably unconvinced. Neither she nor I and certainly not the children would be partaking of my harvest, I was informed, without positive identification from Mme. Sasso. I lugged the basket over to the old woman's house and presented it for her inspection. "Mme. Sasso, can I eat these?" *Egh, oui, certainement,* I could eat them. But first I'd better have a glass of black wine and kiss her good-bye, for I'd be dead in the morning. To this day, I'm half-convinced that the old coquette was merely protecting her turf. Still, you never know unless you *know* you know.

From time to time, we left Mathieu in the care of a widowed octogenarian who lived some distance from St.-Hippolyte, in an old farmhouse outside the town of Fontvieille, not far from Alphonse Daudet's windmill. On one such occasion we had stayed overnight in Mende, the capital of the department of Lozère, a region more familiarly termed Misère, and for good reason. (While in the Lozère, we had lunched at one of those truck stops vaunted throughout France as sources of good cheap food. Our first course, canned tuna with boiled potatoes, was followed by a dish of boiled potatoes with canned tuna. In my experience, French truck stops in general aren't what they're cracked up to be. With few exceptions, the popularity of a given place has more to do with quantity than quality, and the caliber of the provender is far outweighed by the availability of parking space, the pinchability of the waitresses, and the liberality of the bartender.) When I turned up to collect Mathieu, his elderly baby-sitter seated me at her kitchen table, produced a bottle of *marc,* poured me a tot, and placed the bottle before me.

The bottle contained a large pear, patinated like ancient copper, which had been grown inside it by madame's mother in the first year of her—the mother's—marriage. Wondrous is the power of suggestion: in an experiment conducted in New York a few years ago, a group of fashion models, told they were drinking Bloody Marys, got thoroughly squiffy on spiced tomato juice. As I sipped the *marc,* I launched into a flowery dithyramb on the subtle but unmistakable bouquet imparted to the liquor by the fruit, the infinitesimal nuances with which decades of maceration had invested the nectar with its unique mellowness, etc., etc., etc. The Provençaux are a courteous people who never would tell a man he's a damned fool to his face. Madame simply said, "That pear has had no flavor, no aroma, and no effect since before the First World War."

The Provençaux are also an amiable people who mask whatever resentments they may harbor behind a facade of politesse. They dislike Parisians for their perceived uppity ways, for example, but express their contempt with elaborate courtesy, as when an Arlesian tobacconist, pretending not to understand a Parisian's simple, classically pronounced request for a pack of cigarettes, leads the prospective customer on with mock solicitude through five minutes of feigned misunderstanding:

"A packet of Gauloises, please."

"I beg your pardon, monsieur."

"Gauloises."

"Gaulwhat, my dear sir?"

"Gauloises, Gauloises . . ." And so it goes until the tobacconist, bluffing embarrassment, suggests that if the Parisian will kindly make an effort to speak French instead of the foreign language of which he, the tobacconist, regrettably doesn't understand a word, every effort will be made to serve monsieur with all appropriate courtesies.

"Gauloises—CIGARETTES!" the traveler explodes, while the Arlesian once again registers smiling incomprehension.

Finally, the Parisian jabs a finger at the shelves behind the counter. "Gauloises!" he bellows. "CIGARETTES!"

A false dawn breaks over the Arlesian's face. Rolling his *r*'s outrageously and adding an Italianate vowel-ending wherever possible, he pronounces the word in the tones of an ever-so-patient tutor to the language-impaired: "Seegarrrret-tah."

During our stay in the region, I witnessed just one display of open ill temper. It was a pip.

Herb, an American friend who was spending a day or two with us en route to Barcelona, needed some information on train schedules. I drove him to the nearest rail station, a sleepy freight depot at Raphèle, which I'd never before had occasion to visit. The stationmaster, who normally had little to do but watch the infrequent passenger trains roll by, was nowhere in evidence, but a rather wan woman of perhaps thirty-five going on forty-eight stood in the yard of a small house beside the tracks. With a beautician's help and a more flattering costume than the faded housedress that hung shapelessly from her thin shoulders, she might have been pretty, but there was a listless, dispirited air about her that in no way suggested she might be capable of registering an emotion more volatile than simple resignation.

Informed of the nature of our errand, she disappeared into the house, obviously to rouse her husband the stationmaster from his siesta. The man emerged a moment later, clad in trousers and an undershirt, doing up his fly, blinking in the sunlight. Then, having caught sight of two strangers bent on seeing him in his official capacity, he retreated back into the house, reemerging a couple of minutes later, resplendent in brass-buttoned tunic, white gloves, and uniform cap. He received us with rococo flourishes of a sort more appropriate to high-level diplomatic functions than to a mere request for timetable information. He was the personification of the monumental self-esteem characteristic of the least essential of French civil servants. It was quite apparent that our simple transaction would be prolonged and complicated to the fullest possible extent.

But of course, messieurs, this cockalorum assured us, he was delighted to be of service, although his grave responsibilities as *chef de gare* did not, strictly speaking, entail procurement of such information as the dear gentlemen required, since this was a freight, not a passenger, station. There followed some five minutes of lopsided chitchat during which the state of the weather and the nation was discussed, along with the nature of our business in France and the utter dependency for the success of its nationwide operations that the SNCF had reposed in the person of its senior (and only) officer in situ, the selfsame stationmaster. For a time, this recitation was accompanied only by the droning stridulation of the cicadas in the fields beyond the tracks, and the effect of both in concert was altogether soporific, especially in the shadeless light of a sizzling Provençal afternoon. Suddenly, however, from somewhere behind us, two monosyllables rang out like gunshots:

"Thief!"

"Slut!"

The stationmaster went on with his soliloquy as though the explosive nouns had not been uttered, while his visitors turned to see who the alleged thief and slut might be. They were, respectively, a burly, unshaven, shirtless guy in greasy overalls and the stationmaster's wife. They stood glaring at each other from opposite sides of the track while the stationmaster serenely dilated on matters of concern to nobody but himself. *"Ah, oui, messieurs,* it is a heavy responsibility which we of the *chemin de fer* bear, and one little understood by those who do not share it."

"Do you think I don't know who's been stealing my cabbages, you filthy vermin?"

"Shut your face, you broken-down cow, or I'll shut it for you."

"But I am detaining you unnecessarily, dear gentlemen. Tell me precisely how I can be of assistance."

"You can stay off my property and out of my cabbages, you shitty carrion, or I'll see you in jail."

"And I'll see you, you skinny festering cunt, in hell."

"Ah, Barcelona, messieurs, a beautiful city, I'm told, although my responsibilities here with the railroad prevent me from traveling very much myself."

"Don't use your gutter language on me, you pustulated toad bugger. I'll have the police on your scrofulous ass."

"And what have you been bedding down with lately, you misbegotten sixth-generation *salope?* You've put more horns on that fat little fart of a husband of yours than *le Bon Dieu* put on all the goats in the Midi."

"Messieurs, if you will be kind enough to excuse me for a small minute, I will communicate by telephone with my colleague at the station in Arles and secure the precise information you desire."

As the pompous little man bustled off to his office, apparently oblivious to the pleasantries being loudly exchanged some five yards from where we stood, my friend and I turned, pop-eyed, toward the antagonists. The stationmaster's wife had undergone an astonishing transformation. She was fury incarnate. Her vichyssoise complexion had turned a rich tomato bisque. She was literally tumid with rage; her skinny neck had swollen appreciably, like a hooded cobra's, and her carotid arteries stood out in alarming high relief, like stylized vinestalks sculpted on a Romanesque church column. Her body, formerly a hanger for her slack housedress, now filled the garment with unexpected womanly convexities. It was as though her whole being had been transformed into erectile tissue distended by the flood of her wrath. She stood as though rooted in the ground, tilting toward the alleged cabbage thief like a nineteenth-century ship's figurehead, breathing fire and quivering with outrage. She loosed a torrent of profane abuse as creative and mellifluous as any I've heard in a lifetime of hanging out in low haunts.

Momentarily cowed, the man on the other side of the tracks shrugged, turned away, and slouched off toward the horizon. After fixing his back with a curare-tipped glare, the stationmaster's wife also turned and began to quit the arena. The color drained from her face and her form seemed to deflate within its faded wrapper. Then, as if on cue, both combatants froze in their tracks, faced each other again, and exchanged the same compliments with which their colloquy had begun.

"Thief!"

"Slut!"

For a moment, the woman stood transfixed in disbelief, as though never before having been so crudely addressed. Then she erupted in Krakatoan splendor. Mere spoken expletives and violent gestures were no longer adequate to the task at hand; she began literally to sing and dance. High-baroque obscenities poured forth across the tracks with a bel canto fluency that would have brought down any opera house in Europe. Her felt-slippered heels beat a flamenco tattoo on the ground when she wasn't launching herself into grands jetés, and the object of her endearments was gradually drawn into a grotesque pas de deux merely to enable him to stay within cursing distance of the whirling contralto.

As though none of this were transpiring, the stationmaster rejoined us, penciled schedule in hand, blandly launched into another of his fatuous disquisitions, festooning his utterances with garlands of compliments, shooting his cuffs at regular intervals, observing all the fancied solemnities of his office in the midst of a firestorm.

"Now, messieurs, if you will kindly consult the notes that my estimable colleague so graciously has provided, you will comprehend that the most agreeable arrangement for . . ."

". . . your funeral, you pig's turd, where I'll dance all night on your grave, you thieving bastard abortion spawned by a Maltese goatherd and a Sicilian . . ."

". . . a most pleasant journey, esteemed gentlemen . . ."

". . . straight to hell, where you'll recognize your parents and their parents before them by their stench, you loathsome toad-faced fuckpig . . ."

At this juncture, the stationmaster's wife became airborne. As her spectacular aria built to its crescendo, her dance approached pure flight—a state of sustained levitation. In basketball parlance, her hang time was awesome, and the term "hopping mad" in no way describes her brief losses of altitude; she was leaping, bounding, catapulting mad. She had cornered her bête noire on the far side of the tracks, in a sort of gully from which just his head and shoulders were visible to us, and she was harrying him from above, her fingers curved into talons. Again, she was crimson with rage, and her sweat-soaked housedress was plastered to her wrath-distended figure. Somehow, a broom materialized in her hands, and she flailed it at her tormentor in roundhouse sweeps that sent her spinning erratically over the ground like a human tornado each time she missed. Her song became a wordless ululation that set all the village dogs to howling while the embattled cabbage thief bellowed contrapuntally.

The stationmaster bowed us down the platform steps and ceremoniously escorted us to the car. "It has been my pleasure, messieurs, to make your acquaintance," he murmured. "As you have seen, the duties of a *chef de gare* in a way station such as this, though they provide quiet gratification, lack excitement. Your visit here will not be soon forgotten."

At Gwynne's urging, I accompanied Herb, our houseguest, to Barcelona, a morning's ride from Arles. The idea was to scout the city as a possible destination for occasional getaways from the Crau and to return to St.-Hippolyte the next afternoon. In those days, before the advent of casual air travel, Spanish cooking was virtually unknown in America, where it was generally equated with gringo-ized Mexican cookery, to which it bore about as much resemblance as sashimi bears to sauerbraten. I had eaten what passed for paella in a couple of Spanish restaurants in New York, and a dish or two of musty-tasting *calamares en su tinta.* On that skimpy evidence, I had dismissed Spanish food out of hand. I wasn't in Barcelona four hours, however, before it became abundantly evident that the French held no monopoly on the pleasures of the table and that the collective French appetite amounted to pandemic anorexia by Spanish standards.

Herb turned out to be an agonizingly prissy traveler. Michelin in hand, he'd burst before venturing into an unfamiliar john to pee, unless it had been granted the guide's imprimatur. He viewed every restaurant as a probable source of food poisoning and rejected scores of attractive, well-patronized places in the course of an hour's trek through downtown Barcelona. He was the prototypal Felix Unger of the then nonexistent play *The Odd Couple;* my own Oscaresque inclination was to barge into any joint that looked and smelled interesting—the seedier, the better. I was footsore and ravenous by the time Herb consulted his Michelin for the fortieth time. I peered through the window of a restaurant called Quo Vadis, on Calle Carmen, just off the upper Ramblas. Not much could be seen through the glass, which was covered with multi-colored graffiti:

TAPAS VARIADAS

CARACOLES   CIGALAS   CALAMARES   CORDONICES
PERCEBES   MEJILLONES   ALMEJAS   GAMBAS
LANGOSTINOS   BOQUERONES   VIEIRAS   CARABINEROS
CANGREJOS DEL RIO   ALBONDIGAS

"I don't know. It looks sort of, well, unsavory," Herb said, put off almost as much by the graffiti as by the restaurant's absence from Michelin.

Oxymoronic though it may have been, my reply was that I'd had a bellyful of his dithering, that I was starving, that every blessed goddamned restaurant in town looked unsavory to *him,* and that *he* could spend the rest of *his* afternoon in quest of some anemic bloody fucking maiden ladies' tea parlor, but, by God, I wasn't about to follow suit.

We entered and were led past a long bar arrayed with a stunning variety of cooked and raw shellfish, hanging hams, assorted sausages, and all manner of temptations I couldn't begin to identify. I wanted to belly up to that bar more than anything else in the world but decided not to push my luck; Herb, who tended to whinny in moments of nervousness, was acting more like a spooked horse than ever as we threaded our way through a boisterous crowd caught up in what appeared to be a feeding frenzy.

We were led through a doorway at the rear of the bar and seated in a handsomely appointed dining room populated almost exclusively by soigné males—*caballeros* of the sort who spend the better part of their mornings in the care of their barbers. The salient exception, a magnificent young woman, occupied the table nearest ours in the company of six or seven men. Her consort, a damnably aristocratic type who bore a striking resemblance to the film director and actor Vittorio De Sica, conducted a pro forma exploration of a shimmering thigh while he and the others studied their menus.

In such overwhelmingly macho company, any presentable woman would have attracted attention, but this was the most striking, most utterly female woman I'd ever seen: tall, sinuous, and tawny-skinned, with enormous almond eyes, the fine aquiline nose of an Aztec or Mayan princess (or so I imagined), and heavy black hair so glossy that it reflected glints of ambient color. Although her movements were languid, she emanated an electric, pantherine intensity that would impel any male fantasist to check his equipment. I took her to be a world-class fashion model, but she turned out to be a world-champion eater.

If there wasn't a superfluous ounce on the creature, it wasn't for lack of effort; she assaulted her lunch with the purposefulness of a chronically malnourished wolf, successively doing away with a dozen oysters, a tureen of fish soup, a platterful of infant squid, a hunk of beef the size of a brick, a copious helping of potatoes, a mess of dressed greens, and a mountain of wild strawberries mantled in a glacier of whipped cream. She destroyed a pound or so of bread along the way and helped herself liberally to her inamorato's sole, quail, asparagus, and artichokes. At the conclusion of this tour de force, she slithered up from her seat and took a bow of sorts before prowling off to the powder room: she bent over her companion, twined herself around him like so much kudzu, and hungrily nibbled his ear. Somehow, the auricle remained attached to his head.

After sizing up a pair of inexperienced *norteamericanos,* our waitress had unilaterally decided that a portion apiece of *sopa de pescados,* a shared paella, a small salad each, and some wild strawberries would be a more than adequate meal. It was.

After lunch, Herb and I agreed to meet early in the evening and then went our separate ways: he would conduct some scholarly research at a nearby university library while I conducted some research of my own at a succession of *tascas,* or pubs. Tapas, the small dishes served with drinks in such establishments, have enjoyed quite a vogue in the United States of late. At that time, though, they were known to very few Americans. As I had in the penny-candy stores of my tadpole years, I wanted to sample everything I saw in the *tascas,* and I damned near did. The variety seemed infinite, and the profusion of crustaceans in particular was dizzying.

Until then, my acquaintanceship with the order Decapoda had been restricted to *Homarus americanus* and *Callinectes sapidus*—the lobster and blue crab of America's eastern seaboard—and the generic shrimp served in rigor mortis at cocktail parties or, comparably overcooked and stiff, as "prawns" in chop suey parlors or "scampi" in spaghetti houses. In the *tascas,* I found myself stunned by a range of possibilities I hadn't dreamed existed. There were shrimp and prawns of perhaps two dozen distinct species, all served intact (I'd never seen whole shrimp, heads and all, at home), each variety differentiated by size, shape, and coloration. Their freshness was pristine (as was never the case in New York), and the flavor and texture of each sort—*gambas, cigalas, langostinos,* diminutive *quisquillas,* blood-red *carabineros,* flat-bodied *galleras,* or whatever—differed, however subtly, from the others.

Sated as I was, actually and vicariously, by lunch at Quo Vadis, I tried at least a bit of everything in sight, reveling in every morsel and in the *tasca* ethos, which dictated that stripped shells, sucked-out heads, and crumpled paper napkins be discarded directly onto the floor. Awash to my ankles in sea-wrack and paper whitecaps, I was happy as a clam in mud. I'd been introduced to a most exuberant way of eating that suited me right down to the littered ground: a style of gourmandise that couples the most casual sort of bonhomie with, at least for its adepts, connoisseurship of the highest order. The simple purity of shellfish tapas, like that of sashimi, is the form's glory and its great challenge. A squirt of lemon or a thin gloss of oil is about as elaborate as sauces get, with no masking of the principal ingredients and no culinary artifice. The *aficionado de mariscos* is content with nothing more or less than perfection. Unlike the French *bec fin,* he knows you don't fix what ain't broke; you just go for optimal quality, don't mess it up in any way, and don't ruin your enjoyment of it with any affected solemnity. Poor Herb, hunched over his early Renaissance texts, didn't know what he was missing, which was all to the good: he'd have gone into shock in most of the dives I visited.

Eventually, I found myself back on the Ramblas. More specifically, on the Rambla San Jose, spang in front of what remains my favorite food market anywhere the better part of three decades later. The Mercado de San Jose, also called the Boqueria, was then and remains the most compelling facility of its sort that I know of, except perhaps for one in downtown Bangkok.

Drifting from stall to stall beneath the market's vast peaked roof, I began to realize what I'd been absorbing piecemeal and without much awareness on market days in Arles: that there was a fundamental difference between American and southern European attitudes toward food and that most Americans, a generation or more removed from a farming, hunting, and fishing heritage, willfully and persistently kept themselves in ignorance of what they ate, while the southern Europeans faced up with no evasion to the hard facts of the matter. The contrast was underscored in the market by ubiquitous evidence of the Spanish genius for reconciling life and death. At home, the mass slaughter of edible species was effectively put out of mind. The food Americans ate was cosmeticized before it reached the point of sale. A shrimp, a chicken, or a block of frozen spinach was presented not as a deceased organism, but a tidy machined product that entailed as little confrontation as possible with reality on the part of the consumer. The geometry of a cryogenically preserved halibut was much the same as that of a loaf of sliced white bread or a package of processed cheese: as severely rectilinear and unrecognizably organic as mass-production technology could make it. (It was little wonder that Roger hadn't asked about death until he saw M. Trescent's chickens: he'd never seen a chicken identifiable as such in an American supermarket.)

In southern Europe, a dead chicken was incontrovertibly a dead chicken, and a stewing rabbit wasn't Bugs Bunny or a Beatrix Potter illustration, but a ghastly cadaver on an iron hook, its eyes starting from their lidless sockets, its flayed anatomy gruesomely explicit. The southern European confronts the issue head-on, respects what he's compelled to kill, and honors the beings that have died so he may live. He wastes nothing usable, and his meat is prepared with reverence and an understanding that enables the cook to realize its ultimate potential. However convivial the occasion, the consumption of his food is a sacrament and a communion.

The American pays no such obeisance to the dead; he's unaware that anything has been killed. As a consequence, he has little knowledge of or respect for his food. He's unconscionably profligate in its use, cooks it insensitively, and enjoys it only on the most primitive level, his very recent pretensions to epicureanism notwithstanding.

The Barcelona market amounted to a crash course in Spanish gastronomy and a demonstration of the easy, guiltless Spanish acceptance of life's brutality. It was a Monday, and a couple of butchers were doing a brisk business in *toro de lidia,* the meat of bulls killed in the preceding afternoon's corrida. Gwynne and I had been to our first bullfight that Sunday, at the Roman arena in Arles, and had witnessed the killings with an equanimity that surprised me. I had been more put off by the dragging of the carcasses from the ring than by the bloodletting itself, but now whatever misgivings I may have harbored were dispelled by the discovery that dead fighting bulls, unlike losing Roman gladiators and martyred Christians, were put to good, life-sustaining use once the show was over.

At one stall, a buxom country girl sat high above her wares on a crude wooden throne, negligently but deftly divesting live frogs of their hind legs, which she let plop by pairs into a huge glass jar. As she worked, she gazed blankly across the market with bovine placidity, not even deigning to glance at her squirming victims as her thick-wristed, starfish-fat hands groped for and dispatched them. She emanated an earthy, elemental sexuality so disturbing that I took refuge after a minute or two in the blandness of a dairy stall.

The expatriated Spanish restaurateur was then and remains the victim of a bum rap. Of the world's notable cuisines, his emigrates the least satisfactorily. In the United States, for example, neither of its chief glories, its seafoods and pork products, can be imported (practicably in one case, legally in the other), and the available substitutes just don't fill the bill. As a result, the Spanish cook on the wrong side of the Atlantic is forced to play with something like a thirty-six-card deck, lacking face cards and aces. Moreover, his language puts him in a double bind: for the overwhelming majority of Americans, Spanish is Spanish, and no distinctions are perceived among menus as dissimilar as those of the few reasonably authentic Spanish restaurants in operation and those of the far more numerous Mexican, Cuban, and other Latin establishments. Thus misperceived, the Spanish restaurant is expected to be as cheap as the taco parlor and *its* various New World–Hispanic counterparts. It usually is, with predictable results.

If my tour of Barcelona's *tascas* had quickly disabused me of some negative preconceptions based on disappointing experiences at home, the market demolished my remaining doubts. I suppose that had I ever given any thought to the matter, I'd have realized that some cheese must be eaten in Spain, but I hadn't, and the market's dairy stalls left me goggling at the abundance, variety, and quality of their cheeses. Along with an inexhaustible selection of imports from all over Europe, there were countless domestic varieties, many of them superb and most still unknown outside Spain today. There were cow's-milk cheeses like Mahón (from the Minorcan capital), *pasiego,* San Simón, *cebreiro,* León, and the distinctively cone-shaped *tetilla* (literally "nipple") of Galicia, which has been likened to an exceptionally fine Monterey Jack by the relative hand-ful of Americans who've tried it. There were sheep's-milk cheeses like *manchego,* fresh and smoked *queso de Burgos,* and the similar-tasting but differently shaped *pata de mulo* ("mule's hoof") of Valladolid; Roncal from the Pyrenees (a milder, less grainy cousin of parmesan); and *picon,* which at its best rivals the best of the Roqueforts.

The pork butchers' stalls were a high-voltage turn-on, with their subtle regional variations on the *chorizo* theme and their lumpy red *jabuquitos,* pink *salchichas de Cataluña,* pallid *butifarras,* pimento-flecked *sobrasadas de Mallorca,* purple-black *morcillas,* and sinewy, jaw-wearying *bisbes.* There was every conceivable type of bacon, including the long-aged *unto* deemed essential to a proper *caldo gallego,* and various interpretations of *cabeza,* or head cheese. Ser-rano hams were as ubiquitous as prosciutti around Parma. There was silky, truffle-spangled pâté de foie gras from France, mortadella and various salamis from Italy—just about everything that Euro-pean ingenuity has conceived and produced in the history of a genre that antedated Christianity by generations, if not centuries.

Above all, I was charged up by the market's *mariscos,* or shellfish. What I'd assumed had constituted an exhaustive study of the subject in the *tascas* turned out to have barely scratched the surface. There were bins filled to overflowing with *saladas* (small, almost psy-chedelically pink shrimp), *conchas* (chestnut-brown clams that probed the alien air with coral-red "tongues"), and *cacaolillos,* or periwinkles. At a stall presided over by a stout, matronly woman with a radiant smile were *caragulis* (another, even smaller type of winkle), *bigaros* (sea snails the size and shape of golf balls), and *escupinas.* Those last, reddish brown bivalves shaped and sized like cherrystone clams, were spitters, or so I gathered from their name, which I assumed derived from the verb *escupir,* "to spit." At another vendor's, there were thumbnail-size *tallinas,* whose shells ranged from gray-white through yellow-brown to lavender. Although I had no way of anticipating it at the time, these coquinas of the family Tellinidae would, at intervals over the years and in various locations, figure in several of the most memorable and one of the two most erotic meals of my life.

From Galicia, there were *vieiras,* the scallops whose shells symbolize the pilgrimage to Santiago de Compostela, and *percebes,* whose direct personal acquaintance I wasn't to make until years later in Madrid. At one stall, vendors hawked *centollos,* or *shangurros* (alternatively, *xangurros*), huge spider crabs that often weigh in at five pounds or more, and the smaller *nécoras,* whose population is conserved by breaking off a single claw-tipped leg (an esteemed delicacy in Cádiz), and returning the mutilated crustacean to its natural habitat, where the amputated member is eventually regenerated.

Dogging about from stall to stall, I cadged samples of everything that could be eaten out of my hand and on the spot. At one stand, an old woman offered wild strawberries for my inspection. Her entire stock, about two laboriously gathered liters, was displayed in a sturdy rustic basket. On impulse, I cleaned her out, basket and all, for a couple of dollars' worth of pesetas. The plan was to bring a taste of Spain back to St.-Hippolyte the following afternoon. Like a good many of my other plans involving food, it was to go somewhat awry.

With the berries stashed in our hotel room, Herb and I spent an hour or so in dumbstruck contemplation of Gaudí's Templo Expiatorio de la Sagrada Familia, which Gaudí's fellow Catalan Salvador Dalí (perhaps still hungry in 1933, when, before turning himself into a money machine, he extolled the architect's "tender doors of calf's liver") termed "comestible architecture." As the evening wore on, we drifted back to the Ramblas, had drinks at two or three outdoor cafés, and returned to Quo Vadis for dinner. Having found the restaurant more or less in conformity with his exacting hygienic standards, Herb wasn't about to risk breaking any new ground.

After a long afternoon of nonstop noshing, I wasn't the least bit hungry when we got to the restaurant, and the dinner menu generated about as much participatory enthusiasm as an IRS audit. Then, the words "filete de toro bravo" caught my eye, and the prospect of tasting the *toro de lidia* I'd seen in the market had a galvanizing effect on my appetency. "If you do not prefer your meat very rare, señor, you must order something else," the table captain stipulated. "The chef will not broil *filete de toro* any other way." Agreed.

As we waited for our steaks, a certain dead ringer for Vittorio De Sica strolled in, as enviably well groomed and self-possessed as he had been at lunch, accompanied by a stately matron about fifteen years and fifty-five pounds past what obviously had been a magnificent prime. Her frame was as elegantly wrought as that of the afternoon's pre-Columbian stunner, and her features, though less exotic than the matinee attraction's, were superb. The accumulated upholstery, however, was depressing: there, but for the fullness of time and 5,475 meals (not counting the customary Spanish elevenses, high tea, and afternoon and evening *tapas*) went an Aztec princess as lissome as an eel.

Our steaks turned out to be a more persuasive argument for tauromachy than all of Hemingway's pious cant. They were immense slabs of ineffable succulence that stood taller than they were wide: promontories of preternaturally tender beef looming over choppy seas of soufflé potatoes, their highlands lost in clouds of button mushrooms.

The next morning's train was packed, but I found what may have been the last available seat in a second-class compartment occupied by five of the most ruffianly types I've ever seen. The apparent ringleader, an *hombre* who glared at me with what I took to be undisguised menace as I squeezed into the place opposite him, immediately snatched a knife from his pocket, opened it, and muttered something incomprehensible. After a fleeting survey of his dirt-encrusted hands, gap-toothed leer, and five-day growth of stubble, I broke eye contact, feigning a consuming interest in the receding environs of Barcelona. A moment later, the knife was thrust at a point in the general vicinity of my Adam's apple—with a thick round of country sausage impaled on its point. My assassin swigged deeply from a bottle of homemade wine, solicitously wiped its top with a greasy sleeve, and passed it to me. Ten minutes later, full of wine and sausage but lacking six words of Spanish, I was swapping dirty jokes with my fellow travelers, to their apparent hilarity.

What was left of the sausage—as long as a man's arm when *mi amigo* cut the first few rounds off against his thumb—was confiscated at the French border, where we changed trains and I was separated from my buddies, who had turned out to be a crew of itinerant farm laborers. Thirty years later, I can taste both the silty wine and the rough, muscular sausage as vividly as I did then, and I've never tasted anything remotely like either since.

"You're a long way from home," I remarked to the big rawboned American Swede ahead of me in the customs line. He had heaved onto the inspection counter a wooden sea chest stenciled with his name, Andersen, and provenance, a town in South Dakota. After regarding me with unmistakable wariness, he replied that he had been reading Pierre Loti until I interrupted him. He waited for some sign of recognition from me. "Viaud spent time a long way from home, too," I said.

"Let's find seats together," Andersen said, as we changed trains. "I think we can talk." He was a merchant seaman, as it turned out—the master of a freighter then loading in Barcelona, and he was on his way to take in an opera in Marseille before sailing back to the States. He glanced at my basket of berries and produced a short length of rope. Looping it through the handle, he tied the basket to an overhead luggage rack above the seat opposite ours, which was occupied in turn by a prim-looking French blonde in her early twenties and a vulpine, balding, multilingual Italian about ten years older. Neither Andersen nor the Italian wasted time on preambles. Andersen, an autodidact with wide-ranging interests, launched into an impressive variety of esoterica, much of which I missed, as the Italian, a single-minded Lothario, hit on the blonde in three or four languages.

As the basket swayed over his head, Signore Libido embarked on a tentacular examination of his prey and a verbal adumbration of the privileges he was prepared to bestow on his newfound inamorata that very night, if she thought she could bear pleasuring of a sublimity light years beyond her wildest fantasies. (The target of his passion looked to me as though her wildest fantasies might center on a dependable wage earner who snored gently beside her in a flannel nightshirt after an evening of domestic tranquility.) He had just launched into a peroration involving a borrowed château on the outskirts of Nîmes, an abundance of petal-strewn satin bed-clothes, and ineffable ecstasies, when he was interrupted by an audible *plip!* A red droplet appeared on his sweaty brow and trick-led down into his eye. *Plip!* again: the strawberries were deliquesc-ing in the stifling heat of the compartment. In a commingling of accents, the chagrined Italian announced, "Sahmzing ees roh-ten in da stight of Denmarka."

Life went on at St.-Hippolyte, if seldom precisely as planned. Dur-ing the course of the summer, Mme. Orgeas nearly died of mortifi-cation when, after I persuaded her to take a Sunday drive with us to Les Baux, our left rear wheel, immediately above which she had settled her mountainous bulk, collapsed en route, as it tended to do in the best of circumstances. Selectively thinning her small flock of goats, Juliette Treillard had one slaughtered after a final milking, thereby providing us with chops and cheese from the same animal (and Roger with a rare loss of appetite), and persuaded me to ferry another to the foothills of the Alpilles in our car, from which the backseat was removed to accommodate the goat and which stank goatishly for months thereafter.

Thanks to the largesse of another temporary American house-guest, we experienced our first and only Michelin-ordained three-star restaurant, L'Oustau de Baumanière, where we were eaten alive by mosquitoes as we sipped aperitifs beside the pool, and where whatever *we* may have eaten, except for a sweetbread-filled vol-au-vent, escapes my memory. James Beard professed to remember every dish he had eaten during eight epicurean decades. My own gastronomic recall has been somewhat less complete. The meals I remember best during our stay in France were mostly modest, inherently unmemorable affairs: an abundantly cartilaginous *blanquette de veau* at an unprepossessing bistro in the town of Le Luc, roast quail, perfumed by a diet of mountain herbs, in a small inn at St.-Rémy, and a simple *omelette aux fines herbes* at Café Alcazar in Arles. The Alcazar had been the setting for van Gogh's celebrated painting *Café de Nuit* and had undergone some regrettable changes since its immortalization on canvas. Not only had absinthe, the drink of choice during Vincent's sojourn in the Midi, long since been outlawed, but the billiard table of the painting was gone, along with the lurid gaslit color scheme. And although the wall clock in the painting indicates a quarter past twelve, the place, like most places in town, no longer functioned much after dark. Still, the omelets were extraordinary.

During that same summer, Mickey Mantle and Roger Maris mounted their double-barreled assault on Babe Ruth's single-season home-run record, and it was in a café outside Orange, while tracking their progress in the *Trib,* that we learned of Ernest Hemingway's death. Although Hemingway had never been a particular literary idol of mine, he had personified American expatriation in France for me, and his demise seemed to signal the end of an era of which we were belated, marginal hangers-on. With the increasing accessibility of jet travel, the American abroad would soon become a recreational and vocational commonplace.

In the fullness of their season, we gorged on fresh figs, for which we contended with the few birds that escaped du Bellon's notice. (For reasons known to herself alone, Juliette Treillard disdained the produce of her own orchard, allowing us unlimited access to it in return for driving her to the northernmost part of the Crau, where she shamelessly harvested figs from another old woman's trees.) We continued to shop at the market in Arles on Wednesdays and Saturdays, usually breaking for lunch at La Cigale, and it was after one such Wednesday lunch that we returned home to find the women of St.-Hippolyte wailing in chorus. "Oh, *pauvre monsieur,*" Juliette keened, "something truly terrible has happened." Henriette Orgeas blubbered uncontrollably, and Mmes. Sasso and Dijol, along with Marie-Antoinette Treillard, gathered round us to offer their condolences.

Our first thought was of Mathieu, who had been left in the care of the grief-stricken Mme. Orgeas, but Mme. Sasso assured us that the calamity, whatever it was, had nothing "directly" to do with him. Well then, I demanded, what *was* it? More lamentation, but no explanation: no one could bring herself to broach news so dire. I appealed to Juliette, the community's self-appointed spokesperson, whose tears rolled down her nose to mingle with the perpetual droplet at its end. With a trembling hand, she extracted a crumpled envelope from beneath her shawl. Oh, poor monsieur, poor, *poor* monsieur, it was a . . . it was a . . . it was a *télégramme.* She handed the thing over as though it were my death warrant.

The women of St.-Hippolyte stood aghast as I danced a little jig after glancing at the message. "Hey! Look at this!" I cried, passing it along to Gwynne. It was a commission for some children's book illustrations—work that would keep us in food and wine for months.

I drove to Raphèle a few days before Christmas to order a turkey from M. Trescent, and I thoughtlessly specified a large bird. With the butcher's assurances that it would be ready for pickup early Christmas morning, I drove home with visions of a proper holiday dinner—one that would make up for the previous year's fiasco—dancing in my head. I realized later that I should have recognized an ill omen when we bought our tree in Arles the next morning: it was the last available tree in the market and the only two-dimensional Christmas tree I've ever seen. It was a single large bough that looked presentable enough when viewed frontally but took the configuration of a green pipe cleaner in profile. Still, M. Trescent was dependable and had never let us down.

As directed, I turned up at the butcher's early Christmas morning, to join a long line of what seemed like half the housewives in the district outside the door. The other half almost immediately fell in behind me. M. Trescent's window couldn't have looked more seasonally festive, tapestried as it was with pheasant, partridge, turkey, and other birds in full plumage.

The line moved slowly, and it was a good twenty-five minutes before I entered the shop. A beaming M. Trescent and I exchanged holiday greetings. After informing me—somewhat superfluously, I thought—that I had come for my Christmas turkey, the butcher strode across the floor of his shop, reached into the window, and extracted a resplendently feathered bird, which he thrust into my arms. *"Voilà, monsieur,"* he said, still beaming. Was it not a splendid bird?

It was indeed a splendid bird, I assured him—a truly magnificent bird. Arms folded across his chest, M. Trescent continued to beam. Arms folded around the turkey, I felt my own broad grin stiffening into an apprehensive rictus: somehow, I sensed, the transaction had come to a mutually unforeseen impasse. Perhaps, I ventured, monsieur would be good enough to prepare this truly magnificent bird for roasting, so as not to keep the ladies still waiting in line separated longer than was absolutely necessary from their loved ones on this most joyous of mornings.

An expression of profound distress transformed M. Trescent's features. He was of course desolated beyond recovery, but monsieur regrettably had neglected to inform him that the turkey was to be dressed. And much as he would normally desire to accommodate a distinguished patron, monsieur could of course appreciate that the presence outside the shop of so many ladies whose families awaited their return obviated the possibility of obliging him on this particular morning, a morning so steeped in ineluctable tradition and custom.

By the time I got the bird home and heaved it onto the kitchen table, it seemed to have taken on the dimensions of an emu. "Soon's I pluck it, we'll roast it," I announced, never having plucked anything more challenging than a splinter in my life. Seizing and tugging a handful of feathers, I stared in astonishment at a palm lacerated as though I'd grasped a cluster of straight razors. Three-quarters of an hour later, despite having resorted to a pair of heavy pliers, I had made fettucine in red sauce of my hands. More or less holding its own, the turkey was missing patches of hide here and there, but it was mostly fields of jagged stubble, which I supposed would burn off in the oven.

Our oven, to which I hadn't given a thought until I attempted to insert the bird therein, was nothing more than a wall-mounted tin box, roughly four feet off the floor and fueled with bottled gas. As it soon turned out, the volumetrics of the poultry exceeded the capacity of the oven by roughly 15 percent. Angling and repositioning the bird every which way, I couldn't squeeze it far enough into the intended receptacle to shut the top-hinged door. "Bugger won't go in," I panted, putting a shoulder to the turkey's recalcitrant pygidium. The bugger in question not only wouldn't go in—it wouldn't come out, either. It was jammed as immovably as a hippopotamus in a phone booth.

By applying the muddy sole of a heavy work boot to a stubbly avian rump (a maneuver that produced sounds of multiple fractures and assorted internal injuries), I managed to force the turkey into, and close the door on, the oven. Some three hours later, as local custom dictated, there was a knock on the kitchen door; the du Bellons had arrived *en famille* to exchange Christmas greetings and avail themselves of some liquid hospitality.

Oblivious to what had been a gradual fumatory buildup, I threw open the heavy wooden door, crying *"Joyeux Noël!"*

"My God, your house is burning down!" a hazy blue silhouette exclaimed, as opaque billows of smoke rolled out into the yard. "What's happening in here?"

"Just roasting our turkey."

"Just *what?*"

"Roasting our turkey."

One in one's right mind, I was informed as tactfully as possible, did not roast one's turkey. One conveyed one's turkey to either of Raphèle's two bakers, who roasted one's turkey, along with the community's geese and other turkeys, for one, in his bread oven. In sum, one did not incinerate oneself, one's family, one's cat, and one's house in a futile effort to replicate disinterested professionalism while flouting the simplest laws of physics and cookery.

An accomplished actor and a master of irony, du Bellon elevated his nose, pretending to inhale the aroma of our roasting bird. His bit of business was marred to a degree by some strangulated wheezing and coughing, but he managed to gasp, "I think your turkey is done." I thought so too but didn't relish the prospect of extracting the bird from its reeking crematorium while our neighbors looked on. Besides, I was none too confident of the bird's extractability.

Despite the threat of serious lung damage, du Bellon sat on, nursing his drink like a Socrates with a beaker of hemlock, determined to witness the turkey's emergence. After stalling as long as I could, I opened the oven door. The bird had shrunk enough to facilitate its removal from confinement. With an altogether carbonized quarter-inch crust, the thing was rigorously geometric: six blackened, hard-edged sides that in no way suggested a defunct biological organism. It might have been a block of anthracite or a slightly scaled-down Ka'ba.

Du Bellon's tree, of course, was fully dimensional and as resplendent as ours was lugubrious. His smoke-free house was indecently redolent of the fat, magnificent roast goose laid out in state on the dining-room table. I sipped his pastis morosely, slunk back to the disaster area with a hearty *"Bon appétit!"* ringing in my ears, and carved our turkey as best I could, lacking a chainsaw. What little unincinerated meat remained was inedibly desiccated. *Joyeux Noël.*

5

High off the Hog

Gwynne and I had married impulsively and irresponsibly, before we knew each other well enough to know we were mismatched—and before I knew myself well enough to recognize a little rotter who wasn't yet ready to make the commitment I'd pledged, to take on the full responsibilities of fatherhood, or even to hold down a regular job. We had four young sons, including twins, when I moved out, striving mightily to convince myself that I was the more injured of the badly lacerated parties, despite overwhelming evidence to the contrary.

For a time, we'd managed to persuade ourselves (but not our more perceptive friends) that it was a relatively happy, viable partnership, and perhaps it might have been had I not landed a salaried job. As a free-lance, I'd spent the half-dozen years of our marriage working in solitude, insulated from temptation. As a nine-to-fiver with a regular income and a modest expense account, I had access to women, to better restaurants than I previously could have afforded, to better booze and more of it than I was accustomed to. I was able to bib pedigreed French wines instead of carbolic Chilean Rieslings, rotgut putative Chiantis, and similar plonk. (Even in Provence, we had drunk nothing better than the unlabeled *vin du pays* included with our bistro meals or purchased at Juliette Treillard's ramshackle store.)

The extramarital affair that directly precipitated the breakup was the essence of seven-year-itch banality, although I hardly realized it at the time. In any event, it was more or less coterminous with the marriage itself, and I spent the following year in a blue, celibate funk, holed up in a scruffy midtown hotel room not far from my office. During that time, I was a book editor at American Heritage Publishing, which might more accurately have been named American Heritage Partying. With a preponderantly female editorial staff of some two hundred and fifty, most working days at Heritage were somebody's birthday and a good many of the somebodies were some bodies. Between the birthdays and the publication celebrations for books that rolled off an assembly line like burgers at a McDonald's, hardly an evening went by without an office party, and my self-imposed period of penance came to an end when I realized there was more consolation than just free booze to avail myself of when the evening's merriment commenced. For a few months, I pounced on just about anything that moved, impolitically including my boss's mistress. Then I met Curtis, who had been temporarily assigned to a project under my direction. She put an immediate and definitive end to my promiscuity.

When Don Allan's transfer to UNICEF's Beirut offices created the *Gourmet* opening, I chose Le Mistral as the subject of my trial review. I had never set foot in the place (or in any other New York restaurant of its caliber), but it was reputed to be one of the city's cathedrals of gourmandise and its name suggested southern French cooking, with which I was reasonably familiar.

Although it wasn't apparent at the time, the restaurant was poised on the brink of a disaster brought about a few years later by its proprietor's penchant for intramural lechery and extramural high living. Jean Larriaga, whose instinct for self-preservation was somewhat underdeveloped, considered any attractive female who ventured onto his premises fair game, thereby incurring the wrath and ultimate nonpatronage of the ladies' escorts. He ran with a pack of high rollers, including Frank Sinatra, that no prudent restaurateur had any business getting mixed up with, and he spent far too much time flinging hundred-dollar bills around in various nightclubs when he should have been minding the store. Nonetheless, Le Mistral was generally considered one of the city's class acts in the spring of 1972, when I sat down to dinner there for the first time and attempted to eat my way through the menu at one go.

Escargots à la bourguignonne, the dish on which I had come a cropper *chez* du Bellon some years earlier, is an idiot-proof preparation that in this country requires nothing more of a chef than reasonable proficiency with a can opener. My audition piece for *Gourmet* featured a rapturous testimonial to the incomparable quality of Le Mistral's snails, which were no better or worse than those served anywhere else in town, the humblest bistros included. In all innocence, I extolled the plumpness and flavor of precooked tinned gastropods that were no more corpulent or flavorful than any others I might have eaten anywhere in this country. (As I was later to learn, the adjective "plump" is a fixed epithet applied as automatically to snails by all hired bellies as "crusty" is to bread.) With no frame of reference to draw upon, I pronounced Le Mistral an outstanding restaurant of its class. So it happened to be, but I had no legitimate qualifications for judging it as such at the time, having ventured into what for me was more or less virgin territory. On such flimsy evidence, I was deemed a qualified *bec fin* and awarded one of the plummiest gigs in the food-writing game.

Bluffing my way through the first year or so on the beat, I gradually picked up enough experience to legitimize my pronouncements to some degree, but such is the credulousness of readers that even while I was engaged in on-the-job training it seldom occurred to anyone that I might not know what I was babbling about. I'd occasionally be taken to task by some scholar on an obscure point of fact, as when I confessed to total ignorance of a certain Chinese militarist, adding that for all I knew, the dish called General Tso's chicken wasn't named in the soldier's honor but as an aspersion on his courage. My judgment calls, though, were rarely challenged, and the feedback I got from the city's restaurateurs indicated that the magazine's readers considered my dubious opinions infallible and followed my recommendations to the letter. I was told repeatedly of readers who would enter a restaurant, wave away the menu, unfurl a copy of *Gourmet,* and order directly from my review of the place. If I mentioned some modest bottle of plonk, there would be a run on the stuff, to the occasional chagrin of restaurateurs who'd rather have had more attention paid to their pricier selections. Jacky Rouette, then the proprietor of La Petite Marmite, for example, threw up his hands and groaned when I turned up at his restaurant a few weeks after reviewing it. "Nobody has ordered anything but that wine since your write-up," he said. "I thought I had laid in a year's supply, but we're already out of stock."

If the disproportionate impact of favorable ink is somewhat alarming, it's at least understandable; presumably, readers are on the lookout for worthwhile experiences they may have missed. What's baffling, though, is the negative impact of negative reviews on previously well-patronized restaurants. Some years ago, Marian Burros, then the *Times* restaurant reviewer, gave a severe downgrading to the Coach House, a thitherto hallowed Greenwich Village institution that had been packed nightly since sometime during the early Neolithic era. The ink was hardly dry on the page before table reservations were canceled in carload lots, in many cases by regular customers who had dined happily at the restaurant for years. Business fell off by some 80 percent before the operation recovered its equilibrium. Why? What ovine element in human nature impels people to abandon their own convictions at the word of some putative authority anointed merely by access to print? My quibble isn't with the reviewer, whose subjective assessment may or may not have been fair; it's with her readers, who, as I wrote at the time, can be likened to people who fall out of love with their partners because a third party can't understand what they see in them.

The Coach House incident was neither unusual nor quite as damaging to the restaurant as it might have been. Many a flourishing operation has abruptly gone belly-up after a poor review, and fear of incurring the scorn of food writers who may or may not be qualified for their work is rampant among restaurant people. None-theless, supposedly responsible publications make reviewers of candidates with no discernible aptitude for the job and whose appointment in itself is perceived by most readers to be all the certification needed. In print, the blithering of any damned fool can be taken to the bank. Once a reviewer is ordained, it's *sum, ergo cogito.*

As a case in point, a contemporaneous hired belly during my early days on the circuit was the late John Canaday, a pseudonymous mystery novelist and longtime art critic for the *Times.* An estimable gentleman of the old school, he was somewhat out of phase with recent developments in his primary field of expertise and had been shunted to the paper's weekly restaurant-review section, to which he brought the palatal discrimination of a teenager. His idea of serious gastronomy was a plate of refried beans, and his knowledge of anything more sophisticated was spotty, to put it charitably. By all accounts, however, his readers were no less obedi-ent than any other mercenary eater's, and the city's restaurateurs considered his favorable notice money in the bank. To his credit, he was a pillar of ethicality in a field that has attracted more than its share of venal hustlers, and unlike most of his successors at the *Times,* he wrote with a sure grasp of syntax and grammar. Every-thing about him was trustworthy but his judgment, which was trusted unquestioningly by his readers.

It soon became apparent that publishing professionals were as credulous as lay readers when confronted with printed "evidence" of my presumed mastery of the subject of food and its public consumption. The imprimatur carelessly conferred on my stuff by *Gourmet* had made me an instant authority in the field, and I had hardly learned to tell a headwaiter from a busboy before I was commissioned to cobble up nothing less than a history of gas-tronomy for Newsweek Books. Having earlier tossed off a biogra-phy of Robert F. Kennedy in less than a week, I viewed the four months Newsweek allotted me for a survey of eating from prehis-toric times to the present as a piece of cake. All things considered, it turned out to be a pretty good book; given another four or five days, I might have turned out a classic.

Once again, ink begat ink: as a published food historian, I was solicited to contribute articles to a couple of encyclopedias and to various magazines that didn't compete with *Gourmet.*

The perks attached to the hired belly's trade are many and varied. Curtis, who shared my tables and other furniture after my breakup with Gwynne, was my regular dining companion, but she often had business of her own to transact during lunch and dinner. In her absence, I found it startlingly easy to date attractive stand-ins who wouldn't have given me the time of day had I been in any other line of work. As it happened, my life with Curtis was contentedly monogamous, but several of my tablemates made it clear that our evenings didn't necessarily have to end with dessert and coffee, and there wasn't a headwaiter in town who wouldn't have bet his life that I was bedding the various members of what generally came to be known as my harem. When I showed up for the third time in a week at one Upper East Side citadel of haute cuisine with a third different female in tow—a traffic-stopping fashion model—one peripatetic carpet prowler who had observed my comings and goings in half a dozen of his previous places of employment shot me a sotto voce "Jesus, how do you *do* it?"

The plain fact was that the evening's stunner and I not only never had sex together but never even had a conversation. After an entrance that left every other male in sight slack-jawed with disbelief (What's a little creep like that doing with something like *this* on his arm?), I discovered, as did my consort, that we lacked a common language. My casual mention of anything that antedated the mid-1960s, when she had been an eighth or ninth grader, was as incomprehensible to her as matters of import to her generation were to me.

From the reader mail and word-of-mouth feedback I was getting, it was obvious that my constituency had conjured up an image of me that deviated somewhat from reality. As Zanne Early Zakroff, who heads up *Gourmet*'s food department, remarked at lunch one day, many of the people she came into casual contact with took it for granted that, despite what they envisioned as my gross corpulence, I somehow was managing to sleep, just as assiduously as I ate, around. As one of her acquaintances had put it the previous evening, "That guy must be enormous. Does he screw all those women he takes to dinner?"

Although not precisely typecast for the part (I'm about the size of your average jockey and no more than eight or ten pounds heavier), I did nothing to disabuse anyone of the notion that I was some sort of James Bond in the body of a James Beard. If my readers preferred to visualize a 120-odd-pound monogamous nerd as a hugely edacious seducer of scores of glamorous tablemates, I neither confirmed nor denied their fantasies in print. Most of my dinner dates *were* desirable, sophisticated, witty women, and I implied as much in my reviews. Although *Gourmet* cultivated a well-heeled, well-traveled, restaurant-savvy readership, the magazine was also read by a significant number of middle-income boondocks-marooned armchair travelers and vicarious big-city diners out. I did my best to extend the hospitality of my table to them all, to draw them into the totality of the restaurant experience, to allow them to share the companionship of my actual dining companions and our table conversation, which was by no means limited to what was eaten and drunk.

One of the hired bellies of the late 1970s and early 1980s was a woman whose weekly newspaper reviews read as though she marched militantly into every restaurant she covered, tied on the evening's feed bag, and never looked up from her table. After the most perfunctory survey of her surroundings and the service, she would get down to business: a single-minded descriptive evaluation of the grub, munching her way through the menu, dish by dish, relentlessly. Although she employed the editorial (or papal) we, the impression was inescapable that she snaffled her comestibles in solitary splendor and grim silence. She was a professed consumer advocate who had acceded to her post with the declaration that she had no intention of wasting her own or her readers' time on restaurants of no consequence and then proceeded to bash any number of harmless little establishments, many of them essential to specific ethnic or neighborhood communities, putting several out of business in the process.

Mistakenly or not, I considered the quality of a restaurant's food just one factor in a complex equation in which atmosphere, character, panache, and a number of other intangibles came into play. Dining out is not merely a matter of feeding one's face, and anyone who thinks it is is in for a bad time, no matter where the provender is ingested or how well it's prepared. For the tunnel-vision feeder, however developed his palate may be, *any* restaurant and *any* meal might as well be the lugubrious setting and sustenance depicted in van Gogh's *Potato Eaters* or Picasso's *Frugal Repast.* Much of what's derived from dining out depends on what the diner brings to the experience. However adroit the restaurateur, chef, and service may be, however pleasant the setting and attractive the clientele, the whole enterprise can succeed only for those who check their aggressiveness, along with their coats, before being seated and who bring more than just an alimentary canal and a credit card to the table. No matter how prestigious the restaurant and how haute the cuisine, a dinner regarded with the hushed, joyless solemnity of a requiem Mass will not be a good dinner, and the restaurant writer who thinks it will be is in the wrong line of work.

Although I played out the charade of reserving tables in the names of lunch and dinner dates (usually to hear myself addressed throughout my meals by their surnames), it was mostly a ploy for keeping overattentive dining-room personnel at bay. In theory, the hired belly who turns up under an assumed name, or ostentatiously hides under a hat the size of a beach umbrella, does so in order to avoid preferential treatment and be served just as any other customer would be. The reasoning is somewhat specious. A third-rate chef can't be transformed into a latter-day Escoffier at the bidding of an owner or maître d' who has recognized the fat lady in the big hat, and Escoffier himself couldn't have rejuvenated a shipment of rank fish because a known food writer happened to order a portion. Service can be more attentive, to be sure, but that usually entails the obvious neglect of other patrons and works counterproductively to the management's purposes. The writer who is spotted on arrival and finds flunkies flapping around his table like gulls around a mackerel trawler has only to observe the other tables in the room, abruptly deserted by their designated servitors, to form an accurate, negative impression of how "any other customer" is treated. Moreover, the unwanted attention will probably add another demerit or two to the report of a reviewer whose punchlines have been repeatedly stepped on by garrulously solicitous waiters and who has been forced a dozen times to articulate an answer (usually with a full mouth) to "Is everything all right?"

Matters can, and often do, get out of hand when a mercenary eater is recognized. In the normal course of events, however, restaurants are not operated and staffed by faceless zombies or fawning imbeciles, but by hard-working, mostly dedicated, often uncommonly intelligent human beings whose considerable experience of life more than offsets the general sketchiness of their formal education. Most European-born representatives of the breed are multilingual cosmopolites, and many of today's younger American-born owners and chefs have traveled and trained extensively abroad. With occasional exceptions, their acquaintanceship is well worth cultivating, and the restaurant-goer, professional or not, who neglects to establish rapport with them puts himself in the same awkward, ultimately detrimental fix as the partygoer who fails to acquaint himself with the hosts.

As a matter of policy, I always made myself known to the management once I was satisfied that a restaurant merited coverage, made a point of sitting down for a talk with the principals, and passed along whatever information about them I thought might be of use or interest to my readers. I held no copyright on the tactic; two or three colleagues on other publications used it, and my impression is that it served them and their readers far better than did the adversarial posture of the lady in the big hat and her ilk.

(Had she troubled to strike up a conversation with one restaurateur, she might not have castigated his establishment for preparing a gazpacho with white grapes "of all things," thereby imputing culinary heresy to an authentic reading of a Málagan classic.)

It was common knowledge in the restaurant world that some hired bellies could be bought. It was generally agreed that Craig Claiborne and John Canaday (both by then no longer covering the beat) were salient exceptions, but that many others weren't above having their palms greased or otherwise being taken care of. Indeed, so widespread was the assumption that every restaurant writer was on the take that some of the smaller restaurateurs reflexively grew wary when informed that their places were slated for review. Even Nina Migliacco, Irès's successor at my old haunt Tout Va Bien, quailed visibly at what I assumed she'd consider good news. "Jay, how much is this going to cost me?" she asked when I brought her the glad tidings.

Twice, I wasn't asked but told what coverage would cost an establishment. The first time, I received a phone call from an acquaintance who was handling public relations for a midtown Chinese restaurant. The place was reopening after a change of management, and I was invited to a celebratory bash there on the eve of resumption of business. Buttonholed by the PR man the moment I arrived, I spent half an hour chatting with him. The place was packed with some fairly cloutwieldy citizens, to whom he paid almost no attention, which struck me as unnatural behavior for a guy in his line of work. Finally he asked whether we could talk. I replied that I thought we had *been* talking. Yes, I was informed, but not talking turkey. I was led to an unpopulated private dining room, where a fat white envelope lay on an otherwise bare table. "Jay, the owners would like a review in *Gourmet.*"

"Yes, and so would the owners of every other restaurant in town. I'll come in and try the place after it's had time to shake down. If I think it's worth a review, they'll get a review."

My man was clearly taken aback by my obtuseness. "Jesus," he said, "don't you understand?"

"What's to understand? The owners want a review."

"Jay—that envelope. That envelope's for *you*. There's five thousand cash in it."

"Thanks for the drinks," I said. "See you around."

"Wait!" he called after me. "Maybe they'll go a little higher."

Some months later, I had several first-rate meals at the place and reviewed it with genuine enthusiasm. A case of cheap wine turned up at my apartment a few days after the piece was published. By my calculation, my uncompromising stand had saved the owners four thousand nine hundred and seventy-some bucks.

Another payoff in the same amount was offered to me by an Upper East Side Italian venture a few years later, again through an intermediary. The would-be conduit in this case was a longtime friend, a woman I'd met years before I became a hired belly and before she had a brief, disillusioning fling as a restaurateur. Gently turned down, she proceeded to tell me the facts of life as she had learned them from some of my colleagues. She had a sordid story to tell, involving one prominent restaurant writer's rating scale: three to five thousand, depending on the warmth of the published praise, payable in advance to the reviewer's spouse, who might waive some of the payment in return for the sexual favors of a kitchen scullion of the same gender. Except for the erotic proviso, the story was later corroborated in all its particulars by a number of restaurateurs in whom I had complete confidence.

Spurning bribes was no safeguard against imputations of venality—or so I discovered when an anonymous charge was mailed to Alexander Liberman not long after he became *Gourmet*'s nominal editorial director after its sale to the Condé Nast publishing conglomerate in 1984. The allegations were relayed to Jane Montant, who confronted me with them. The writer was, or professed to be, a restaurateur whose establishment I had pointedly ignored (according to him) year after year, although he and his clientele considered it the equal of, or better than, dozens of similar places I had reviewed. In confabulation with a number of his colleagues, he had learned (he claimed) that I covered restaurants only in exchange for "cash or large-breasted women."

Perhaps naively, I believed that my prompt disclosure to the magazine's executive editor of the two overt attempts to buy my ink had established my journalistic ethicality, but I'd neglected to take into account Jane Montant's ready acceptance of hearsay as proof positive. The matter came down to my word against an anonymous libeler's "they say." The mere fact that neither the corporate editorial director nor the editor of the magazine summarily disposed of an unsigned accusation wasn't encouraging.

Offers of outright payola and various quid pro quo arrangements were easy enough to deal with, but an assortment of fringe perks was more problematic. For me, they constituted a gray area in which sensibilities could easily be offended and called for a degree of perhaps compromising diplomacy to be exercised on a case-by-case basis. With very few exceptions, the temptations were either proffered or delivered after the fact by either of two ethnic groups of restaurateurs—the French and the Italians. The French were easier to deal with by far. Aside from the odd, unsolicited case of wine delivered as a token of appreciation for a beneficial review and too cumbersome to return, most French restaurateurs issued a vague pro forma invitation to return for dinner on the house at some unspecified time, an invitation about as sincere as the three-piece-suiter's let's-have-lunch brush-off. The Italians, on the other hand, almost unfailingly tried to express their gratitude in more tangible and more heartfelt form and clearly would have been offended had their overtures been spurned.

On a tip from Jean Larriaga of Le Mistral ("There is only one Italian restaurant worth going to in this city"), I had investigated and enjoyed a certain family-owned Neapolitan establishment in Midtown. It was a hangout of movers and shakers, with a fair proportion of reputed Cosa Nostra luminaries scattered among world-class entertainers, media superstars, corporate heavy hitters, and international political headliners. After a succession of anonymous visits, I introduced myself to the proprietors, interviewed them over lunch, and batted out a highly favorable review. A few days after its appearance, I received a handwritten note from one of the owners. "Dear Jay," it began, "I hope you don't mind my using your first name, but we now consider you a member of the family. If there is ever anything—ANYTHING [underscored three times by a pencil that had torn through the paper]—we can do for you, just let us know." I spent a few delicious days drawing up lists of people who had seriously bugged me in one way or another over the years. It was an offer I almost couldn't refuse.

Regretfully, I soon found myself avoiding favorite establishments that I would have liked to patronize in a nonprofessional capacity. In effect, I was eighty-sixed from them by my own published prose and by various restaurateurs' subsequent refusals to accept payment for my meals. However well intended, a headwaiter's discreetly murmured "There is no check" amounted to self-imposed future banishment for me, and the number of restaurants to which I couldn't return as a paying civilian expanded inexorably at a rate of three each month. After a couple of years on the job, I was effectively barred from all the best places in town.

Subterfuge cut no ice. Mendacious advance notice that a table reservation was being made for business purposes, that the meal would be an expense-account write-off, and that a check was expected at its conclusion almost invariably resulted in the nonpresentation of a tab and a lot of unavailing protest. Even on the rare occasions when my plastic was picked up, I'd be informed on the way out of the restaurant (usually with a conspiratorial wink) that all evidence of payment had been destroyed and that I could thereby be reimbursed for a lavish meal on which I hadn't spent a dime, cash tips excepted. I was being paid to gluttonize by the magazine. If the restaurateurs had had their way, I would have been paid by them to gluttonize on my free time. Ruefully, I stopped taking my extracurricular dinner dates to Lutèce, Le Cirque, and most of the city's other showcases of chic. My assurances that this or that obscure ethnic hole in the wall, with its garlic reek, thread-bare napery, and Upper West Side Koren-cartoon clientele, was the momentary locus of the town's hottest action were not warmly received by prospective tablemates.

Delusionally or not, I was convinced that acceptance of the odd free meal or case of wine or the like could in no way affect the probity of my restaurant evaluations. Whenever practicable, I avoided whatever dubious goodies were proffered. In the interests of simple tact, however, I was none too rigorous about spurning a drink or a dinner or some other token of gratitude: an elaborately framed engraving, after Gérôme (a painter I've always despised), of Caesar being hailed by gladiators in the Colosseum; a set of bed linens more appropriate to an Alpine chalet than a Manhattan apartment; a battery-operated Japanese letter opener that defied all attempts at identification for a month and a half and was put to use just once, a dozen years ago, when its function was finally determined.

If I felt mildly queasy as the recipient of the restaurateurs' unwanted largess, a good many other foodies didn't. Wine and booze addressed to me at the magazine's offices was routinely forwarded to my digs by editors who apparently saw nothing questionable about receiving baksheesh once editorial coverage was a *fait accompli.* Other hired bellies not only accepted miscellaneous gifts and free feeds without even a token show of resistance, but viewed them as an inalienable right to be exercised in perpetuity.

The owners of one big-ticket Italian restaurant on the Upper East Side had their premises invaded, year after year, by two of these parasites. One was a marginal nonentity whose review of the place "never brought in a single goddamn customer" according to one of the owners, but who regularly regaled parties of six or eight there without once going through the motions of attempted payment. The second of these vultures, who commands a considerable national readership and whose ink has undeniably generated some business at the restaurant, would drop in every few weeks, order the best of everything for his several tablemates, and not only disdain a pro forma request for the tab but saunter out at the meal's end, leaving a crew of stiffed waiters in his wake.

The place in question has been a haunt of mine almost since the day it opened a decade ago, and I haven't been allowed to spend a penny there since the end of my tenure with *Gourmet*. Periodically, one of the owners joins me at the bar, often to fulminate about the pair of freeloading albatrosses hung round his neck. "Those sons of bitches have been taking advantage of us for years," the man I'll call Franco will say. "I wanted to cut the bastards off five, six years ago, but my wife overruled me. Now, goddamnit, the next time one of them comes in, he's going to get a check and pay it. And if I never see him again, good riddance."

"But Franco, you haven't let me pay for a single drink in three years."

"With you, it's different. You always paid until *we* decided not to take your money. Besides, your write-up *made* this restaurant. You've paid us thousands of times over for your few lousy drinks."

I'm in disagreement with Franco on a few points. I didn't always pay (although I always tried to) before being put on the comp list; I don't believe any review, however laudatory or widely read, contributes significantly to the long-term success of any restaurant; and my drinks have been neither few nor lousy, but innumerable and expertly mixed.

In general, restaurant owners stoically suffer the impositions of journalistic cadgers out of fear of published retribution or, at best, noncoverage. Occasionally, however, one will get his back up. Some years ago, Michael "Buzzy" O'Keefe, the proprietor of The Water Club, flatly refused to serve Mimi Sheraton, then the *Times*'s mercenary eater, and Harry Cipriani barred the doors of his second Manhattan venture, Bellini By Cipriani, to one of Sheraton's successors, Bryan Miller, after Miller had made his displeasure with another of Cipriani's restaurants a matter of public record.

More recently, Joseph Scognamillo, the co-owner of Patsy's, was sufficiently steamed by a negative Miller review to buy a full page in the *Times* and turn a number of his regular patrons loose on the journalist. The restaurant has been a haunt of major celebrities and assorted power brokers since the 1940s, with evidence thereof, in the form of autographed eight-by-ten glossies, prominently displayed on the walls. In his review, Miller had expressed open skepticism about the legitimacy of the display while committing several errors of simple fact and generally giving the kitchen the back of his hand. In rebuttal, Frank Sinatra, Burt Lancaster, and a clutch of corporate heavy hitters aired their contempt for the reviewer in a flurry of letters to the editors of the *Times,* the owners of the restaurant, and Miller himself. The collective howl of protest failed to dislodge Miller from his post (as Scognamillo had confidently predicted it would), but industry scuttlebutt had it that the *Times* thereafter kept him on a much tighter rein.

To the best of my knowledge, the most audacious attempt by a restaurateur to settle the score with a hired belly was initiated by Frank Valenza, whose shockingly pricey restaurant, The Palace, became a cause célèbre during the mid-1970s. Valenza, an actor manqué, was considered a somewhat loose cannon in restaurant circles, and the project he outlined to me one evening certainly seemed to confirm the widespread notion that he harbored suicidal tendencies. After phoning for an appointment, he turned up at my pad armed with a tape recorder and asked what I knew about bribe taking by restaurant writers.

At that time, I didn't know much. I told him about the two unsuccessful attempts to buy my coverage, adding that I assumed other writers had been offered similar inducements and that I'd often heard that at least two influential reviewers were or had been on the take, but that I had no hard evidence of consummated cash payoffs. "Well, I *have,*" Valenza crowed, "and I'm working on a book that'll get one corrupt bitch off our backs once and for all." He refused to name the corrupt bitch in question and took his leave when it became apparent that I had little fuel to add to his fire.

Some years later, when I began work on this book, I called Valenza to inquire about the progress of his exposé. "I had to drop it," he replied. "The bitch stopped reviewing restaurants." By then, the identity of Valenza's target was clear. While she was active on the local journalistic scene, her stuff had exerted more immediate impact on the city's restaurants than any other writer's. I've described her modus operandi earlier in this chapter. I regret her departure from the scene only because it deprived Frank Valenza of his chance to make real waves in a small puddle. As he put it, "Who wants to read about someone who's no longer reviewing restaurants?" I find his rhetorical question somewhat unsettling as I set these lines down.

Of the perquisites that come with the food writer's territory, some are decidedly dubious, and some of the more desirable benefits are more than offset by concomitant social disadvantages. After a prolonged succession of restaurant meals, the body and mind cry out for surcease in the form of a relaxed home-cooked dinner, the more unpretentious the better. The certified *bec fin* soon discovers, however, that unless he cooks it himself, no such dinner will be forthcoming. His perceived lofty gastronomic standards effectively exclude him from the dinner parties, however casual, of those who flock all too eagerly to *his* table. "I wouldn't dare cook for you" becomes a doleful refrain, repeated ad nauseam, by friends with whom the hired belly would be only too happy to eat a scorched greaseburger after weeks of indulgence in engorged goose livers, arterially congestive sauces, and excessively perfumed delicacies.

The many dinners to which he *is* invited are just what he longs to avoid on an evening off: uptight restaurant functions (as often as not, constrictive black-tie solemnities at which there is no chance of getting an honest-to-God drink, putting one's elbows on the table, or talking baseball); insufferably pretentious wine tastings; fulsome testimonials to the culinary prowess of some fatuous chefly jackanapes whose sainted *mère* would be outraged by the pretty pictures he paints on a plate.

Of the readily available perks, the most desirable by far was the opportunity for subsidized travel. The many junkets that came my way not only amounted to paid vacations, but could often be converted to significant supplementary income as a result of the travel articles I was able to base on them. Moreover, I soon discovered that a modicum of proficiency with an idiot-proof camera could augment my earnings considerably if I illustrated my pieces with my own photographs.

Of course, the sponsors of any press junket expected some return on their investment: to wit, quantities of ink favorable enough to impel paying customers to follow in the footsteps of the freeloaders. The trips were usually paid for by publicly financed promoters of regional tourism, chambers of commerce, or the like, occasionally by commercial consortiums, with the collaboration of the appropriate national airline. Now and then, an independent operation—a distillery, winery, hotel, or restaurant—would offer to foot the bill, but I avoided any quid pro quo entanglements with producers and suppliers of specific goods or services. For that matter, I made no advance commitments to any sponsoring group with a vested interest in press coverage, and almost none of my junketing resulted in any sort of immediate payback. Over the years (often long after the fact) I'd lace my stuff with references to my travel experiences when I thought they'd shed some light on matters at hand, but such piecemeal coverage, whatever its cumulative impact may have been, wasn't precisely what the organizers had in mind when the invitations were extended.

There seems to have been no commonly held standard of travel-related ethicality among the magazines I dealt with. Some wouldn't allow a writer's expenses to be paid by anyone but the magazine itself. Others subsidized most travel assignments but allowed their correspondents to make arrangements of their own on an ad hoc basis. Still others routinely arranged to have all tabs picked up by interested third parties, sometimes without the writer's advance knowledge. One such publication sent me off to Spain a few years ago, ostensibly to write a generic piece on the Rioja wine country. It wasn't until I arrived there that it became glaringly obvious that a particular winery was paying all the bills and expected exclusive, laudatory coverage. Fortunately, the winery in question was one of the region's finest, and I was able to give it a fair proportion of ink with a reasonably clear conscience. Not long thereafter, the same magazine proposed that I write travel pieces on Hong Kong (with which I was fairly familiar) and Singapore (where I'd never set foot). Again, there was no indication that the trip would be paid for by anyone but the magazine itself or that I was expected to shill for any specific enterprises. It didn't become apparent until the eve of my scheduled departure that a couple of hotels would be paying the freight and were not in the business of dispensing free lunches. I didn't take the trip and haven't heard from the magazine since.

"A Gastronomic Tour of Tuscany," my first overseas freebie, had been organized by a marginal press agent of the old school, a broken-down boozer whose acquaintanceship with fine Italian dining was roughly paralleled by my knowledge of quantum mechanics. The eclectic cast of characters he had assembled for the trip included Joe DiMaggio; Sebastian Leone, then the Brooklyn borough president, and his wife; a number of the organizer's longtime drinking buddies; a stupefyingly gorgeous young woman of noble Russian extraction who had something to do with the importation of Italian marble into the United States; and Curtis and myself. It was one of the most congenial groups I've ever traveled with, and the trip was the most well-organized I've ever taken.

We forgathered in a VIP lounge at Kennedy Airport, where DiMaggio held himself somewhat aloof from the assembled company, looking to me like a colossus excised from Mount Rushmore. Although not otherwise much impressed by celebrities, I've been a devout baseball buff since early tadpolehood. Seen up close, DiMaggio seemed about forty times larger than life: an immense, room-filling presence, a legend in the flesh. And that, as it turned out during the next week, was precisely the way he saw himself. Joltin' Joe had just one topic of conversation, on which he was the world's supreme authority. He was the living archive of his own diamond exploits, and his recall of his superlative thirteen-year tenure with the New York Yankees during the club's second dynasty was total, down to the precise location, velocity, and trajectory of every pitch he'd ever seen. He'd been the best in his time at what he did, had married the object of Everyman's fantasies, had become the curator of a historic relic. In Tuscany, he was immediately recognized and lionized—but only as a former spouse of Marilyn Monroe. Wherever we went, women flung themselves at him. He brushed them off with godlike disinterest. He drank nothing stronger than mineral water and ate sparingly and austerely while his traveling companions swilled and gorged. Imprisoned in his own legend, determined not to betray an iota of tarnish or clay-footedness, comfortable only talking baseball with his male fellow travelers, he seemed the loneliest man I've ever known.

If any female on earth could have penetrated DiMaggio's reserve, I'd have bet on the young woman I'll call Natasha, who was not only a sheer physical wonderment, but an immensely worldly creature of uncommon intelligence and wit. At breakfast in Florence one morning, she confided to Curtis and me that her project for that evening was the seduction of the Yankee Clipper. Over orange juice the next morning, Curtis asked a somewhat shaken Natasha how the previous evening had gone. "I struck out," she replied.

As our mixed bag ate and drank its way through Tuscany, my notions of gastronomic finesse underwent considerable alteration. I had eaten in the region some years earlier, but not as extensively or purposefully and with a lack of appreciation imposed by my ignorance of the underlying logic of one of the world's most elegant regional cuisines. As an article of faith, I'd always taken French food to be incomparably better than any other that Western civilization had to offer, but that faith was badly shaken by the purity and naturalness of Tuscan cookery, which contrasted strikingly with the muddled excesses, obfuscations, and illogic of northern French cuisine in general and haute cuisine in particular. Superb culinary technicians though they may be, the French, I began to realize, don't have much respect for what they cook and eat. Metaphorically considered, their dishes are larded with adjectives and adverbs, whereas the Tuscans make do with the noun and the verb. Wherever possible, the French have traditionally gilded the lily, altering the textures, flavors, appearance, and aromas of their primary ingredients, pureeing whatever they were too lazy to chew, smothering delicate seafoods in cow-derived sauces, debasing the essential character of whatever they put in their mouths. The first concern of any French cook—especially any professional chef—is with mutation: What can I do with this thing that will make something else of it? Except in a few enclaves of Austro-Hungarian influence, the first concern of any Italian cook—and Tuscan cooks in particular—is the uncompromising preservation of a primary ingredient's integrity: What is the least I can do to this food in the course of preparing it for the table?

Writing on the cookery of his native France in his book *The French,* Sanche de Gramont (now anagrammatically Ted Morgan) refers to the "urge to refine the physical world," conceding that "the danger is overrefinement, yew trees tortured into fanciful shapes, elderly ladies drenched in Arpège, and recipes that call attention to their own cleverness." The Tuscan cook harbors no such urge and stands in no such danger. His respect for the innate goodness of natural ingredients of the highest quality obviates the possibility of abusing them with excessive artifice. He views the physical world as a state of ultimate refinement to which human cleverness has nothing to add, and he honors the palatal perspicacity of those who sit at his table when he serves them the season's earliest fava beans raw and in the shell. The French made a feeble attempt to amend their culinary ways during the heyday of the so-called *nouvelle cuisine*—a cuisine the Tuscans had anticipated in all its essentials at least as long ago as the dawn of the Renaissance.

I've never much cottoned to *crostini alla fiorentina,* the chicken-liver canapés served throughout much of Tuscany as an accompaniment to aperitifs or as a sit-down antipasto. (When James Beard confided to me in the last year of his life that he no longer had a taste for chicken livers, I wondered what had taken him so long.)

We had our share and more of these *crostini* throughout Tuscany, but otherwise we ate better than I've eaten on any subsequent food writers' junket. In general, such trips are designed to showcase a particular region's emblematic dishes, which various individual restaurateurs serve meal after meal, ad infinitum and ad nauseam. Until I recently spent a week touring the Istrian Peninsula, for example, *jota* was a dish I'd thought I could never get enough of. A full-bodied, stick-to-the-ribs Slavo-Italian soup of dried beans, potatoes, sauerkraut, and pork scraps, *jota* is vaunted from Trieste down to Pula, near the southwestern tip of Istria, as a surefire hangover antidote. Blessedly immune to hangovers (not from lack of effort), I had been introduced and become addicted to the soup in the early 1970s, at Giordano, a West Side Manhattan restaurant run by transplanted Istrian siblings. I had learned to cook up a fairly creditable version of the dish, which improves from day to day with refrigerator storage, and I usually had a batch on hand for all occasions. I'd never experienced the stuff in its region of origin, though, and looked forward, as we crossed the border between Italy and northwestern Yugoslavia, to unlimited indulgence in *jota* in its definitive, homegrown form. Something like fourteen copious helpings of *jota* later, I never wanted to see a bowl of it again, and it wasn't until I was back home for at least a week that I was able to cook up another potful of the stuff.

The ubiquitous *crostini alla fiorentina* excepted, our meals in Tuscany were superbly orchestrated, with no redundancies from one to another. Years after the fact, specific dishes stand out with startling clarity: a sweet, docile, deceptively lamblike roast filet of Chianina beef delicately perfumed with wild rosemary; a splendorous panoply of infant *frutti di mare* at a Tyrrhenian fishing port; a quintessential reading of *pappardelle alla salsa di lepre* at La Cisterna, a small hotel-restaurant in the haunting medieval hill town of San Gimignano, once a mighty Renaissance power and now a somnolent relic of a long-forgotten power struggle that viciously pitted Guelphs against Ghibellines, leaving a few poignant frescoes and truncated towers to be remembered by. As we overlooked the local vineyards basking in the honeyed sunlight from the dining room of La Cisterna, we drank the previous year's Vernaccia, a liquefaction of the air we breathed. Joe DiMaggio, ulcerated as a result of the stresses of his famous fifty-six-game hitting streak, stuck to his customary mineral water and pushed his food around his plate.

6

Egg
on My
Face

The persona I tried to project, in print and at table, was that of the suave, cultivated man-about-town, the embodiment of savoir-faire. Image and reality were somewhat at odds, however, and my propensity for gaffes of one sort or another was in no way ameliorated by a couple of minor physical disorders that cropped up periodically and easily could be mistaken for breaches of decorum.

I had contracted malaria while stationed in India, a mild case that originally laid me up for just a few days but that resurfaces from time to time as bouts of extreme dizziness, ghastly pallor, and profuse sweating, occasionally culminating in a complete swoon. The attacks are infrequent and last no longer than ten minutes or so, but for some reason they invariably take place in theaters or restaurants, never in private. The affliction democratically draws no distinctions between good and bad restaurants, modest and grand establishments, or one cuisine and another. At various times, it has struck in a Spanish restaurant in Barcelona, an Italian restaurant in Milan, and in Greek, French, Chinese, Italian, and American restaurants in New York.

Not long after landing the *Gourmet* gig, I took a party of four to Molfeta's, a cheap, nondescript Greek place on the West Side. Curtis, two other women, and I were just attacking the *mezadakia* when the malaria attacked me. Excusing myself as urbanely as possible while a Niagara of sweat cascaded down a face several shades whiter than the tablecloth, I tottered off to the john, locked the door behind me, and leaned weakly against a wall. From some-where in the distance, I heard a hollow object landing in a body of water: a simultaneous *thonk* and splash, as though a bucket had been nudged off a wharf. I came to with my head and one arm wedged in the toilet bowl, which smelled as though it hadn't been flushed since its last use. There's nothing for upholding one's *amour-propre* like resuming one's place at the dinner table drenched in *eau de toilet*.

If my sorry condition drew little general notice in a place like Molfeta's, where the customary reek of garlic would have drowned out the emanations of a musk ox in rut, an attack some years later at one of the city's pinnacles of social and gastronomic splendor, Le Cirque, raised a few eyebrows, notably those of the owner, the impeccably soigné Sirio Maccioni, who had invited Curtis and me for dinner and installed us at the best table in the house.

Even at the top of my form, such as it may have been, I was never completely at ease at Le Cirque, where Richard M. Nixon received a heartfelt round of applause not long after his ignominious depar-ture from the White House, and where the cost of what any other of his fellow Republicans wore on a given evening exceeded that of my entire wardrobe. Although I dressed presentably enough on a freelance writer's income, I was all too well aware that I was out of my financial league there. Any veteran waiter in any big-ticket restaurant can assess a man's accoutrements to within a dime of their purchase price, and my off-the-rack pinstripes and Florsheim shoes just didn't cut the mustard in the midst of Savile Row threads and custom footwear. My Pulsar wristwatch, with its base metal bezel and Taiwanese leather band, may have been as accurate as a Jaeger le Coultre Reverso or a five-figure Piaget, but it lacked a certain cachet.

I took consolation in the certain knowledge that I had a much better idea of what I was eating than any of these rag-trade nou-veaux riches and their assorted beminked, bejeweled, belimoed consorts; these Old Money, Wall Street white-breaders; and these show-biz luminaries (including Woody Allen, who sat at the table next to ours on the evening in question, brooding morosely over his victuals, casting a pall of gloom over a six-table radius, dressed like a campus radical at a diplomatic function). I was treated deferentially as a friend of the boss and presumptive wielder of inkly clout, and I tended to overtip (a sure sign of a negligible bank balance). But I knew that the dining-room personnel had me pegged, and knew they knew I knew it, which had a dampening effect on my spirits. The aroma of proximate wealth has *always* had a dampening effect on my spirits. It's not that I covet it myself; it's just that I don't want those who have it sticking it in my face.

The chef had joined us briefly to outline the menu he proposed for the evening, which I don't recall in its particulars but remember as a prospective sampling of the highlights of his repertory. My subsequent recall of this abortive grand occasion (it was Curtis's birthday) mingles horror and blankness in roughly equal proportions. If I remember aright, we were happily tucking into something involving the livers of force-fed geese when the sweating, the pallor, and the faintness commenced. *No one* sweats at Le Cirque, and anyone who dines at Le Cirque sweats only at his country club. *Everyone* at Le Cirque displays an epidermis tanned mellowly enough to set off a king's ransom in state-of-the-art orthodontics. The merest hint of a lack of self-possession at Le Cirque is equated with garlic breath, flag burning, and moral turpitude of any and every stripe. I remember hearing Curtis moan, "Oh, no, not tonight," excusing myself from the table, and making unsteadily for fresh air. I remember remembering an upchucked portion of shredded pig's ears, in similar circumstances, outside a Szechuanese restaurant in east Chinatown a couple of years earlier. I remember debouching from Le Cirque at the peak of the evening, vaguely aware of a line of limos at the curb discharging pampered, impeccably coiffed, manicured, and garbed citizens into the restaurant and the posh Mayfair Regent Hotel in which it's situated. Then I went blind. Had I been able to see, and seen myself reeling along the sidewalk, I'd have assumed that I was bombed out of my skull.

Some semblance of vision returned by the time I groped my way to the hotel entrance. After sweating out the next ten minutes miserably enthroned in an off-lobby men's room, I toweled off as much wetness as I could and reeled into the lobby itself, where I slumped shivering on a sofa, now looking, I suppose, like a junkie in dire need of a fix. It was the most severe attack I'd ever had, but I thought the worst of it was over when the shakes subsided, and I returned to the restaurant determined to tough out a meal for which I now had no appetite. A glance at my plate brought on a fresh outbreak of the sweats. After one look at me, Curtis said, "I'm taking you home." In no shape even for a pro forma protest, I was led, shambling erratically, to the door. The situation was explained, with profuse apologies, to Sirio, who graciously shrugged off the incident, but whose quizzical expression suggested that he and I diagnosed my condition somewhat differently. The irony of it all was that I hadn't even had a proper drink—only a couple of ritual sips of champagne, for which I have a chemical intolerance.

The discovery that I could no longer drink champagne—or, worse, eat crustaceans—with impunity had occurred during my third or fourth year as a mercenary feeder. Stepping out of bed one morning after a night on the town, I emitted a yelp of anguish, glanced floorward to see what I had stepped on, and found it to be my own right foot, swollen to twice its size and alarmingly inflamed. The thing (it seemed an alien presence) throbbed so excruciatingly that I thought I'd somehow managed to break an ankle in my sleep. (Unlikely as the possibility may seem, I didn't dismiss it out of hand: as a teenager I *had* sustained a hairline fracture of a collarbone in the presumable safety of an otherwise unoccupied bed.)

Because I couldn't begin to get the offending foot into a shoe, let alone walk on it, a doctor was summoned and persuaded to make one of the last house calls in the history of the city. He arrived, took a cursory glance at the inflamed extremity, and confidently announced that I had eaten lobster and imbibed champagne the night before. Technically, he was only half-right: I had washed down a brace of lobsters with a bottle of still white wine. "No difference," I was told. "There's the same uric acid content in both. You have gout."

"Gout?"

"Yes, gout. From now on you'll have to cut way down on crustaceans and white wine. You'll have to go easy on the organ meats and spicy foods, too."

I was given a shot in the rump and a prescription for some pills usually given to ailing racehorses and left to brood on the cruel injustice of it all. For years, lobsters, shrimp, crabs, crayfish, and the like had constituted the better part of my diet. Suddenly, my chief sources of both protein and gastronomic delight had become major occupational hazards, as had the vinous accompaniment of choice.

Giving up wine was painful but possible, and from then on I made do with a mere sip or two of those I ordered—just enough to enable me to taste them in the line of journalistic duty. Giving up the shellfish, on the other hand, was clearly unthinkable, both from personal and professional standpoints, and I continued to indulge in them, on a somewhat curtailed basis, sometimes with no ill effects, sometimes suffering swift retribution.

My inability to drink white wine in any quantity was a social and professional handicap soon perceived in some quarters as an oafish refusal to comport myself in a civilized manner. The problem became particularly acute on various gastronomic junkets to Italy, where sparkling or still white wine is the ceremonial aperitif of choice, automatically served (with no alternatives countenanced) at any formal gathering. Aside from its chemical incompatibility with my bodily well-being, white wine as a preprandial quaff has always struck me as something like kissing one's sister. For my generation, at least, it's as welcome, when a dry martini is wanted, as an interior decorator on a football field.

Although I was less circumspect about the matter, I wasn't alone among my colleagues in my insistence on an honest-to-God drink before dinner. One of the most respected hired bellies during my early days on the beat was seldom altogether coherent by the time he got to his table; another highly regarded writer for a national magazine still refers privately to strict wine bibbers as "pussy drinkers." Don Allan, my predecessor at *Gourmet,* seldom forked his hors d'oeuvre into his face before downing a third martini, which in no way impeded his performance at table or compromised his judgment of the restaurants he covered, and I've seen more than a few hard-drinking chefs tasting and fine-tuning their most delicate sauces while sozzled half out of their minds.

In print, I made no secret of my fondness for real booze, occasionally groused about poorly made drinks, and sometimes singled out a particularly adept bartender for special praise. In my view, beverage service was an integral component and criterion of a restaurant's performance *in toto,* and a mixologist of particular distinction was no less worthy of kudos than a great chef, an outstanding headwaiter, or any other member of a smoothly functioning team. Not all my readers held the same view, and some took me severely to task for allegedly anesthetizing my palate by partaking of a cocktail or three before a meal. In one of my books, a little-noted volume called *Winning the Restaurant Game,* I tried to put these puritanical objections to rest:

> Short of inflicting measurable brain damage on oneself, there is nothing reprehensible about taking strong waters as a prelude to a meal, the precious carping of prigs notwithstanding. Any set of taste buds likely to be rendered comatose by a couple of dry martinis wasn't much of a set of taste buds to begin with.

Possibly because the book's sales were negligible, the prigs continued to carp.

Even before the days when the nation's nonsmokers began to campaign militantly for their perceived rights, I was less forthcoming about my tobacco habit than about my enjoyment of alcohol. While I never believed that smoking impaired the appreciation of my own food, it was obvious enough that anyone's fumatory emissions might have a deleterious effect on some nearby stranger's enjoyment of his truffled fettucine or pedigreed wine. Hence, I deemed it prudent to shed no light on my own use of the weed. As it turned out, there can be fire even where there's no discernible smoke. In the course of some routine observations about one restaurant's service, I noted that water tumblers were kept filled and dishes and ashtrays promptly cleared. Nothing was written to indicate that ashtrays at my own table were put to any use or required clearing, but I received an irate three-page screed a few days after the review's appearance. The remonstrant was certain, he wrote, that anyone with as discriminating a palate as mine would never sully it with noxious nicotine inhalations, but he demanded to know how I could even tacitly condone the use of tobacco by *anyone* in a public restaurant whose patronage I recommended.

My reply, to the effect that I had merely noted the efficiency of the busmen, which didn't necessarily constitute an endorsement of individual or communal gasping, brought another six pages of vituperation by return mail. My correspondent was canceling his subscription, and the faster I puffed myself into the grave, etc., etc. Ashtrays were never again mentioned under my byline.

In general, the condemnation of smoking by the magazine's readers had little to do with environmental or health concerns, but purely with palatal sensitivity. Their attitude seemed to be that it was perfectly all right for any suicidal idiot to risk lung cancer, emphysema, or the pollution of the atmosphere, but to risk the diminution of some rarefied taste experience by making a chimney of one's nose and a tar pit of one's palate threatened the very foundations of civilized existence. It was unanimously agreed that the subtle nuances of a great sauce or the elusive complexities of a distinguished wine couldn't possibly be apprehensible to a smoker. Any smoker who believed otherwise was simply deluding himself.

In theory, the argument seemed logical enough. I had given up smoking on several occasions, and each time my perceptions of what I ate and drank seemed to register more vividly for a day or two after my head had cleared out. Another forty-eight hours or so, however, and the sensation of heightened clarity would subside, leaving my comestibles and potables tasting and smelling just as they had when my diet included a heavy admixture of carbon monoxide. Eventually, I concluded that some compensatory mechanism enables the nose and palate to make whatever adjustments they require to remain in good working order. Still, I harbored some feelings of guilt about my own publicly unacknowledged use of cigarettes. Or such was the situation until I was invited on a tour of the Cognac district toward the end of my tenure with the magazine.

It's accepted as axiomatic among junketing foodies that there is no free lunch; however splendorous the food and wines and accommodations may be, however warm the reception and enchanting the region, sooner or later the piper must be paid. Like my earlier trips to Tuscany, the Cognac tour was a salient exception. The organizers, who represented Courvoisier, apparently had a quota to fill, and I was as up-front as I could be about the uncertainty of my ever being able to devote any ink specifically to what they referred to—in reverential tones usually reserved for terms like "the Godhead"—as "the Product." They assured me that no strings were attached, and off I went.

Our group—a small one—spent a couple of days in Paris, where Curtis, who coincidentally and independently happened to be on a business trip, joined us for a superb dinner the first night, at one of those obscure establishments that Parisians jealously manage to keep to themselves, undiscovered (or at least undisclosed) by even the most assiduous Michelin and Gault Millau moles. (The evening's *pièce de résistance,* for which "sublime" would be damnation with faint praise, was a dish of duck gonads, lightly glossed with a hauntingly perfumed reduction of the deceased birds' essences and euphemistically termed *"ris de canard"* in deference to the sensibilities of the American women present.)

As has been well advertised in song and story, Paris is the city of lovers. It's also the city of Parisians, and for people who fall into neither category or lack manifest evidence of either qualification, Paris, to my mind, can be hell on earth: the coldest, most inhospitable, cruelest town anywhere. I had been there alone several times since Gwynne and I had been captivated by its seedier charms in the early 1960s and had been treated as an undesirable everywhere I went. Occasions that in the companionship of an intimate might have seemed a delightful indulgence in stolen pleasures—a dozen oysters slurped from their shells while shivering in ankle-deep rain-water near the Gare St.-Lazare or a thin, gristly, intensely sapid *steak au pommes frites* at a nondescript back-street bistro—turns to ashes in solitude, and a late-evening pastis in a blue-collar bar can be an absolute nightmare for a stranger whose comprehension of pointedly xenophobic French is presumed to be nil.

In Curtis's company on an otherwise dismally cold, wet day, however, Paris was everything it was supposed to be. Our time was unstructured until my departure for Cognac the next morning, and we were free to roam about the Left Bank on our own, as though in the throes of first love, searching out the little streets, the cozy cafés, and the small hotel that had been her haunts twenty-odd years earlier.

Circumstance, association, and anticipation do as much for French food as the chef who prepares it. With rain streaming down the windows of a cramped bistro redolent of damp wool and stewing meat—a cheap, quick-turnover office workers' and sales clerks' pit stop—a decent, modest lunch can seem as memorable as an unstinting blowout in some three-star mecca of higher gastronomy. I mopped up the remains of my *tripe à la mode de Caen* with something like reverence, while Curtis sighed rapturously over a pork chop she'd hardly have noticed anywhere in her native Michigan.

The Courvoisier château and adjoining distillery and warehouses perch alongside the Charente River in the town of Jarnac. The visiting foodies were ensconced in the château, where I was assigned the most splendacious guest room I've ever occupied. The company's public relations people, virtuosos in the art of the soft sell, spent the next few days wining and dining us with the easy affability of polished hosts concerned only with our comfort and enjoyment, seemingly disinclined to let any hint of commercialism mar a purely social occasion. Of course, if it would interest or amuse us, they'd be delighted to show us the workings of their operation, from the harvesting of the grapes (then in full swing) to the final realization of the Product, but only if . . .

But of course we were interested (a few of us, not including me, genuinely: when you've seen one distillery and one winery and one grape harvest, you've seen them all, possibly excluding Villa Banfi in Italy, a state-of-the-art vinification facility that, in its immensity and technological sophistication, bears an eerie resemblance to a major oil refinery). After dutifully slogging through muddy vineyards, tasting the raw juice of freshly pressed grapes, and inspecting various distilleries and warehouses (our hosts' and others), we were conducted into the holy of holies, the Courvoisier tasting room, and it was after an hour or so in that sanctum that my guilt about smoking was dispelled for once and for all.

The professional taster and the hired belly are different breeds of cat. The taster—whether of wines, brandies, teas, coffees, or whatever—is an indubitable expert: a supremely confident, bloodhound-nosed sensor whose palate and taste memory are unerring, whose visual acuity enables him to differentiate among minute nuances of color and tone indiscernible to the common run of mortals. The hired belly, on the other hand, is an imprecise slob who masks wildly capricious evaluations behind a screen of usually ill-chosen adjectives. The taster's livelihood and the survival of his employers depend on degrees of exactitude as different from the restaurant critic's as a lapidary's are from a jackhammer operator's. At best, the hired belly formulates and articulates a highly debatable value judgment. The professional taster's word is law.

The resident Courvoisier taster, a product of generational fine-tuning, spent an hour or so going through his exquisitely refined paces for the edification of the assembled American rubes. The hairsbreadth distinctions he drew between one minute sampling and another were altogether lost on his listeners, notwithstanding their transparent pretensions to the contrary. The guy was simply infallible, his every pronouncement writ in stone.

Needless to say, tobacco was taboo in the tasting room, a laboratory in which fanatical antisepsis obtained. When the session broke up, I hustled into an anteroom, intent on pulmonary pollution. The taster was already there, stoking his pipe—a big-bowled hayburner of the sort his fictional compatriot, Georges Simenon's redoubtable Chief Superintendent Maigret, stuffs with cheap shag when mulling conflicting evidence. "But, monsieur," I protested, "how can you reconcile an indulgence in tobacco with the sensitive demands of your vocation?"

Wreathed in clouds of noxious smoke, the taster informed me that a compensatory mechanism enables the nose and palate to make whatever adjustments they require to remain in good working order.

"What about the Russian Tea Room?" Curtis suggested.

"You know I've always detested the place," I replied.

"For God's sake, you haven't been there in years, and everyone else loves it. Why can't you give it a fair try?"

Okay, I'd give it a try—on the condition that she make a late-ish dinner reservation, because it was then midafternoon and I was out on the East End of Long Island, some three hours from West Fifty-seventh Street if the usual square-wheeled train got in on time.

It's true that I'd never liked the restaurant. It seemed to be the lunch haunt of choice of various authors I'd had to deal with in the past, and although I'd found it possible to eat well there by restricting my intake to caviar, my none-too-lavish expense accounts had obviated the possibility of making a square meal of caviar alone. Besides, I'd always found the service lousy (unless your name happened to be something like Nureyev, Baryshnikov, or Rostropovich) and the décor blowsy. Still, Curtis's point was well taken; the restaurant was a venerable institution, and the thousands of world-class performing artists who flocked there over the years couldn't *all* be gastronomic ignoramuses. I resolved to show up with an open mind and in an equable mood.

My resolve began to falter the moment we were seated—at the worst table in a half-populated room—and a matronly waitress brusquely informed us that our meal would have to be ordered forthwith; the kitchen was closing, and if we craved sustenance of any kind, we could forego cocktails until she got the food to the table. It was a Saturday night. Curtis, who was then an upper-echelon book editor, had invited her assistant, an attractive young woman, along. Both were dressed for what had been planned as a festive night on the town, and none of us expected to be hustled through a mediocre meal by a thickset woman who glared alternately at us and her watch as we ate.

"I'm sorry," Curtis said, pushing her food around on her plate. "Let's get out of here."

I signaled for the check and tabled my plastic. Both were snatched up and carried off. Ten minutes went by. Fifteen. Twenty-five. Finally, the woman returned, empty-handed. "Go see the manager," she snarled.

The manager, one of those supercilious ponces whose days are made by sneering at their betters, informed me that my card was no good. What did he mean, no good? Did I not understand English? He meant precisely what he said: no good. How had he come to this conclusion? He had run a check on me with American Express, that's how. Well, American Express was mistaken, probably a computer glitch. "American Express is not mistaken. Your card is no good."

The rhinoceros was obviously spoiling for battle. He announced once more, not only to me but to the few remaining diners within shouting distance, that my plastic had been invalidated, doubtless for good cause. "All right," I said, "I'll pay cash. Let me have my card back."

"Your card has been destroyed."

"What the hell do you mean, my card has been destroyed?"

"I mean your card has been destroyed. Shredded."

I demanded to see the remains. The remains were "inaccessible." I could pay up and clear out.

"Look, you creep, either I see that card, or what's left of it, or you can *eat* your fucking check."

"You can *pay* your fucking check, you deadbeat, or I'll call the police."

"Go ahead, call the police, you festering pustule, and you'll be looking for a job tomorrow morning." I decided to play my trump card: my business card, with the talismanic *Gourmet* embossed thereupon. My breast pocket turned out to be devoid of authentication; in my rush to the restaurant, I had neglected to provide myself with any.

The manager and I had been exchanging increasingly heated pleasantries for twenty minutes or so when my tablemates joined us to find out the cause of the delay. They were informed that their escort was a cheap con artist and prospective jailbird whose imminent arrest could be avoided only by immediate quittance of his lawful obligations and prompt departure from the premises.

"This cheap con artist just happens to be the highly respected New York restaurant critic for *Gourmet* magazine," Curtis remonstrated.

"Sure, lady, that's what they all say."

The manager was challenged either to call the cops or produce the "destroyed" credit card. When advised that he was risking a major lawsuit, he drew in his horns a bit. I suggested that he put through another call to American Express and let me talk to the representative who had misinformed him. Grudgingly, he dialed the number and handed me the phone. With profuse apologies the voice on the other end conceded that a mistyped digit was responsible for the contretemps. The phone was handed to the manager, who listened, crestfallen, for a few minutes, hung up, and produced the "destroyed" card. "You're lucky to get it back," he said, his sneer still indelibly stamped on his face.

I was just signing the long-withheld tab (pointedly omitting a tip) when Rudolf Nureyev entered the restaurant. Although the kitchen had ostensibly closed an hour earlier, he was led in stately procession to his customary table, where he settled down for a leisurely late supper. Until now, I've never expended any ink on the Russian Tea Room.

As I was to learn later, there are a number of bona fide deadbeats who palm themselves off, with varying degrees of success, as known hired bellies. Not long after the Russian Tea Room incident, I received a call from a restaurant press agent. (I knew he was a press agent when he addressed me by my first name, even though we'd never met.) "Jay, I want to thank you," he said.

"Thank me for what?"

"For deciding to review Pier 57."

Pier 57 was a Brazilian seafood house that I'd tried several times and found wanting. I told the caller that I had no intention of reviewing the place and had no idea why he thought I did. "But you called and reserved a table for six for tonight," he said. "You said you'd be writing a review and expected the meal to be on the house."

I explained that I didn't operate that way. Steamed at the free-loader who was using my name, I decided to stake out the joint that evening and nab him in flagrante. Together with Zanne Zakroff, the director of *Gourmet*'s food department, I took up a strategic position at the bar, near the entrance, where the imposter couldn't possibly pass undetected. He never showed up.

A few weeks later, I received a call from one of the owners of an Italian restaurant in Greenwich Village—an unpretentious little place, Volare, that I was genuinely fond of and had reviewed a couple of months earlier.

"Jay, did you make a reservation for a party of eight for this evening?"

"No, Tino, I didn't. Why do you ask?"

"Because someone called and reserved a table in your name. I didn't think I recognized your voice, but thought it might have been a bad connection."

"Tino, whoever he is, he's not me. I'm tied up this evening and can't get down there, but make sure he pays for everything he orders."

I called Tino the next morning. "Jay," he said, "you won't believe this. This guy was a gigantic black man, maybe six-foot-seven. The guys with him looked like a basketball team. He ordered the best of everything and ran up the biggest tab I've written since we opened the place. Then he puts down a credit card with your name on it. Of course I ran a check on him, and he turns out to be perfectly legitimate. He's some high roller from Chicago, and American Express tells me they constantly get calls about him from restaurant owners who think he's pulling a scam. What the hell's he doing with the same name as yours?"

What, for that matter, was I doing with the same name as his?

One of the first of the city's restaurants to substitute computer printouts for waiters' hand-scrawled checks was Maurice, a hushed cathedral of gourmandise in the Parker-Meridien hotel. I was presented with a foot-long strip of paper there one afternoon after a light lunch—an accounting that seemed to contain at least twice as many line items as it should have. "The waiter's brought us the wrong check," I muttered while fumbling for my reading glasses. When I could see properly, I found that the notation PRBL had been inserted between each pair of drinks or dishes we'd been served. "What are all these pribbles doing on my bill?" I demanded of the table captain. "We didn't order any pribbles and weren't served any pribbles."

"Pribbles, monsieur?"

"*Oui,* pribbles."

The man examined the offending document and returned it to me with the sort of quizzical expression that might be reserved by members of Mensa for readers of the *National Enquirer*. "Your 'pribble,' monsieur, is your previous balance."

The hours between lunch and predinner cocktails—a doggerel day afternoon—produced these lines for my lunchmate, Gail Zweigenthal, *Gourmet*'s executive editor:

> *The prbls are coming! If you harken, you'll hear*
> *Their humming and drumming—they're drawing quite near!*
>   *The odious prbls,*
>   *They munches and nbls!*
> *The prbls are coming, I fear.*
>
> *The prbls are coming! If you harken, you'll hear*
> *Their strumming and thrumming—they're drawing quite near!*
>   *The bellicose prbls,*
>   *They argues and qbls!*
> *The prbls are practically here!*
>
> *The prbls are coming! If you harken, you'll hear*
> *Their frightful yum-yumming—they're drawing quite near!*
>   *The hideous prbls,*
>   *They drools and they drbls!*
> *The prbls are coming, my dear.*

Plagued by insomnia since early childhood, I seldom sleep longer than three hours on a given night, and I often get no shut-eye at all. My nocturnal hours are mostly spent reading, smoking, and tippling small doses of gin in an unavailing quest for oblivion. As a result, something like a mild form of narcolepsy occasionally catches up with me around lunchtime: a sudden, irresistible descent into deep sleep, sometimes in midsentence, after a night spent wakeful as a barn owl. It usually happens during a heavy meal in a poorly ventilated dining room. A tablemate's discreet nudge will ordinarily bring me back to life, thoroughly refreshed, when I've nodded off, but I have managed to slumber through a couple of courses from time to time when large groups were engaged in animated conversation. I attached no importance to my soporific lapses (which weren't all that frequent) at a time when the nation's chief executive was catching his z's during cabinet meetings. Still, they weren't enhancing my image as the consummate man-about-town.

I was certainly wide awake and fully conscious of what was expected of me as a putative sophisticate one evening at Il Nido, which at that time epitomized the then-emergent Italian *alta cucina* and was frequented by some of the city's savviest, most extravagantly self-indulgent eaters. In season, the restaurant specialized in the dauntingly pricey white truffle of Piedmont *(Tuber magnatum),* which to my taste is the sexiest edible known. French partisans of the black Périgord truffle *(Tuber melanosporum)* will hotly contest this assertion, and the late Waverley Root, whose book *The Food of Italy* remains the definitive work on its subject in English two decades after its original publication, considered the black Umbrian truffle of the same species, which has a negligible following in Italy, "the tastiest I know."

French claims about the superiority of the black truffle can be dismissed as simple chauvinism, but Root's case is more difficult to diagnose. His only references to specific uses of the white Piedmont truffle involve cooking the tuber, whether in wine or with cheese, abuses few of its more devout fanciers would countenance.

During the first few years of the restaurant's operation, Il Nido and its soigné *padrone,* Adi Giovanetti, were more or less synonymous with the white Piedmont truffle, then relatively unfamiliar in this country. I had praised the place to a longtime friend, Ed Giobbi, a respected painter, sculptor, and printmaker better known outside the art world as an avocational cook and cookbook author. One morning, he called to invite me to lunch at Il Nido, on condition that I select the menu for what would be his eldest daughter's twenty-first birthday celebration. I thought I knew precisely what to order; the truffle season was at its height. A phone call to Adi elicited assurances that the entrée I'd chosen—one of his signature dishes—would be available and would be served in its ultimate manifestation.

Four of us met at the restaurant, and Gena (the birthday girl) immediately asked what I'd decided on as the main dish. "A mushroom," I replied.

Puzzlement. "A mushroom? You've got to be kidding. *A* mushroom?"

"Yes, *a* mushroom. That's what you're getting, baby. Happy birthday."

Gena eyed me warily, intrigued but half-hoping I was putting her on. Her father gave me the fish eye too, perhaps suspecting that I'd somehow managed to procure some hallucinogenic fungus and had persuaded Adi to serve it. "A mushroom," Gena repeated softly.

And that's what each of us got: a single beefsteak-size porcini mushroom, quickly seared in olive oil, spangled with minced garlic and parsley, and topped off as it was served with a blizzard of raw white truffle shavings. My confidence in my choice was somewhat shaken as Gena inspected her portion in manifest dismay. She was clearly impressed by the size of the thing—it could have been worn as a beret—but there it lay on the plate, mantled in what appeared to be detritus swept up from some cabinetmaker's workshop floor. She sniffed it tentatively while I held my breath, and an expression of rapture lit up her face. Ten minutes later, she basked in the afterglow of what all four of us agreed was a virtually orgasmic experience.

A couple of years later, on the evening of one of my more maladroit performances, the same dish and setting again led to erotic associations, but a bit more crudely. As I envisioned it, the scenario was to be a reprise of Gena's birthday lunch, but with a different cast of characters: Curtis, myself, and a fastidiously prim closet gay who had written a couple of well-received cookbooks. Again, the famous truffled porcini was the *pièce de résistance,* and up to a point, the evening was eminently civilized. Curtis had prevailed on me to refrain from my wonted indulgence in off-color stories, rough language, sexual innuendo in general, and any references to my dentist, who, because he also happened to be gay, I had dubbed "the tooth fairy."

Throughout dinner, I had, I thought, comported myself like a perfect gentleman, the soul of tact, the embodiment of urbanity. Our prissy guest had been suitably impressed by the correctness of my haberdashery, wine choices, and dealings with the flunkies who hovered around our table. He had pronounced the *funghi porcini con tartufi* "exquisite" and the evening "memorable." At the appropriate juncture, I signaled discreetly for the check and suavely extracted my plastic from a breast pocket, a maneuver that, unbeknownst to me, launched into space a small blue packet that landed in an ashtray, directly under the nose of our guest, the prig.

This was before the advent of AIDS, a time when condoms were still requested sotto voce at the neighborhood pharmacy and were hardly a subject of polite conversation, let alone open media attention and advocacy. Still playing the role of polished raconteur, I gradually began to realize that a pall had settled over the table, that neither of my companions was paying the slightest attention to whatever it was I was babbling about, and that both wore expressions of utter consternation. The table captain arrived, proffered an Amex receipt for my signature, and murmured, "Shall I remove the ashtray, sir?"

The ashtray? Of what concern was the ashtray, since we were about to leave, and . . . Oh, Jesus!

With my customary savoir-faire, I pocketed the offending item. Yes, by all means, remove the ashtray.

Tuber magnatum, the white truffle, and sex have been inextricably linked for me since my first whiff and taste of the subterranean aphrodisiac. At one time or another, just about every edible substance except Cream of Wheat has been touted as an aphrodisiac,*

---

*The first time I dealt in print with this subject, I cited oatmeal as the exception. Since then, a New York radio gonzo, Don Imus (a.k.a. Imus in the Morning) has contended that the veteran character actor Wilford Brimley copulates with his daily bowl of Quaker Oats.

but the white truffle is the single food I'm convinced is unfailingly and ineluctably erogenous.

A day or two before Christmas one year, Adi invited me to Il Nido, ostensibly for a cup of Yuletide cheer, and sent me home with a colossal truffle. Buried in pounds of raw rice, the thing was the size of Einstein's brain and of such pungency—clearly detectable through a metal-capped glass jar—that an ecstatic moan involuntarily escaped a young woman in the elevator of my apartment building. It was the first time I'd seen anyone ravished by groceries.

Everything eaten *chez moi* during the holidays was liberally truffled, and, although I had a number of gastronomic heavy hitters over for various meals, the gigantic tuber hadn't undergone significant diminution by New Year's Eve. Salient among the week's visiting trenchermen was Rusty Staub, then the right fielder for the New York Mets, a literal heavy hitter and an apprentice epicure of cetacean appetency.

I had met Rusty a few years earlier in the kitchen of Ponte's, a riverfront haunt of professional jocks, rag-trade nabobs, and assorted wiseguys, where he was sedulously taking notes and depleting the house supply of prosciutto while the chef demonstrated the technique of stuffing a breast of veal. I had heard about his culinary propensity (when traded from Montreal to New York, he reportedly had bitched about having to lug "all those pots and pans" across the border), and knew he planned to open a restaurant (which he did, and which I reviewed, a few months after we met. Otherwise undistinguished, the place qualified for coverage in *Gourmet* by virtue of the best Canadian baby-back ribs and the only shrimp-stuffed mirlitons served in the city).

We had become friendly over the years, and he had transported my four young sons to nirvana one evening when he installed them at the coveted front-window table of his restaurant and spent a couple of hours talking baseball with them. I tried to reciprocate during the Christmas season in question by having him over for Sunday brunch and serving him homemade fettucine with a sauce of four cheeses and cream, garnished with lightly poached eggs, bits of torn prosciutto, and copious shavings from the inexhaustible truffle. It was his first encounter with the white tuber; several years and a good deal of serious eating around Europe later, he still describes the dish as "awesome." If I say so myself, it was.

The plan for New Year's Eve was to shave truffle over everything but the ashtrays, reserving the last couple of ounces for brunch à deux the next morning with a certain young woman who was providing me with a modicum of consolation during one of Curtis's increasingly frequent entanglements with other men. Traditionally, my New Year's Eve bashes have revolved around a buffet of twenty-odd dishes of varied provenances, almost all of which would in no way be diminished by a liberal overlay of truffle. The exception this particular night was a large crock of *kimchi,* a hellaciously incendiary Korean mixture of pickled vegetables, which had been ripening on a kitchen shelf for the better part of a week.

With several parties on his annual New Year's Eve rounds, Rusty usually hits my place first, an hour or so before it begins to crowd up, while he still has a clear shot at the arrayed comestibles. He was the first guest on the evening in question, and, characteristically, waded straight into the buffet. He has uncommonly small hands for a guy his size, but in the presence of food his grasp exceeds his reach. In informal situations, what the French term *la fourchette d'Adam* is his eating implement of choice, and he considers anything that isn't soup to be finger food. Randomly sampling whatever came to hand, he dredged fistfuls of a rabbit salad, Chinese hacked chicken, prosciutto, bourbon-basted baked ham, galantine of duck, caviar-lashed white beans, *cima alla genovese, orzo* with oxtail sauce, roasted peppers, *tortilla español,* gravlax, venison chili, pigeon pâté, a potato salad garnished with seared, pepper-encrusted raw steak, an octopus salad, *trippa all'arrabiata,* barbecued pig, *ceviche* of scallops and red snapper, assorted sausages, *insalata di mare,* stuffed mussels, and a few other *spécialités de la maison* before noticing the crock of *kimchi.* "Wait!" I yelled as he lowered a meathook into the vessel, withdrew about half a pound of the inflammatory veggies, and conveyed them to his open maw. With his eyes pinwheeling in their sockets and steam hissing from his ears, he emitted a strangulated shriek and spent the next ten minutes gasping and weeping. "Jesus!" he finally moaned. "Why didn't you stop me?"

Stop him, indeed. Stopping *Le Grand Orange* when he's homing in on provender of any sort would be just a little more impossible than stopping a bull rhinoceros in full charge.

During the nights preceding the party, I had toiled in the kitchen between the hours of dusk and dawn. Fueled by a fifth of gin each night, I was more or less totaled by the time the festivities got under way, and I gratefully accepted a guest's offer to carve the prosciutto, the single item on the menu I hadn't produced myself. The prosciutto had been cured on Long Island by Dante Laurenti, who had mastered the art on his native turf, just outside the town of Langhirano in the Italian province of Parma, which, despite some dissension on the part of fanciers of hams cured at San Daniele del Friuli, is generally conceded to be the ultimate source of air-cured pigs' asses in the known universe. At that time, several years before the importation to the United States of the real McCoy was legalized, Dante was the house prosciuttist and general *salumiere* for a superior Upper East Side restaurant called Felidia, of which we'll hear more later. He was and remains one of a scant handful of restaurant-associated specialists this side of the Atlantic, and he's easily the best of those whose handiwork I've sampled. I had jumped at the chance when he invited me to observe the entire curing process, from its inception to its conclusion the better part of a year later. I was especially eager because I was scheduled to spend some time in Langhirano that spring, where I could compare Dante's transplanted technique with the traditional procedures at their source. The resultant article, one of my best pieces, was reported to have generated more favorable reader response than anything else *Gourmet* published that year, and it copped first prize in an international food journalism competition sponsored by a not-altogether-disinterested consortium of Parma ham and cheese producers.

Delighted by his fifteen minutes of narrowly parochial fame, Dante had one of his prosciutti—about a fortieth of his year's output—delivered to my pad in time for the party. I borrowed a marble-based stainless steel carving cradle from his employers, mounted the ham on it, and installed a very impressive display on the buffet table. Enter the volunteer carver, the nerdly adjunct of a spectacular redhead—a woman who played a starring role in my carnal fantasies. Her consort was a southerner, ergo (I assumed) a connoisseur of ham. Moreover, he was a surgeon, ergo a man to whom a meat knife could be entrusted with confidence. The son of a bitch turned out to be the clumsiest butcher since Gutzon Borglum raped Mount Rushmore, and he worked on roughly the same scale. A culinary strip miner, he hacked massive ragged slabs of shocked meat from an entity meant to be divided with lapidary finesse into translucent petals. Thick, stodgy rhomboids of impermeable flesh were hewn away and scattered about, as though awaiting baptism in red-eye gravy. I disarmed the geek summarily and did what I could to camouflage the disfigurement. Naturally, Dante walked in before I had a chance to accomplish much cosmetic surgery.

Pamela, my inamorata pro tem, was never in better form than she was that night. A gifted sculptor of diaphanous outdoor, often waterborne, installations, she had designed and crafted some striking costume jewelry during the previous few weeks, and she arrived wearing a basic black frock that set off one of her own dramatically volumetric necklaces to perfection. The bauble attracted considerable attention, as did its wearer, the ubiquitous truffle shavings, the two young women who swooned amidst shattering glassware in the crush of bodies, my brand-new Himalayan Christmas kitten, and the Salmanazar of Moët that Alan Stillman, the principal owner of the Manhattan Ocean Club, had sent over as a token of his appreciation for my recent review of his restaurant. (The bubbly, the equivalent of nine bottles and a slight improvement on the two cases of discount Freixenet iced down in my bathtub, was opened at the stroke of midnight and drained within five minutes.)

By late morning of New Year's Day, I had cleared away the night's mess while Pamela slept and had done the prep work for our brunch. Its potential for activating my goutiness notwithstanding, a hoarded bottle of Roederer Cristal was chilling. Thin squares of crustless toast had been thickly paved with a few ounces of beluga caviar withheld from the madding crowd, a dozen quail eggs had been gently poached in a pair of improvised foil molds matched precisely to the dimensions of the toast, and a quartet of hen's eggs was approaching room temperature. Redundant as two types of egg (not including the sturgeon roe) may seem for a two-course meal, the quail ova, which were to be overlaid on the caviar, and the hen's eggs, to be lightly scrambled and heavily truffled, would bear little resemblance to each other in their final manifestations, and I had no intention of denying us either in what I consider its most exalted treatment.

When Pamela had showered, I suggested she remain in the buff, as I was, during our modest repast. "Would you mind if I wore my necklace?" she asked.

"Not if I'm allowed to wear black tie."

And so we toasted the New Year, naked as Chaucer's worm except for our festive neckwear, and tucked into the goodies.

The consumption of *T. magnatum* as a prelude to lovemaking, especially when significant expanses of skin are exposed to its invasive pungency, is in effect a stage of the act itself, just as sex after truffles seems a continuation of their ingestion. I've sometimes imagined that eating the white Piedmont truffle—which happily entails suffusion amidst the mingled bouquets of humus and dew-dabbled dog shag and spiderweb, of earth and garlic and bodily concavities permeated with leaf-mould—is as close as mere mortals can come to intimacy with dryads. Our viands that morning tasted of sex; the afternoon's kisses, of truffle. Happy New Year!

*   *   *

In my professional-cum-extracurricular experience, I found that, except for soulful eye contact, discreet hand holding, and the odd under-the-table caress, whatever amatory pleasures even the most romantically designed restaurants afforded were merely anticipatory. Dining tête-à-tête in public has its limitations: candlelight flickering over a silver ice bucket beside the table may be a powerful sexual stimulant, but headwaiters take an inhibitively dim view of consummation within their domains and aren't much more encouraging about overt foreplay. In such circumstances, Joan Greenwood and Albert Finney came about as close as it's possible to come, so to speak, with their famous oyster-slurping duet in the film *Tom Jones,* but their lascivious shellfish consumption was only surrogate sex, sexy as it may have been. It wasn't until *La Grande Bouffe* was filmed in a more permissive decade that comestibles and substantive carnality were physically united, although not in a public restaurant.

Neither of the two most erotic eating experiences during my years as a hired belly took place in restaurants either, but one did occur while I was on assignment in Málaga, on the Costa del Sol, a few years before the brunch with Pamela. It involved a mess of shellfish, specifically *tallinas. Tallinas,* or *tellines* in French, are thumbnail-size bivalves of the family Tellinidae, a second cousin of which, the coquina *(Donax variabilis),* is prevalent but unaccountably spurned as a food resource along Florida's southeastern coast. I had introduced Curtis to them in Aigues-Mortes, the rampart-girdled esturian port of embarkation, in southwestern Provence, for the Sixth and Seventh crusades. Although the town's emblematic dish and sole claim to gastronomic fame, the mollusks are prepared there just as they are wherever I've found them along the Mediterranean—with oil, parsley, and immoderate amounts of garlic—and a similar critter is given essentially the same treatment, with minor variations, in Hong Kong, on Taiwan, and in Thailand.

Whether they're called *tallinas* or *tellines,* they're at their best when eaten alfresco around midday, when a high sun envelopes them in a shimmer of nacreous iridescence and fresh air mitigates the breath-stopping acridity of untamed garlic. Because the minuscule clams pop open and are served almost as soon as their pan hits the fire, the pungent lily remains raw, its reek unmodulated, which seemed to preclude any indulgence by Curtis in Aigues-Mortes's locally renowned specialty; her tolerance for garlic, even it its mildest forms, was nil. Her tolerance for sunshine, on the other hand, was limitless, and she basked with the equanimity of a lizard in the torpor of an otherwise deserted place St.-Louis, where the heat of the paving stones burned through the soles of my boots. She sipped from a tumbler of sun-mulled white plonk and suggested we have a little something to eat.

"Here, in Aigues-Mortes?"

"Yes."

"*I* might have a little something to eat, but *you* can't. All they serve in this place is *tellines*—garlic with a light shellfish garnish."

"What sort of shellfish?"

"A sort of miniature clam that . . ."

Curtis, a tidy size three who had once put herself on the outside of seven dozen freshly raked Long Island cherrystones faster than I could shuck them, summoned a waiter and ordered two portions of *tellines* and another round of *blanc ordinaire*. A portion of *tellines* is not a dozen clams on the half-shell but, traditionally, a capacious bowl brimming with fifty or sixty sweet-fleshed morsels, each to be sucked from the shell, with plenty of bread on hand for moiling about in the sauce. Oblivious of her nemesis, the garlic, Curtis snaffled her portion with startling dispatch and unseemly glee, ordered another, and declared that even the overheated local swill was elevated to something like nobility in the context. The garlic produced no ill effects.

Málaga, a year or two later. Curtis is once again catching a few rays, this time in the Plaza de la Merced, while I follow my nose to a nearby market, a clangorous concrete shed where stentorian fishmongers bawl their wares, their bellowing ricocheting from wall to wall in a continuum of white noise. I sniff and poke at the bounty of the Mediterranean in the state of euphoria that lively seafood markets always induce in me. At one stall, I find a mountain of *tallinas* and, with no thought given to simple practicality, buy a kilo.

The sun worshipper is still at her devotions when I return to the square. Her initial excitement at the display of my booty gives way to consternation: How do I propose to cook the things? Oops, hadn't thought of that. We're staying at the Parador del Gibralfaro, perched high on a hillside on the outskirts of town, overlooking the *plaza de toros* and, directly beyond it, the harbor. Hell, I decide, we'll just have to have them raw on the half shell, and we set out in search of a small thin-bladed knife.

Our room at the *parador* debouches onto a terrace screened off for absolute privacy, on which the sun worshipper lies supine, unencumbered by a stitch, as I begin shucking and hand feeding her our *tallinas.* She insists, equitably, that they be consumed in alternating sequence. On one of my turns, a *tallina* poised by the edges of its fragile shell between forefinger and thumb squirts from my grasp and plops onto her bare belly, where it nestles snugly, shell side down, in her navel. Accident becomes design: I spend a languorous hour tonguing sweet bits of flesh from the center of her topography, as oleander and bougainvillea cascade down surrounding walls, before we break for a proper lunch on the public dining terrace.

Like our improvised hors d'oeuvre, lunch is a plethora of miniature sea creatures, a delicately gilded *frito* of infant calamaris no bigger than our *tallinas,* whole octopuses the diameter of small change, thumb-long flatfish, tiny whitebait, and krill-size prawns all eaten intact, heads, bones, and shells included. Sparrows alight on our napery, gleaning crumbs of gray Spanish bread, while the sun lasers down, obliterating thought, and the sea stretches to the horizon in numbing blueness. "There are still a few *tallinas* in the room," Curtis says. And we have them as before, washed down with splits of champagne from the minifridge, while bulls are slain in the arena below and the Mediterranean slumbers, tautly overarching thousands of years of trade and strife and imposed acculturation. Sated with food and death and history, we seek each others' bodies, our lovemaking intensified by the mass graves we've made of our bellies.

East Hampton, Long Island, a year later. We've invited Bill and Gloria Durham for Easter dinner. Weary of the equally predictable *gigot d'agneau* and *jambon en croûte,* I've opted for a departure from the norm. In keeping with a personal tradition, blown eggs, elaborately decorated with antique collage elements (In your face, Fabergé!), ornament each place setting, their effect diminished somewhat by Curtis's cynical observation that they couldn't have had much of a sex life, having been laid and blown just once. Otherwise, all goes swimmingly through aperitifs, hors d'oeuvre, and soup. I bear the main course to the table in triumph, and Gloria bursts into tears: "You bastard! You've roasted the Easter Bunny!" I cobble up a quick *omelette aux fines herbes* for the offended party, who refuses to partake of my superb *lapin rôti,* but everyone has lost whatever appetite he or she may have had, and the meat is picked at in lugubrious silence.

East Hampton, again, the following Christmas season. Curtis has abandoned me for some Wall Street hustler, and I'm going through the motions of prepping my annual New Year's Eve bash in Manhattan, minimally consoled by the presence of a former friend's wife in the midst of a messy divorce. I've spent the past several hours hacking meats, blending herbs and spices, shelling pistachios, chopping black walnuts, beating eggs, and all the rest of it for a lavish game pâté crammed with microchips of truffle and soused in rare old Armagnac. The thing is close to a yard long and designed to serve seventy as one element of a thirty-dish buffet. Extracted from the oven, it's weighted down with a slab of marble surmounted by a substantial boulder and left out on the deck to cool while we repair to a local Chinese joint for dinner. We return to find the weights distributed over the deck and the aluminum mold licked clean, with a single, mocking pistachio left centered in its bottom. One or more raccoons have gorged themselves on the goodies, leaving for my contemplation a single sneering reference to my competence and sanity or lack thereof. Little bastards!

Restaurants are notoriously more volatile than almost any other commercial enterprises, and they have an alarmingly high incidence of premature mortality. Because the exigencies of monthly magazine publication dictated that copy be turned in three months before publication, I was dogged constantly by the possibility that some place I'd praised in manuscript might fold before my encomiums got into print. Every precaution was taken to forestall such an eventuality (occasionally to the detriment of worthwhile but shaky-looking ventures that might have been saved by favorable ink but went belly-up for lack of it), but none were glitch-proof. I had come perilously close to recommending a defunct restaurant during my early days on the beat, and I was effectively blown out of the water on a couple of later occasions.

In the first of these episodes, my bacon was saved at the last possible moment by sheer chance and a craving for a dry martini. Strolling down Second Avenue one afternoon, I had nipped into a Chinese restaurant called Lantern Light (itself now long defunct) for a quick juniper consommé, not because the resident mixologist was particularly adept, but because I just happened to be passing the place in the throes of a mighty thirst. I had expended some ink on its behalf a few months earlier and was joined at the bar by the owner. In the course of some trade gossip, he remarked that Panchito's Mexico City, which was located nearby, was going belly-up within the month. When the shock wore off, I dismissed the news as groundless scuttlebutt: Panchito's was about as good as New York Mexican restaurants got in those days (or these days, for that matter), a lot more presentable than most, and was packing the house every night. Of more immediate personal concern, my review of Panchito's was slated for imminent publication. Oh, no, I was assured, this was no idle rumor. My informant had been offered the location himself and had written evidence to that effect. Panchito's closed even as I lost a weekend cobbling together a substitute review that got into print by the skin of its teeth.

I wasn't that lucky when a Greek place in Midtown abruptly folded a day or two after my dithyrambic effusions hit the newsstands, when the owner's wife eloped with the chef. The incident provoked more irate mail than I received in aggregate while covering upward of five hundred other restaurants during my tenure with the magazine. My correspondents unanimously demanded an explanation of how I, a putative authority on restaurants, could have failed to recognize a case of terminal illness; could have directed them to a place so patently awful that it had succumbed to its own inadequacies; could have, in my obtuseness, failed to see handwriting that must have been writ large upon the wall. My explanation, that neither I nor the most perceptive observers of the visible evidence could have foreseen the proprietor's cuckolding, abandonment, and reaction thereto, cut little ice with my accusers.

It was a couple of years later when I happened on one of those rare finds that gladden the heart of any hired belly: a previously undiscovered and unreviewed little gem of purest ray serene. It was a startlingly inexpensive Japanese restaurant on the Upper East Side. The elderly sushi chef, a world-class virtuoso and former professor of the art at a leading Tokyo culinary institute, crafted the most poetic exemplars of the genre in my experience. The entrées of choice were various lobster preparations, each made with a whole specimen of appreciable size and irreproachable freshness, and each bearing a sticker price of about eleven bucks, appetizer, soup, salad, and dessert included. The service bordered on the reverential, and not least among the understated physical amenities was a backyard dining garden as enchanting by night as a setting from *The Tale of Genji*. The consensus among the several guests who shared a succession of meals there with me was that the place was too good to be believed. As it soon turned out, it was.

The venture, I was assured by a savvy female manager after I'd set up an interview, was a labor of love: a cultural mission inaugurated by a dedicated Japanese academic of independent means who didn't care a fig for bottom-line practicality. I burbled in print like the new parent of a firstborn, scattering superlatives all over the place. I pronounced the establishment the find of a lifetime, a sapphire amid the garlic and mud of the pullulating Upper East Side restaurant scene. On the morning of the day the review appeared, Zanne Zakroff called about lunch. I suggested we hit the great discovery before the hoi polloi trashed it.

As it turned out, it had already trashed itself: the service and sanitation would have mortified the manager of an inner-city McDonald's. The distinguished sushi chef had been replaced by a callow youth with hands of stone. Lobster had been banished from a now altogether lackluster menu. The cooking was abominable, and the prices had been jacked up accordingly. The cultural ambassador had sold out, and the resultant shambles had been taken over by a gang of contumelious thugs. I rushed an explanatory disclaimer into print at the first opportunity. Three months after the original review, it didn't much matter.

A dose of irony completed the dismal experience a few months later. This is how I described the incident in a piece in a giveaway restaurant guide:

> The flier had been slipped under my apartment door during an apparent saturation papering of the neighborhood. Circulated on behalf of a nearby Japanese restaurant, it reprinted the better part of a review that had appeared in a national magazine. The reviewer painted word pictures of such a swell-sounding place that I'd have been there in a flash, grappling with the lobsters he so temptingly described, had I not been privy to certain disconcerting information. By genetic accident, I was more intimately acquainted than anyone else with the reviewer in question, who happens to inhabit my skin and answer to my name. Consequently, I knew a thing or two about both the restaurant and the review that no casual reader of the flier could be expected to know: I knew the restaurant was an egregious

bummer and the review wasn't worth the shoddy paper it was reprinted on.

If you're wondering how or why I could have bestowed an enthusiastic endorsement on a meretricious little dump, my reply is that I couldn't and didn't, but that any restaurant review, honestly formulated though it may have been, can be suborned by happenstance the reviewer can neither anticipate nor control; by alterations unwittingly set in motion by the review itself; or by the simple passage of time. As a cautionary example, the case in point merits further inspection. What happened was this:

Reviewer stumbles on what he deems a terrific new neighborhood restaurant, finds succession of subsequent visits increasingly rewarding, and lavishes adjective-encrusted hosannas on his find. Exigencies of monthly magazine publication entail "lead time" (i.e., interval between delivery and publication of copy) of some fourteen weeks. On or about publication date, reviewer revisits restaurant, discovers that abrupt, unanticipated change of ownership has made sow's ear of silk purse, and so notifies readership at earliest possible opportunity. Earliest possible opportunity: two issues later, when reviewer's sincere recantation is buried somewhere in back of book, at bottom of monthly reviews. World little notes nor long remembers what he says there.

Circa one year later: Reviewer opens apartment door to find cat chewing literature transmitted thereunder. Extracted from feline clutches, literature informs reviewer (and neighbors for miles around) that he considers certain Japanese restaurant, now extant in name only, to be not merely cat's masticatory but cat's absolute, unequivocal pajamas. Moral: *Caveat lector.*

7

The Customers

Always

Write

They laughed when I sat down to the typewriter. Or so I gathered from much of the reader mail I received while covering the restaurant beat. However seriously a hired belly may take his mandate and his craft, his stuff is not enduring literature but ephemera of the most transitory sort, and if he can't lighten up and have a few chuckles on the way to nowhere, he and his readers are in for a grim ride. In my view, anyway, a given season's hot new yuppie hangout, chefly wunderkind, or salad leaf of choice were hardly matters of cosmic import, and the impulse to treat them with a certain playfulness was irresistible. Add to that an incurable penchant for wordplay of any kind—puns, anagrams, palindromes, spoonerisms, double entendres, limericks, and the like—and the resultant belletrism may have lacked the sprightliness of, say *Das Kapital* or Pater's reflections on Pico della Mirandola, but I gave it my best shot.

Always delighted to stumble on some serendipitous find that lent itself to recombination of its elements, I gleefully reported that a Turkish restaurant called Genghiz Khan's Bicycle "was named after a comedy by Refik Erduran, about whom I've been able to discover only that he's a contemporary Turkish playwright and that 'naked furrier' is an anagram of *his* name." An exchange in a Midtown Chinese place was duly noted in one review ("'Wonton?' asked the waiter. 'Not now,' I replied, completing the palindrome he unwittingly had begun"), and the colossally proportioned *spécialité de la maison* served at Keen's inspired a salvo of hyperbolic wordplay: "The Mutton Chop, which may or may not be hoisted onto the plate with the aid of a forklift, is one awesome hunk of meat for which no comparable examples come to mind. To the dilettante bank robber, it would be a Willie Sutton Chop; to the average check kiter, an E. F. Hutton Chop; to a marginal publisher, an E. P. Dutton Chop; to a weekend figure skater, a Dick Button Chop; to any reasonably appetent diner, the ultimate Glutton Chop."

When favored by a somewhat clubfooted muse, I'd resort to verse:

> *La Tulipe is La Tulipe,*
> *The cuisine is refined and the prices are steep.*
> *(One doesn't find grub like that on the cheap.)*
> *La Tulipe is La Tulipe.*
>
> *La Tulipe is sober, staid,*
> *All understated till the bill must be paid,*
> *But when you get home and the evening is weighed,*
> *La Tulipe was La Tulipe.*
>
> *La Tulipe is quite reserved:*
> *Orders are taken and dinner is served*
> *With solemnity that at times has unnerved*
> *Diners new to La Tulipe.*
>
> *La Tulipe is La Tulipe,*
> *Not superficial but studiedly deep;*
> *Some praise it highly and others say "[bleep]."*
> *La Tulipe is La Tulipe.*

Occasionally, the problem of confronting a blank sheet of paper would become its own solution:

Typist's block never has been one of my problems. Having watched "Good Morning America," done the crossword puzzle, composed and discarded three letters to the editor, played with the cat, riffled through three or four magazines, dealt a few hands of solitaire, rearranged the living-room furniture, emptied and refilled the ice trays, taken a single shirt to Wong's laundry, discussed the weather with the elevator operator, filled out a Publisher's Clearing House Super Triple Sweeps entry card, brewed a second cup of tea, checked the fridge to see how the ice cubes were coming along, and re-read Christopher Smart's "Of Jeoffry, My Cat," I went promptly to work on my next book: *An Introduction to Herb Cookery.*

Halfway through the opening sentence ("I met Herb and Madge Cookery for the first time in Appleton, Wiscon . . ."), the phone rang. Was I free for lunch? "Gosh," I demurred, "I dunno. I've really been churning out the prose this morning and hate to break the momentum. Oh well, how about La Table des Rois? It's just down the block from your office, so we can make it a quickie."

"La tahb des wha?"

"Yes, that little place just down the block from your office."

The volume of reader mail my *Gourmet* pieces generated exponentially exceeded anything in my previous experience. Admittedly, a few letter writers were not amused by what one characterized as "a frightful ratio of egocentric verbiage [that] goes beyond anyone's standards of good taste [and from which] one emerges . . . wondering if it really was an article on the ostensible subject, or, if it was yet another feature on Jay Jacobs by Jay Jacobs." The overwhelming majority, however, were so unrelievedly effusive that I sometimes wondered if it was really my stuff they were burbling about and, if so, what they were smoking. Otherwise seemingly responsible citizens confessed to elaborate fantasies that ran the gamut from the purely gastronomic to the plainly erotic, and a few children seemed as disoriented as their elders: "Dear Author in school I had to write about a famous person I rote about you I think you are a kind Person an a great Author when I grow up I want to be a great American like you I wish you an your family good health my Teacher said you are to busy to answer"

Wrong, Teach. I wasn't too busy to answer the boy, who lived in

New Bedford, Massachusetts, not far from where an authentic great American, Wade Boggs of the Red Sox, was setting a sterling example for the youth of the region. Nor was I too busy to reply to a Connecticut subteen's plea for guidance toward realization of his dream to join the ranks of the hired bellies. Would I have replied if he had been saddled with a name like Mortimer Mulch, instead of the richly cadenced syllables his Fairfield County parents had conferred on him? I really don't know, but this was my response:

> *Dear Channing Matthew Lindsay Stave:*
> *O! What a rogue and peasant slave*
> *Am I, to let your earnest query*
> *Go long unanswered: I was weary,*
> *Bilious, nauseous, and neuritic*
> *From working as a rest'rant critic.*
>
> *O, Channing Matthew Lindsay Stave,*
> *I think you must be very brave;*
> *You must be very bold—nay, bolder—*
> *To think that when you're somewhat older*
> *You'd like to eat and write about it.*
> *The job sounds pleasant, but I doubt it*
>
> *Will still seem to the grown-up Stave*
> *Precisely quite the work you crave.*
> *For you may find food criticism*
> *Isn't worth a family schism;*
> *That your mother and your father*
> *May, if you ask them, say they'd rather*
>
> *See Channing Matthew Lindsay Stave*
> *Put the upbringing that they gave*
> *Him to more profitable uses*
> *Than judging birds' nest soups and mousses,*
> *Or tasting crêpes and scaloppine,*
> *Sushi, couscous, and linguine.*

Dear Channing Matthew Lindsay Stave,
No one has yet seen fit to pave
With gold the road that gastronomic
Writers tread. Be an atomic
Physicist, physician, banker,
Even though you think you hanker

To write on food, Dear Channing Stave.
It's not the gastronome who'll save
Mankind by judging five-course dinners—
Food critics don't make peace prize winners.
And, though they dine on milk and honey,
By and large, they're short of money.

Yes, Channing Matthew Lindsay Stave,
Your prospects will, I fear, be grave
If you seek wealth and public favor
By writing of the foods you savor.
Though this may leave your feathers ruffled,
Oysters, caviar, and truffled

Pheasant, though you're led to rave
About them, don't dear Channing Stave
(Though you are talented and able),
Put lots of bread upon your table.
So heed my counsel and stay healthy.
Get wise, kid: if you can, get wealthy.

Still, Channing Matthew Lindsay Stave,
When you are old enough to shave
(And wish you once again were younger),
Though far from wealth, you won't know hunger
If, while risking family breakups,
You take my job.
      Your friend,
      Jay Jacobs

The most poignant letters that came my way all seemed to come from the more remote boondocks of western Canada, where *Gourmet* apparently had more subscribers per capita, caribou included, than in any major metropolitan area. However the missives were phrased, they were invariably wistful confessions by women of various ages to the improbability of ever experiencing a big-city night on the town, or the company of an attentive male, except vicariously through my accounts of what they took to be nonstop high living. As one lady from Saskatchewan put it, "I feel as if I have a standing dinner date with you every month (actually three dinner dates) . . . and I thoroughly enjoy every one of them."

Married, single, or somewhere in between, my Canadian correspondents all seemed to have been exiled from their dreams and to have made me a fantasy surrogate for the men from whom they'd been estranged in actuality or in effect. I derived no pleasure from my role as their imagined consort and found many of their letters wrenching: "A number of years ago, in Alberta, a neighbor lay dying of cancer; when I offered her books to read, she asked if she could borrow my accumulation of *Gourmet* magazines—and she spent those last months reading your column and escaping, in her mind, to the wonderful places you write about."

Not all my correspondents were resigned to fantasy; a good many offered to share my table in the flesh, either as my guests ("If you're ever stuck for a dining companion . . .") or hosts ("Although this may be an unusual request I was wondering if you would be our guest for lunch or dinner at a restaurant of your choice"). Once in a while, I'd take the bait if their letters seemed to betoken good company, with mixed results over the years. In some cases, the volunteer tablemates were clearly disappointed by my lack of resemblance to whatever images they had conjured up, and they were never heard from again. In others, my own preconceptions broke up on the rocks of stark reality, but every now and then one of these encounters would be marked by a genuine mutuality of interests, tastes, and attitudes and would lead to a lasting friendship.

Albert Aschaffenburg and I hit it off from the moment we first met for lunch. Albert was the courtly, infinitely gracious second-generation New Orleans hotelier whose domain, the Pontchartrain, is the flat-out sweetest of the planet's smaller hostelries. He had written two or three years earlier to express his interest in my restaurant and travel pieces and to invite me to join him and his wife for dinner the next time they were in town. After setting up a date a few weeks later, I had been forced to beg off at the last moment when some sort of UFO lodged in Curtis's eye, necessitating immediate medical attention, but I arranged with the restaurant of Albert's choice, Aperitivo, to bill me for whatever wines were chosen in my absence. It seemed a minimal gesture after standing up my host on the shortest possible notice, but Albert sent an effusive note of thanks, adding that he was now more set than ever on meeting me.

Conflicting schedules delayed the meeting each time Albert came to New York, but we finally got together for lunch at the Bull and Bear, and I resolved at once to enjoy the man's company at every possible future opportunity, whether on his turf or mine.

Win a few, lose a few. I lost one *big* when I agreed to a blind lunch date with a woman from Washington, D.C., who described herself in well-turned phrases as a much-traveled upper-echelon business executive and experienced food lover who moved in the best Washington circles. She was not considered unattractive, she added with implied understatement, but she wasn't just another pretty face: she was a member of Mensa, the rigorously exclusive society of accredited superbrains.

I was then sizing up Le Périgord Park, a stately cathedral of epicureanism, for possible coverage in the magazine and had turned up there several times during a ten-day span in the company of various women whose comeliness had impelled the maître d' to put them on display at the most visible table in the house. When I arrived a few minutes early for lunch with the Washingtonian, I was shot a knowing smirk by the headwaiter, who ushered me to what had become "my" table, clearly expecting me to be joined there by still another in an improbable succession of traffic stoppers.

Clearly consternated, he reappeared a few minutes later with the Venus du jour waddling in his wake. She certainly hadn't misrepresented herself in some respects: her experience of the pleasures of the table had been so extensive that I mistook her for a sumo wrestler in drag, and I suppose she *wouldn't* have been considered unattractive by a similarly cross-eyed hippopotamus of the opposite sex. She grunted a perfunctory greeting and fell on her *salade de foie gras Pompadour* with the purposefulness of a ravening hyena. She polished off a roast pigeon as though it were a hummingbird, wore out a team of busmen, who rushed breadstuffs to her in relays, and, unable to decide which dessert looked most tempting, ordered a portion of everything from the trolley. She munched her way through the meal in concentrated silence, sluicing down the victuals with whatever came to hand—a first-growth Médoc, the remnants of a Scotch sour, the dregs of my own dry martini, a gallon or so of mineral water—and made no attempt at conversation until coffee and brandies were served. *Then* it turned out that she did indeed have a mind, but there was only one thing on it: immediate, sustained postprandial sex, either at her hotel or my apartment, or, if need be, in the form of manual stimulation right there at the table. I extracted my person from her clutches as gracefully as I could, mumbled something about urgent business elsewhere, paid the bill, and fled.

I can't remember how long you have unknowingly been a part of my life through your reviews in *Gourmet,* but for the last six or eight years I've pounced on the monthly editions and turned immediately to your columns. (My Virginia-bred mother gave me a subscription for Christmas when it was clear that I would top six feet and not fit the mold of the debutante: It was her last-ditch effort to civilize me. Despite her good intentions, I am not the average Southern Belle but am perhaps salvageable nonetheless.

At any rate, every Christmas and every birthday since, when asked what I wanted, I have replied "dinner with Jay Jacobs." For years I have been disappointed.

The letter went on to explain that the writer was pursuing a master's degree at SMU in Dallas but frequently had run the marathon and other road races in New York. "This October," it went on to say, "I will again be in New York and as I can no longer rely on my family to arrange my life, I am taking the risk of being very improper and forward, and coming right to the point. Is it possible for a total stranger, albeit with decent table manners . . . to accompany you on one of your restaurant visits?"

The letter was headed and signed "Terrell Vermont" (which sounded more like a place than a person to me), and I found its self-deprecating tone and Old South propriety appealing. Still, I'd been quite gun-shy since the encounter with the edacious Washington nymphomaniac a few years earlier. Moreover, I reasoned, the prospect of sharing a table with some carb-loading female jock who topped out at two yards plus and might turn up in a sweat suit and Nikes wasn't altogether reassuring. Who the hell, in short, needed this? Against my better judgment, I wrote to this Terrell Vermont, suggesting that she call when her travel plans were settled—if she really wanted to waste an evening with a guy her parents' age, half her size, and a dead ringer for Kermit the Frog.

We met a couple of blocks from my digs at a favorite haunt of mine, Felidia. I was bracing myself for the worst at the bar, where the presiding genius, Sime (Sam) Peroš concocts the known universe's most singular dry martini, when a vision of loveliness, smartly dressed and luminously radiant, pronounced my name in the honeyed accents of the Deep South. I had envisioned a gaunt, ropy athlete (she had been good enough at what she did to collect appearance fees from major race organizers on two continents) of single-minded devotion to the mortification of the flesh and, a longstanding subscription to *Gourmet* notwithstanding, an ascetic contemptuous of any sort of gastronomic indulgence. To my astonishment, she turned out to be a witty bonne vivante, an exceptionally knowledgeable food buff, and—literally and figuratively—a thoroughly rounded human being. It soon developed that we shared a passion for the exploration of obscure ethnic food markets and restaurants, many of the same writers, and the same sort of risqué stories and racy language. Respectively committed to other partners, we were platonically in love.

Two or three years before we met, Terrell had contracted leukemia and fought it to a standstill, but she had had to give up competitive running. Shortly after our first meeting, she moved from Dallas to Atlanta, where she hooked on as a hired belly with a local food publication. On her occasional trips north, we'd prowl the markets of Chinatown, Ninth Avenue, and Little India together, dine out together, and cook together on Long Island's South Fork, where she reveled in the bounty of my garden and my various shellfish harvests. She came to think of me as a sort of culinary and journalistic mentor, and thanks to the perspicacity of Myra Appleton, who was then the nonfiction editor at *Cosmopolitan* and to whom I introduced her, Terrell published her first pieces in a national magazine. Our friendship was and remains perfectly unclouded but was to lead to one of the eeriest, most improbable coincidences a couple of years after I received her first letter, when I received another unsolicited mash note from another road runner.

During the interim, it was business as usual, with just enough put-downs mixed with the praise to keep my perspective from getting altogether skewed. Although surprisingly little exception was taken to most of my judgment calls, I knew for certain that any review of a restaurant of uncommon merit—a place that even the most obtuse of my fellow mercenaries had lauded unstintingly— would produce at least one piece of mail from a reader who couldn't disagree more vehemently with my findings. Any hot-dog stand, according to one of these billets-doux, was preferable to Lutèce, and only an idiot like me could be taken in by the most brazen con game in town. The Four Seasons (a lunchtime haunt of the city's most recognizable movers, shakers, and media luminaries) was strictly for impressionable yokels, and my testimonial to its excellence established me as the hayseed apotheosized. My tribute to the superiority of La Côte Basque was the most egregious example of the blind leading the blind ever to grope its way into print. If I *really* thought Le Cirque was any better than a third-rate neighborhood taco parlor, I didn't have a brain or a taste bud in my head.

On mercifully rare occasions, I'd be taken to task for alleged or actual lapses of usage or grammar, factual inaccuracies, or locutions that over-prim readers found offensive ("A vulgarism like 'veggies' has no place in serious food writing"). I and the copy editors were certainly asleep at the switch, but half a dozen subscribers were wide awake when "comprised of" inexplicably found its way into type. How I managed to toss off, and the editors miss, "good but unprepossessing" still baffles me, and it baffled a veteran trade book editor, the late Dan Wickenden, who wrote, "Is it possible that you've been led astray by Mimi Sheraton, who persists in using unprepossessing when she clearly means unpretentious or unassuming? Such blunders are characteristic of her disheveled prose, but they have no place in your own elegant commentaries."

James Beard appeared to be in full possession of his faculties when I interviewed him several times during the eighty-second and penultimate year of his life. His recall, from his earliest childhood onward, seemed astonishingly complete, especially on the subject of his native Oregon, and I assumed there was no need for verification of his references to the geography of a state he knew like the back of his hand. My two-part profile of Beard was published to more acclamation, both within and outside the professional food world, than anything I'd done before or have done since, and I was still savoring the afterglow when a letter from one Elizabeth C. Bennett of Grants Pass, Oregon, informed me that while she too had found the profile enjoyable and instructive, she "was surprised to learn that since [she] was on the Oregon coast [a year earlier, the town of Gearhart had] been moved to Tillamook Bay from its former location about fifty miles north of the bay."

When I observed, in a review of Café des Artistes, that in one of a cycle of dining-room murals painted by Howard Chandler Christy the "indigenous Seminoles" who greeted Ponce de León's arrival in Florida included a number of blonde chorus girls wearing nothing but lipstick, an Amerindian scholar was quick to point out that Seminoles were not indigenous but were latecomers to the region.

I'd like to believe one New York City reader was being deliberately obtuse when she began three closely typed and loosely reasoned pages with "I suspect that you are being deliberately obtuse when you claim not to comprehend the meaning of the phrase 'priced accordingly' when used on restaurant menus." I hadn't claimed not to comprehend the meaning of the phrase; I had contended that it was meaningless as it stood. Of course I knew—as did anyone else except, apparently, the letter writer—that in its common menu usage it was shorthand cant for something like "Our market costs fluctuate; your lobster is priced accordingly." Still, there was a you-know-what-I-mean lazy-mindedness about it that I'd always found mildly irritating, and I'd vented that irritation in a few tongue-in-cheek lines at the end of one review:

The dictionaries I use give such adverbs as "correspondingly," "consequently," "harmoniously," and "agreeably" as definitions of the adverb "accordingly." The locution "priced accordingly" has been appearing on menus with increasing frequency of late, as in "Plat du jour—priced accordingly." I'd dearly like to know what this is supposed to mean. Since *nothing* is priced harmoniously or agreeably these days, those possibilities can be dismissed out of hand. I suppose, say, a lamb chop or a flatfish can be priced consequently (we serve it, consequently we price it) or correspondingly (you eat it, correspondingly you pay a price for it), but I doubt that those possibilities are precisely what the menu prosodists have in mind. Any forthcoming enlightenment on this matter would be appreciated accordingly.

Accordingly, the correspondent in question took it upon herself to provide some enlightenment:

> To my mind [she wrote, claiming a faculty to which she had no clear title], the term merely signifies that the dish will be priced as a person might "reasonably" expect in light of the type of restaurant and the ingredients used in making the particular recipe. The word "reasonable" is a legal term of art used extensively in the Uniform Commercial Code.

I didn't, and still don't, know what legal terms of art are, but I suspected that anyone who did was predisposed to elaborately convoluted argle-bargle that ultimately led nowhere. With resolute avoidance of anything pertinent to the matter at hand, the exegesis continued:

> Clearly, offerings of lobster, caviar, *foie gras* or filet mignon, will be priced higher than *cassoulet, choucroûte garnie* or roast chicken. Similarly, a more expensive restaurant will price its specials—even those with less costly ingredients—more expensively than other dining spots. Obviously, you will pay more for poached salmon at Le Cirque than you will at a casual . . . place like Confetti, more at Confetti than at a Greek coffee shop [Greek coffee shops where poached salmon is served were left unspecified]. The higher prices are not merely a matter of snobbery . . . but really a reflection of "ambiance." A nebulous concept, perhaps, but to be fair, ambiance costs. The diner must bear the expense of the high rent where a restaurant is in a high rent district, of a large, skilled staff, costly decorations, fresh linens, flowers, and of an uncompromising use of quality ingredients.

"So," the lady concluded, with the irrefutable logic of the clinically brain-dead, " 'priced accordingly' reflects two factors: what you are eating, and where you are eating it. Nothing tricky about it, in my opinion."

My favorite letter of misdirected complaint came from a reader with somewhat inflated notions of both current familiarity with the poetry of John Masefield and the volume of response a hired belly can expect after an alleged misquotation:

> I imagine this may be only one of thousands of letters you have received, or will receive, concerning your inexcusable misquoting of John Masefield's *Sea-Fever* in the July *Gourmet.*
>
> To make two mistakes in two lines of a poem so famous that most schoolchildren know it by heart is utterly inconceivable to me. And then to put the poet laureate's name beside it only adds to the insult.
>
> How long would it have taken you to look up the poem in any anthology? Or ask the office help to do so? And what was the editor doing? Assuming, no doubt, that as an old pro you did not require checking on. I have seldom seen in print anything as *un*professional or irresponsible.

Unlike "most schoolchildren," I *didn't* know the poem by heart, but I *had* consulted a couple of anthologies before quoting its opening stanza in a review of Riveranda, a pleasure-yacht-cum-restaurant that toured the Hudson and East rivers during mealtimes. Admittedly, the late poet laureate's immortal lines were put to somewhat irreverent use in the review (they were followed by some parodic doggerel), but I was sure I'd transcribed them verbatim, with their punctuation intact down to the last comma. Rechecking my sources, I found no discrepancies between them and the transcription, and I concluded from the letter's internal evidence that the writer must have been an elderly lady with a failing memory who herself hadn't bothered to verify her charges before firing off her complaint. As gently as I could, I wrote back to disabuse her of the notion that "thousands" of Masefield buffs had, or would, register protests (hers was the only one) and that any more than one present-day schoolchild in a million might have memorized the poem, which, I added, had been quoted with scrupulous accuracy, as the accompanying photocopy from Bartlett's *Familiar Quotations* would attest.

With rare exceptions, my refutations of readers' complaints elicited either stony silence or pigheaded bluster that ignored whatever hard evidence was marshaled in my defense. The Masefield partisan, however, was surprisingly gracious in defeat:

> It was most kind of you to write as you did. Please forgive the crabby carpings of a homesick Nova Scotian landlocked for the summer in central Florida. You are quite right that Masefield will survive [the aforementioned parody], and so shall you.

Although I'd been a moderately active supporter of the feminist movement almost before it was recognized as such and was living with one of the most quietly effective campaigners for equal rights in the then notoriously inequitable world of book publishing, I took more heat from militant young feminists than from all other letter writers combined. Everything else equal, I've always preferred dealing with attractive women to dealing with plain or emphatically unattractive women, and I have never considered myself unusual in this respect, among either males or females. In my coverage of restaurants, I routinely noted the presence of personable dining-room workers of whatever gender, along with any other elements—flowers, costumes, artwork, food presentation, and the like—that might appeal to the readers' aesthetic sensibilities.

Well, nobody accused me of lusting after the flower arrangements or anything else on which I cast an admiring eye—unless the object of my appreciation happened to be a comely female. Any mention of an attractive woman—and most women restaurant workers, recruited from the ranks of theatrical aspirants, were uncommonly easy on the eyes—would impel a few of her outraged sisters to take pen in hand. "Male chauvinist pig" was perhaps the mildest of the epithets addressed to what was perceived as a fantasy (if not de facto) rapist chronically compelled to flaunt his machismo in an attempt to allay his underlying sexual insecurity; a monster who regarded all females as pieces of meat; a potential (if not actual) child molester.

The last charge, leveled in response to a travel piece on Bangkok, came from a Cambridge, Massachusetts, admirer. In the course of reviling me for my use of "dozens of sexually descriptive terms, almost all negative towards women," she seemed particularly outraged by a passing description of a typically enchanting Thai child of five or six. "What I found most outrageous was his remarks about the sexuality of girls: 'Another small girl, an irresistible beauty, sits patiently beside a display of nut brittle of some sort, lotus seed perhaps.' "

The article in question centered on one of Bangkok's major food markets (populated almost exclusively by women and preschool girls), but it included accounts of several excursions around the city, in the course of which Thai males, who are inclined to advertise their masculinity as loudly as possible, were described in all their macho bravado. The letter writer studiously ignored all references to these he-swaggerers, choosing to single out instead such "negative" descriptions as "a scaled-down Cambodian Venus in skin-tight jeans," "primly sexy Western-style skirts" (articles of clothing, not vernacular allusions to women), and "a synthetic redhead wearing a black wetlook jumpsuit."

The Bangkok piece generated a good deal of mostly favorable comment, but a few zingers rebuked me for offenses other than my alleged prurience. One San Franciscan, for example, was "tremendously offended" and "incensed" by an admixture of hard reality in what she obviously had expected to be one more travel article in the magazine's patented see-no-evil style. I had found Bangkok an enchanting city for the most part but had been somewhat less than captivated by its notorious traffic congestion, unbreathably polluted downtown air, abject shantytowns, clusters of rag-clad beggars, and the Thai Public Health Ministry's own discouraging statistics on widespread malnutrition in some rural areas. With rigorously Cartesian logic, the San Franciscan implored Jane Montant to remind me that "sensitivity to poverty, which one hopes moves people to action, is crucial," but that any expression of such sensitivity in a travel article is "outrageous." "Please be more sensitive," the letter writer perorated. "I think part of appreciating another country's culture involves more than noting its aesthetics."

Say what?

To spare my readers possible embarrassment on foreign soil, I'd taken some pains to comment on the Thai ethos without sermonizing too obviously. Among other things, I'd pointed out that an impulse to tousle one market child's hair had been nipped in the bud when I suddenly remembered having read somewhere that the Thai consider the touching of their heads by strangers an insupportable breach of etiquette. "He touches a young girl's head," the Cambridge letter writer wailed. "The Ugly American lives. Can't you send someone who is more sympathetic to the tradition of a country to report on that country?"

"My dear Jay" was the salutation. The writer was the pop-music lyricist Sammy Cahn, whom I'd never met but who "look[ed] forward to meeting [me] for a drink" at the earliest opportunity. Sammy (as he signed the letter) had been excited enough by my review of one of his favored haunts, Le Premier, to stud his missive with the fully capitalized interjection BRAVO!, progressively increasing the number of exclamation points with each use, until BRAVOs were popping all over the page like firecrackers on Mott Street during Chinese New Year. Good old Sammy had made a point of including his home telephone number in his letter, but I hadn't yet called him when a dinner date and I chanced to drop into the St. Regis Hotel a week or so later to discover that none other than my newfound buddy was playing a gig there. The evening's last set was breaking up just as we entered the lobby. A door opened, and the performer stood just outside it, pressing the flesh of his departing parishioners. As the last of the congregation filed out, I propelled my consort of the evening Cahnward. "Sammy, it's Jay. If you're free for half an hour, why don't we have that drink now?" The man's brow furrowed in Jay-who? what-drink? puzzlement. At the addition of my surname, his pasted-on smile faded, to be replaced by a bemused who-the-hell-is-this-guy stare. "Well, Joe, it was good of you to catch my act," pal Sammy murmured, scuttling crabwise past me to freedom. I'd finally discovered what makes Sammy run.

Like any other hired belly's, a fair proportion of my mail (roughly forty pieces per week) came from mercenary flacks— mostly marginally solvent, none-too-presentable PR scroungers and assorted hangers-on who operated out of their hats, couldn't put a simple declarative sentence together without misspelling half its content and appending an exclamation point to it, were congenitally incapable of doing their homework, and invariably added "and Associates" to their own names although they operated in unassociated loneliness.

As a general rule, the restaurants promoted by these hucksters were in bad trouble for good reason, but there were exceptions enough to warrant occasional investigation of a paid shill's recommendations. Over the years, however, experience taught me that the overwhelming majority of these tipsters never represented anything but flat-out, unreviewable losers, and all communiqués from certain touts—typically headed with something like "From Arnie Glotz Associates; FOR IMMEDIATE RELEASE" (premature ejaculation?)—were automatically consigned unopened to the overflowing wastebasket.

Some of the larger corporate restaurants relied on in-house promoters in their dealings with the food press, usually with no more effective results than the city's mom-and-pop ventures derived from their freelance hustlers. I still prize and occasionally consider framing a 1986 letter from the manager of The Post House, an Upper East Side establishment that I'd reviewed a few weeks earlier. "Dear Mr. Jacobs," it began. "In the five years since we opened, the critics have said some nice things about The Post House." After quoting several of the nice things the critics had said about his place of employment, the manager unfurled the evidence he deemed best calculated to wring some favorable ink from me. "And now, Jay Jacobs of *Gourmet* says that we are 'a haunt of dedicated carnivores and lobster-grapplers, but hardly to the exclusion of more sophisticated diners." He went on for three paragraphs, always referring to me in the third person, to tell me what I'd already written, and he concluded by suggesting that I come in and see for myself what I'd already described.

Not long thereafter, I found myself describing something I not only *hadn't* seen but didn't know existed. Leafing through the *Times* on the way to the crossword puzzle one morning, I was startled by an endorsement, attributed to me, of a cookbook I'd never heard of. Its author was a very young French chef, a fatuous, epicene little twit from Provence who a year or so earlier had been the subject of what may have been the most hostile "favorable" review *Gourmet* ever published.

The kid was talented, no doubt about it, but I was turned off by several of his conceptually flawed original creations, and his relentlessly arch menu prose set my teeth on edge. While conceding that his restaurant's virtues marginally outweighed its deficiencies, I had taken quite a few potshots at the precocious *gros bonnet,* the stunningly ignorant *patron,* and several of the more outré *spécialités de la maison* and menu locutions: "If the chef chooses to perceive his anglerfish as being equipped with sheep's legs *(gigot de lotte),* I suppose he's entitled. . . . I haven't tried the *gigot de lotte . . .* and have no intention of doing so. As Chef B—— described what appears to be an original inspiration, it's a fillet of anglerfish sculpted to resemble a leg of lamb (the chef neglected to say why) and napped with the natural juice of a genuine roast leg of lamb (which joint the chef normally refrains from disguising as a fillet of anglerfish). When told that his stroke of ovine-piscatorial genius sounded slightly bizarre, the chef looked hurt."

Perhaps more pointedly than may have been necessary, it was noted that the chef's *"petit pot-au-feu"* was "no more a *pot-au-feu* than the chef is a member of the Jets' defensive line." It also was noted that "The menu all but minces with 'littles' (as in *'petite nage,'* *'petit coq,'* *'petite garbure,'* *'petit gateau,'* *'petite bouillabaisse,'* and *'petite omelette'*)," and that the chef's *charcuterie de la mer* translated as "pork butcher's meat of the sea."

Buried in the midst of a fairly rough going-over was the observation that one dish, *confit de canard,* was "in a class by itself." That was the phrase, with the clear implication that it had been applied to a book of which I was altogether unaware, that appeared over my name in the *Times* ad.

As the letters kept coming, the realization dawned that just about anything I wrote, however innocuous it may have seemed to all concerned with its publication, was bound to put *somebody's* nose out of joint. The more paranoid among the feminists could be counted on to fulminate at length about my alleged sexism when any mention was made of an attractive female, but other complaints were less predictable. When, for example, I remarked that restaurants of a certain type were "proliferating like gerbils," neither I nor my editors expected to be rebuked by a self-appointed arbiter of journalistic decorum who was "appalled" by a reference to a rodent in an article on fine dining. My immediate reaction was to try to persuade André Soltner and Jean-Jacques Rachou (respectively, the chef-owners of Lutèce and La Côte Basque) to put *blanquette d'ecureuil* on their menus, or to get Larry Forgione, of An American Place, to include an authentic Brunswick stew on his, but a paucity of squirrel purveyors put an end to the scheme.

I should not have been permitted to sneak my leftist political views into a restaurant review, according to one censor, who was outraged when, in the course of some observations on a trend toward more casual garb during the 1980s, I remarked that even the president of the United States dressed like a cowboy on occasion. And according to a member of the military stationed in Colorado, I had editorialized inappropriately, if not unpatriotically, in a review of Le Périgord Park in which this passage appeared:

The clientele is made up of conservatively turned-out citizens apparently unconcerned with economy dining. Most dinner entrées [in 1983] range from thirty-five to forty dollars, and, although the price theoretically covers the cost of the whole meal, supplementary tariffs abound, and a starter of domestic duck liver commands the sort of cash outlay more familiar to Pentagon officials than to most of us. (According to one slightly misguided guidebook, "prices are almost reasonable at Périgord Park." All things considered, so is the present defense budget, which provides for a standing army almost as large and well trained as the restaurant's.)

Like Terrell Vermont, another, somewhat more diffident letter-writer, Susan, was a distance runner, although she had run with the pack, not as a subsidized competitor, in the New York City Marathon. She was a native Bostonian who lived in Manhattan, not far from my own place. She had never before (she added in a post-script) written a fan letter.

Then miserably estranged from Curtis, with my famous harem of dining companions marrying off one after another, I replied to Susan's letter in the hope that another *Gourmet*-subscribing runner might turn out to be another Terrell. Susan and I met one evening, during a violent cloudburst, at a then new place called Sandro's, conveniently located a couple of blocks from my apartment. Drowned-rattedness notwithstanding, with her drenched brunette locks plastered to a swarthy Italianate face straight out of a Bronzino portrait, she was one of the most vulnerably appealing women I'd ever met. Oh Lord, I thought, just keep the letters from the distance runners coming. We dined on infant squid the size of fingernails and other obscenely indulgent delicacies that escaped my notice while I gazed, drowning, into the most gorgeously troubled eyes I'd ever seen.

Such as it was, the ensuing relationship with Susan was a bit more problematic than my platonic liaisons with Terrell and the assorted odalisques who shared my tables. Consigned by an otherwise involved Curtis to bachelorhood, I was horny as a bull rhinoceros but was stonewalled by my newfound inamorata, who restricted our intimacies to adolescent fumbling in the vestibule of her apartment building. A virtuosic tease, she would make all sorts of inflammatory body-language promises during dinner but would invariably ice up after suffering some hallway foreplay at the evening's end. "I'd ask you up but . . ." became the inevitable refrain at the conclusion of our nights out, the *buts* ranging from the putative disarray of her apartment to the proverbial headache and including four or five menstrual periods every month. In the supremely ironic misadventure of my life, she finally invited me to dinner at her place, just when I was crippled by a particularly excruciating attack of gout, which for the first time was centered not in a foot but a knee. To my astonishment, I was invited to spend the night in her bed, where we built up a pretty good head of steam before the moment of truth arrived at long last. Unthinkingly assuming the conventional position, I shrieked as the agony in my knee transferred itself, in the form of a white-hot seizure, to my cerebellum. The lady's born-again virginity remained intact.

Some months later, our grotesque relationship still unconsummated, Susan called to invite me to a Sunday outing at Old Bethpage Village, a Williamsburged reconstruction of a nineteenth-century Long Island farm community, where the advertised plat du jour was a down-home clam chowder served in plastic cups. It was the most pathetic, watered-down reading of one of America's two great soups (the other being an authentically dirty gumbo) I'd ever tasted, but the afternoon was pleasant enough. We drove back to Manhattan in fine fettle, visions of long-deferred sexual congress dancing in my head. Somewhere along the Long Island Expressway, I made casual reference to a phone call I had received from Terrell the night before.

"Terrell? Who's Terrell?"

"A friend."

"A woman friend?"

"Yes."

"How do you know her?"

"Well, curiously enough, we met the same way you and I did— after she wrote me a letter."

"Where does she live?"

"In Atlanta, at the moment."

"Are many southern women named Terrell?"

"Not that I know of."

"Does she look like Susan Anton?"

"Dunno. Who's Susan Anton?"

"Is Terrell from South Carolina?"

"Well, yes, originally."

"Spartanburg?"

I took a long look at Susan, whose appearance others besides myself had likened to a Renaissance *signorina*'s, but who, I now realized, could easily have passed for a Gypsy. She was peering through a windshield, not into a crystal ball, but she was obviously on some paranormal wavelength. "Yes, Spartanburg," I conceded, frost forming on the back of my neck.

"Is her father a lawyer?"

"Well, yes, I think he's a fairly prominent jurist, but how the hell . . ."

"Was Terrell married to John S——?"

Phew! The magic spell was broken. Terrell, I cackled, had never been married to John S——, whoever he might be, or to anyone else. Susan begged to differ: not only had Terrell been married to John S——, but the groom was a cousin of Susan's, and Susan and Terrell had met shortly before the marriage, at a country club in a Boston suburb.

The odds against the possibility of such a farfetched concatenation of coincidences seemed overwhelming, and I just couldn't credit the notion that two magazine subscribers, both distance runners from different parts of the country, could have independently chosen a hack journalist as a literary hero. "Terrell's last name is Vermont, not S——," I submitted weakly.

"I only knew her by her married name," Susan replied.

Pleading the usual sudden headache, Susan dropped me off at my apartment building, and I put through a call to Atlanta. It was none of my business, of course, I told Terrell, but had she by any chance ever been married? Well, yes, she had, but it had been such an unpleasant episode that she had pretty much put it out of mind and seldom voluntarily alluded to it. Was the guy a Bostonian named John S——? "Hell, Jay, how do you know that?" Told how I knew, she said, "Jay, I can't believe you've been dating that creepy cousin of his. I thought you had better taste than that."

8

Eating My Heart Out

Whatever a hired belly eats is eaten on the job. Once he becomes a mercenary feeder, all his eating experiences—past, present, and future—are or will be stored in his data bank, to be retrieved and put to use as needed in the assessment of other eating experiences undertaken for specific journalistic assignments. James Beard termed this accumulation of retrievable sensory impressions "taste memory" and claimed (quite persuasively) to be capable of summoning up at will precise recollections of every individual dish—of every apple, pear, or pickle—he had ingested during eight decades of virtually nonstop gourmandizing.

To a greater or lesser extent, everyone who has eaten enough to survive earliest infancy possesses a taste memory that even in its most rudimentary form facilitates the choice of what is to be eaten, its immediate qualitative evaluation (this meat loaf sucks; it's not like grandma's), and some retrospective reassessment of earlier eating experiences. The starving Southeast Asian or Ethiopian, unable to reconcile relief supplies of alien grain with his taste memory of home-grown rice or wheat, hasn't much choice about what he eats and eats the unfamiliar food grudgingly and miserably, his appetency dulled by memories of marginally happier times, when his food tasted of his own turf and not of Arkansas or Nebraska.

The guy who pulls his rig into a truck stop and tucks into a platter of bacon, eggs, and fries has a general, somewhat idealized idea of what his breakfast will taste like even before it's slammed onto the

Formica. His taste memory has provided him with certain specific expectations, and if the rashers are scorched or the eggs frazzled, his generalized recall of more satisfactory renditions tells him so. It's a consensus of critical opinion, based on commonly held taste memories, that enables Mom's Diner to prosper while Joe's Eats, a half-mile down the pike, languishes.

I certainly couldn't lay claim to the sort of taste memory that Beard appeared to share with a relative handful of the most exquisitely attuned palates and noses on the planet; deprived of my notes, I couldn't have recalled *what* I'd eaten on any given bibulous evening before the morning after, let alone how well or poorly it had been prepared. For Beard and most other food writers, taste memory was an evaluative tool brought into play when particular foods or dishes demanded a basis for comparison. It enabled the writer to envision a specific palatal experience in its optimal form, to juxtapose current and past sensory reactions, and to pronounce judgment according to how closely they coincided or diverged. It rarely loosed a torrent of ink or inspired prose of any great distinction, but rather it served a simple utilitarian purpose.

If most food writers haven't yet begun to exploit the associative literary potential of taste memory, one ringer, Marcel Proust, just about exhausted the possibilities when he got enough mileage out of a bit of cake dunked into a teacup to rattle on through the seven volumes of *A la recherche du temps perdu.* To be sure, Proust's mnemonic inspiration strayed a bit from the simple palatal experience that triggered it. Indeed, he had nothing much to say about his tea ("a thing I did not ordinarily take") except that it was warm, and nothing at all of a critical nature about the famous morsel of madeleine, which for all anyone knows may have been made with stale butter and eggs.

Although Lord knows I was no Marcel Proust, I shared his worst deficiencies during my stint as a hired belly: an inability to concentrate solely on gustatory experience and an inability to shut up. In my ostensible restaurant reviews, I muddled along the meandering paths of free association, sniffing like a dog up an unfamiliar gutter at whatever presented itself along the way: the odd literary or anecdotal allusion, ad hoc references to the company I kept, and various other extrinsic considerations. As a case in point, this is how I began a typically rambling report on an Upper West Side seafood house, managing to fill upward of four manuscript pages before getting down to some semblance of business:

A few issues back, in her report on a Los Angeles restaurant called The Maryland Crab House, my West Coast colleague, Caroline Bates, described "plain, old-fashioned premises permeated with the sweet smell of steamed crab . . . and reverberating with the din of hammering mallets and laughter [as] crab eaters whack away happily at heaps of cooked crabs, sending bits of crab shell flying through the air, squirting crab juice on their neighbors, and littering tables with crab armor and cartilage." Mrs. Bates took the words right out of my mouth. Until I read her piece, I had planned to apply substantially the same description to Sidewalkers', an enormously engaging half-year-old seafood restaurant at 12 West Seventy-second Street.

To roughly half its clientele, Sidewalkers' is a single-entrée restaurant. The entrée of choice is the so-called "Maryland Crab-bash," a gloriously raffish exercise in hand-to-hand combat and, to my low taste, one of the supreme eating experiences this side of paradise. It's an experience, however, with which few newcomers to the restaurant appear to be familiar. Hence, I'll ask Marylanders and other initiates to bear with some background.

The crab in question is the Atlantic blue crab, on the subject of which there is no more imaginative, witty, or readable an authority than William W. Warner. This is how Warner introduces the critter in his definitive book on the crabs and watermen of Chesapeake Bay, *Beautiful Swimmers:*

The Atlantic blue crab is known to scientists as *Callinectes sapidus* Rathbun. It is very well named. *Callinectes* is Greek for beautiful swimmers. *Sapidus,* of course, means tasty or savory

in Latin. Rathbun is the late Dr. Mary J. Rathbun of the Smithsonian Institution, who first gave the crab its specific name.

Dr. Rathbun, known as Mary Jane to her Smithsonian colleagues, has often been called the dean of American carcinolo-
gists, as experts in crabs and other crustaceans are properly
termed. Before her death in 1943, Mary Jane identified and
described over 998 new species of crabs, an absolute record in
the annals of carcinology. In only one case did she choose to
honor culinary qualities. History has borne out the wisdom of
her choice. No crab in the world has been as much caught or
eagerly consumed as *sapidus.*

To its legions of passionate admirers, no crab in the world—indeed,
no other crustacean of any kind—rivals *sapidus* for sweetness, texture, or culinary adaptability. To the purists among them, no other
culinary manifestation of *sapidus* remotely compares with the crab
when it is steamed live beneath a light encrustation of spices blended
in conformity with venerable Maryland tradition. This is the preferred treatment at Sidewalkers', where only the heavier, meatier,
larger-clawed males of the species ("jimmies" in the parlance of the
Chesapeake Bay watermen, who refer to the females as "sooks")
are served, and where their preparation is something like an exact
science.

Although the male blue crab is one of the gentlest, most touchingly solicitous amorists in the animal kingdom, the tender side of
his nature is known to the object of his conjugal affection alone. In
his dealings with the rest of society, he is one of the most ornery,
bellicose, dauntless beings in all creation. A jimmy at bay, taking up
a defensive stance in, say, the corner of a kitchen sink, is the personification of murderous rage and a force to be reckoned with.
Literally foaming at the mouth, with claws agape at their fullest
extension, he is one bad actor, and woe betide the adversary who
takes him lightly. Put him and several of his fellows into a steamer,
and they'll rend one another limb from limb—again quite literally—

before succumbing to the inevitable. Having cooked up many a sapid but dismembered mess of *sapidi* in my own kitchen and been served some equally unsightly messes in various East Coast restaurants, I asked Arnie Benson, the owner of Sidewalkers', how his cooks invariably manage to send their steamed crabs to the table intact, with claws tucked demurely under their chins and legs folded in precise symmetry.

"It's simple," Benson replied. "Before we steam them, we soak them in an ice water bath, with just a touch of vinegar added to the water. It has an anesthetic effect on them—just puts them right to sleep. They just tuck themselves into their normal sleeping position and dream whatever crabs dream about."

Thus sedated, jimmy is smeared with a blend of Old Bay seasoning (a commercial preparation much favored in the Chesapeake Bay area), mustard, cracked pepper, and several grades of coarse salt. Then he's steamed for eighteen to twenty-two minutes, depending on his size, in a specially designed device whose sloping cover prevents condensation from dripping onto his carapace and diluting the spice mixture. After the crabs have cooled sufficiently to be handled, they are borne to the dining room on a tray and slid directly onto a table covered with white butcher's paper and furnished with wooden mallets and stacks of paper napkins. Clean white waste receptacles are dispersed around the table, within easy reach of the diners, and bibs are provided for those who want them. If instruction in crab dismantlement is required, the server demonstrates the art at this juncture, then discreetly withdraws as the carnage begins.

Even for the most proficient initiate, there's an inherent sloppiness about the Crab-bash. Decorum is out of the question, and the only way to enjoy the ritual to the utmost is to throw yourself into the spirit of the occasion. Dress casually, roll up your sleeves, and wallow gleefully in the mess you're making. As the menu gloss at Sidewalkers' puts it, "The Baltimore style of cooking and eating crabs . . . makes you, the eater, an integral part of the seasoning process. . . . When you eat . . . the spices cover your fingers and coat your hands, as well as your lips, ensuring that each piece of crab meat will be heartily seasoned by the time you swallow it.''

As originally submitted, the review contained a parenthetical afterthought to the menu copy: "You, the eater, it goes without saying, will be heartily seasoned for some time to come. Several hours after enjoying one crab-bash, I dropped into a favorite watering hole on the East Side of town. When the manager, who grew up in Maryland, joined me at the bar for an exchange of pleasantries, I waggled my fingers under his nose and asked what they smelled like. 'Oh, man!' he exclaimed. 'They smell like home.' " Predictably, the passage was deleted by some hygienist on the magazine's editorial staff.

According to its proprietor, Sidewalkers' was the city's only crab house when it opened in 1983. When I took issue with Arnie Benson's claim, pointing out the existence of an older establishment on the Lower East Side, he sneered, "That's no crab house. They *boil* their crabs." Whether or not it was indeed unique in town, Sidewalkers' was the sort of place I was happiest reviewing. It specialized in a critter for which I harbored particular affection and which was relatively little known or served in recognizable form anywhere but a few pockets of enlightenment along the eastern seaboard, a critter I had often extracted from its natural habitat, that had periodically avenged itself for my predation by laying me up with gout, and that I had read up on fairly extensively. *Sapidus* and its method of preparation at the restaurant lent themselves generously to my discursive style, and I could figuratively sink my teeth into the subject with the same enthusiasm as I did literally.

In their near-infinite variety, aquatic foods in general struck a more responsive chord in me than anything else. Nothing much could be written about a beefsteak that wasn't already common knowledge (or at least nothing printable by a writer whose name didn't happen to be Upton Sinclair), and the classics of haute cuisine were equally well known and well documented. These subjects required nothing more than simple evaluation of the quality of a given restaurant's raw materials and execution, larded with a few of the threadbare adjectives hired bellies mercilessly inflict on their constituencies in piece after piece, year after year.

Whether or not the magazine's readers shared my view, I found the taxonomy of edible marine and freshwater creatures endlessly fascinating and elegantly precise, unlike popular nomenclature, which was often ambiguous (e.g., "striped bass" or "rockfish," depending on local usage, for *Roccus saxatilus,* or worse, the slovenly food writer's "bass" for any of various, wildly disparate saltwater and freshwater denizens).

With scattered exceptions, finfish and shellfish, separately or in combination, have played the starring roles in the truly memorable meals of my life (relatively few of which have been prepared by vaunted chefs or served in the more celebrated showcases of higher gastronomy), with *Callinectes sapidus* not the least among the featured actors.

In *Beautiful Swimmers*—far and away the finest, most felicitously written book on a single food resource I know of—the author describes the courtship and mating ritual of the blue crab in prose as hauntingly evocative and as affecting as the Song of Solomon or the most erotic of Shakespeare's sonnets: quite an accomplishment when the description is applied to a stalk-eyed embodiment of otherwise unremitting cussedness. As Warner details jimmy's elaborately solicitous concern for the sook of his choice, foreplay is accomplished "very patiently" while the male makes a protective cage of his body, positioning it over his moulting inamorata and tenderly cradling her while she is most vulnerable to predators. For the nubile sook (termed a she-crab during her immaturity), this is the final and most painful ecdysis of her lifetime: she "busts," or divests herself of her shell, a process that takes two or three hours to accomplish, then rests in the guardian embrace of her mate until her strength returns. She reproduces several months later and dies, leaving a presumably grieving widower to live out his allotted three years or so in bereavement.

I had crabbed for several years with some regularity on the South Fork of Long Island, using an amateurish but productive technique contemptuously referred to by the professional watermen of Chesapeake Bay as "chicken necking." The procedure is accomplished by driving a series of stakes at five-foot intervals into a shallow bottom, tying a line several yards long and baited with a ripe chicken neck or fish head to each stake, and flinging the bait-weighted line out into deeper water. The line hangs slack until an invisible crab unwittingly signals its interest by pulling the line taut (Caller on line three!), whereupon line, bait, and crab are teased slowly shoreward to the shallows, where the crustacean is scooped up with a dipnet.

Deliberately or not, the seventeenth-century English dramatist Thomas Shadwell had as much to say about gastronomic as about social deprivation when he wrote "I am, out of the ladies' company, like a fish out of the water." Although many varieties of fish and shellfish are marketed live, life per se is no indicator of quality or freshness. Any sea creature begins to undergo change for the worse the moment it's removed from its natural environment, and the longer it breathes an alien atmosphere and is deprived of nutrients, the more drastically its condition will deteriorate as it undergoes changes of body chemistry and loss of muscle tone that directly and adversely affect its flavor, aroma, and texture.

In my fairly extensive experience, the best way to eat mollusks is right where they live: in the water that nurtured them, within instants of their capture, sans terrestrial embellishments of any kind. (You don't, goddamnit, dig clams or oysters in lemon orchards.) To bring to the surface, shuck, and gullet down a bay scallop or a topneck while immersed chest-deep in its native element is to experience sensations otherwise reserved for the starfish, the gull, and other seafood purists and denied the patrons of the finest restaurants. At times, I've considered attempting to ingest *Callinectes sapidus* or *Homarus americanus* in more or less identical circumstances, but I was dissuaded by considerations of simple practicability and by my own cowardice in the face of clearly superior firepower: a crustacean determined not to be eaten at a particular moment gives pause even to the most resolute prospective eater.

If the crabs we ate weren't eaten *vivant,* in the absolute prime of their lives (as certain shrimp have been consumed by certain Chinese exquisites since time immemorial), Curtis and I came about as close to the ideal as we could when we chicken necked. As soon as we'd hauled in a half-bushel or so of midsummer-plump blues of optimum wingspan, we'd rush them home in minutes, steam them immediately in nothing more elaborate than their own piss and vinegar, dump them on newspapers spread on the deck, and blissfully whack away at them and each other for a couple of hours. Unspiced and unsauced in any way, they were as good as mortal eating gets in an imperfect world, and my inability to walk on hideously distended feet for a week or so thereafter seemed a small price to pay for the ineffable gratification of experiencing *sapidus in excelcis.*

I had never witnessed "doubling"—the cradling of the sook beneath the jimmy—while crabbing and didn't stumble on the phenomenon for the first time until one August afternoon when, while wading through transparent shallows on my way to a particularly fertile bed of hard clams *(Mercenaria mercenaria),* I glimpsed peripherally a live manifestation of what I had previously known only as an illustration in Warner's book.

His dun carapace virtually indistinguishable from the silt in which he hunkered, there was jimmy, standing guard on tiptoe over his armorless mate, who peered out warily from between his folded chelae, thinking sweet thoughts while awaiting coitus. In a purely reflexive split second, I shot my clam rake into the water at an oblique angle, pulling it back and snaring the lovers even as they whispered sweet nothings into each other's ears. Less than ten minutes later, I stood, still dripping, before the kitchen range, while Romeo and Juliet sizzled in a black-iron skillet. Their fatal tryst imparted incomparable sweetness to their flesh, providing unspeakably brutal me with a standard of perfection against which all subsequent sautéed crabs would be measured, to the detriment of the pretenders. Lord, what a lunch it was!

The common freshwater crayfish is one of the world's most widely distributed crustaceans and one of the least appreciated in the United States, saliently excepting Louisiana, where the beast is justly venerated and answers to such names as crawfish, crawdad, écrevisse, and mudbug. As a member of the order Decapoda, it belongs to a gastronomically beneficent fellowship that includes the crabs, shrimp, prawns, and lobsters and extends honorary membership to squid and cuttlefish but excludes a third group of eminently edible cephalopod mollusks, the octopuses, whose eight limbs fall two short of the association's admittance requirement.

As luck and my own poor planning would have it, none of my trips to Louisiana have coincided with the crawdad's seasonal availability there. Except for two epic orgies, my crayfish eating had been limited to a few decorous experiences in Europe until the mid-1980s, when the widespread proliferation of the so-called, outrageously overhyped Cajun-Creole restaurants generated some limited interest in—and slightly increased retail distribution of—the crustaceans outside their normal purlieus. I also had been tantalized on occasion by inadequate hints of écrevisse in a few of Manhattan's better French restaurants, usually in the form of some sauce-smothered puff pastry creation flecked with a few bits of shriveled tail and crowned with a single intact specimen in full armor, the garnish offered as a spurious earnest of what the dish clearly was not. Aside from full-grown lobsters and blue crabs the size of defensive linemen, East Coast decapod crustaceans served in anything less than genocidal numbers are more frustrating than no crustaceans at all.

I was unable to form a conclusive opinion of the crayfish served in season during the early 1980s at an atypically glamorous Upper East Side Chinese restaurant called Auntie Yuan. The eponym was a nonexistent surrogate for the Chinese-born owner of the place,

David Keh (of whom we'll hear more later), and its manager, Ed Schoenfeld, an autodidactic Sinologist who spoke Cantonese with a Brooklyn accent. Schoenfeld, who bore a distinct if somewhat startling resemblance, in the context, to a Hassidic rabbi, was the first, and possibly last, exponent of Chinese *nouvelle cuisine* in the city. He had devised an imaginative, if somewhat anomalous, menu made up in large part of dishes to be found in no other Chinese restaurants or, in one case, no other restaurant of any kind in the city. This unique offering was displayed, wriggling, for my inspection one evening by Schoenfeld himself, who ceremoniously placed a dripping cardboard carton on a thitherto pristine tablecloth and opened it as though it were a reliquary. (One way or another, it was highly unlikely that your napery would remain dry when Ed was in residence and table hopping. A notorious schmoozer with no inhibitions about crashing anyone's party, he was a "spitter" in theatrical parlance and a torrentially voluble monologist. He put on the performance of his career one night when he insinuated himself into what had been planned as a tête-à-tête with a blind date and held forth, cascading over the linen, until he was bluntly invited to bugger off halfway through the entrée.)

"Crayfish!" I exclaimed as Ed unveiled his treasure trove.

"Crayfish, schmayfish," he replied. "These, my friend, are *soft-shell* crayfish."

I had often wondered whether lobsters in moult could be eaten as crabs are during *their* ecdysis. I had concluded there was no theoretical reason why they couldn't be, but the hypothesis had gone untested over the years for lack of opportunity. Eventually, I learned that *Homarus* doesn't shed its exoskeleton until its replacement is far too leathery for human consumption. Somehow, I had never entertained similar speculation about crayfish, but I now realized that putting myself on the outside of a mess of Auntie Yuan's soft-shelled mudbugs would be as close as I would ever come to the realization of an old, impracticable dream.

(According to Norma S. Upson, the author of *The Crawfish Cookbook,* crayfish "are, in fact, a form of *freshwater lobster!*" On purely visual, miniatured evidence, they would seem to be, and elegant biological distinctions have never got in the way, for me, of simple sensual enjoyment. If it looks, walks, and quacks like a duck, it's a duck on my dinner plate, whatever the learned taxonomists may consider it; if it looks almost precisely like a scaled-down specimen of *Homarus americanus,* regardless of its freshwater provenance, so much the better, whatever its formal designation.)

The enjoyment of crayfish is a cumulative process that entails wholesale procurement of the raw materials, rapid dismantlement of them after they're boiled, and nonstop ingestion over an appreciable period of time. The true believer doesn't savor the objects of his affection singly, episodically, and ruminatively, as does the oyster fancier or the connoisseur of escargots; he feeds his face as though engaged in a race against the clock. For him, unbridled gluttony is prerequisite to maximal arousal of the taste buds, and it's no mere coincidence that cold beer in inundatory volume is the washdown of choice. The keepers of the faith in this country are overwhelmingly good ole boys for whom the service of a *few* 'dads would be an egregious solecism, as would be the pouring of some distractingly nervous little lapdog of a white wine that constantly had to be assured that it was cherished and understood.

As befitted the solemnity of the occasion, no lesser a personage than Ed Schoenfeld himself, his beard spangled with the detritus of various dishes tasted in the line of duty, bore my sautéed crayfish to the table and reverently set them down before me. There were six of them, fetchingly arranged on a black plate. They were accompanied by a small glass of Graves of impeccable pedigree. They were history before I was able to form any palatal impression of them.

It hadn't been until the early 1970s, when we traveled to Curtis's mother's place, a former working farm in rural Michigan, for the Christmas holidays, that I had encountered crawdads in meaningful numbers for the first time. Warned that Delta, Curtis's mother, was a self-educated polymath who had unaccountably neglected to familiarize herself with the supreme achievement of modern Western culture, the dry martini, I arrived laden with several bottles of Gordon's gin, the equivalent of a thimbleful of dry vermouth, and the remnants of a jar of olives that had been rusting in my refrigerator since the early days of the Eisenhower administration. Delta, with whom I fell in love on sight (thereby reducing by a few hours the time it had taken me to fall under the spell of her daughter), wasn't deterred for an instant by my proposal that she join us in celebration of a rite as alien to her previous experience as human sacrifice or the chanting of mantras. Tentatively sipping her drink, she reacted as though she'd stepped on a third rail, but she somehow managed to smile through the shock. Preoccupied by introductions to various members and friends of the family, I didn't become aware of the emptiness of Delta's glass for some time. Would she like a refill? Oh, yes, by all means: she had already acquired a taste, she claimed, for the most austere cocktail that depraved human genius had ever devised. After mixing and handing her a refill, I looked on in disbelief as she stirred a couple of spoonfuls of sugar into it, knocked it back as though it were nothing more potent than pineapple juice, and extended her glass for replenishment.

A narrow creek runs along the edge of Delta's property, at the bottom of her sloping lawn. I was poking along its snow-covered bank the next morning when I spotted a pair of lilliputian lobsters scuttling along its muddy bed. Had I given any consideration to the question, I'd have thought crayfish hibernated during the Michigan winters, but I hadn't, and there the critters were, going about their errands as though on a day in May. In a state of considerable excitement, I made a few inquiries up at the house, where Curtis's brother Mike and a few of his cronies were sitting around the kitchen table analyzing the contents of a couple of six-packs. Hell no, nobody around here had ever gone after them mudbugs. What in hell would they do with 'em? When told what I intended to do with 'em, they stared at me as though I'd confessed to some unspeakable perversion that confirmed their worst suspicions of New

Yorkers. "Goddamn asshole," a guy in a hunting shirt and feed-lot cap muttered when he thought I was out of earshot.

Chicken necking is supposed to work as well with crayfish as it does with blue crabs, but it requires a dipnet, which I lacked. After taking inventory of a catchall garage, I improvised a trap of sorts by cutting a couple of square feet from a beat-up old window screen and attaching a length of twine to each of its corners. I slogged through semithawed snow, stripped down to my skivvies, and waded into the creek. Baited with a scatter of kitchen detritus, the rudimentary trap settled on the bottom, its string-ends gathered in my hand. Out of their muddy burrows came the crayfish to congregate on the rusty mesh, to be hoisted from the water and dumped into a bucket. An hour later, blue with cold, shuddering uncontrollably, standing on unfeeling feet of stone, I filled Delta's kitchen sink with the creatures, which everyone present except Curtis regarded, as they did me, with the utmost disdain.

After another hour of thawing in a hot bath, I returned to the kitchen, commandeered the biggest pot in Delta's *batterie de cuisine,* and announced that lunch would be served immediately after a round or three of martinis. For most of the assembled company, I was informed, lunch would be served, after a few more rounds of Bud, at Elias Big Boy, the local mecca of epicureanism, where the *spécialité de la maison* took the form of a double-decker greaseburger paired with a stack of ketchup-blanketed cordwood fries. Morbid curiosity delayed the departure of Mike and his colleagues, who were clearly skeptical about my announced intention to follow through on my threat to cook and serve the despised mudbugs.

Aside from a few insignificant variants, the staples of Delta's larder were the staples of the region: flour, sugar, lard, miniature marshmallows, and Jell-O. Unimaginative cook that I was, none of these raw materials seemed very promising in conjunction with crayfish, but a ransacking of the pantry turned up a few marginally usable items: a half-empty jar of bay leaves that had moldered in a cupboard for a generation or two and a few equally fossilized herbs and spices. I concocted an improvisatory crab-boil mixture and pitched it into the pot, along with the crawdads and a cup or two of tap water. The dry components of the recipe represented nothing more than wishful thinking: whatever flavors and aromas they originally may have possessed were by then the most attenuated of memories. But more than any seafood I know of, with the possible exception of octopus, crayfish are gifted with a genius for self-seasoning. Cooked with the barest minimum of ancillary ingredients, their own bodily chemicals imbue them with complexities and richly orchestrated subtleties beyond the imaginings of the most gifted sauciers.

The pot didn't stay on the fire long; the abuse of crustaceans by overcooking in this country, at home and in restaurants, is scandalous. Shrimp that should be as supple on the plate as in life are routinely served in catatonic rigidity; crabs are murderously overboiled, their precious body fluids (to paraphrase General Buck Turgidson of *Dr. Strangelove*) thrown out with the bathwater; and lobsters, which logically should die in the element that nurtured them, are subjected to dry heat that shrivels their sweet flesh, fusing it inextricably to shell that stinks like the aftermath of an industrial fire.

Taking her cue from Curtis, Delta, God bless her, sat down in a state of happy expectancy, as did I, when the 'dads were piled on the table. Mike and his contingent ostentatiously passed, mildly interested in the geek activity but in no way inclined to participate. Following the example Curtis and I set, Delta snapped the tails off a few crawdads, stripped them of their shells, ate them, and sucked sweet essences from their severed heads. The Michigan rednecks were obviously shaken: here was one of their own, a respected senior citizen and pillar of the community, eating mudbugs with manifest relish. Tentatively, the guys gathered a little closer to the table, sizing up one another for any signs of weakening resistance, challenging one another to take the plunge. Someone said, "Aw, hell," and a hand at the end of a flannel sleeve snaked its way between Curtis and her mother to the center of the table. It hovered over the crustaceans for a moment, then withdrew a single speci-men from the outermost edge of the sprawl, as though raking in a single poker chip from a hefty pot.

The ice thus broken, the other guys followed suit. Someone allowed as how the damn things *weren't* bad eating, and someone else seconded his vote, and all of a sudden guys had pulled up chairs and were engaged in a devil-take-the-hindmost feeding frenzy. My satisfaction at having converted them was dampened somewhat by the concomitant reduction of my own share of the spoils, but mar-tyrdom, I figured, comes with the territory. When it was all over, their verdict was unanimous: it had been one hell of a feed.

It damned well had been, and I was a lot better equipped to pronounce judgment than they were.

Oddly enough, supposedly adventurous big-city diners can often be more resistant to unfamiliar eating experiences than the most ob-tuse heartland rubes. Or so I discovered the next time I got a crack at crayfish in appreciable quantity.

Our phone rang early one morning, just as Curtis was about to leave for work. The caller was Irwin Berman, a young surgeon whom I'd met a year or so earlier when some superficial whittling of my person was required. As it turned out, we shared a common interest in art—I as an art journalist; he as an avocational painter and collector—and similar mating propensities. His wife, Linda, a transplanted southerner, and Curtis would easily have passed for sisters of each other and of the actress Angie Dickinson. Once acquainted, the four of us dined out together frequently when I needed tablemates while casing out prospective review subjects.

Irwin's first words on the morning in question were, "Do you and Curtis like crayfish?" Do we ever! Why? Why? Because a colleague of his was attending a medical conference in New Or-leans that morning and would be returning to New York late in the afternoon with as many pounds of fresh-caught bayou 'dads as he could carry, all of which would be cooked up by Linda for the delectation of a few chosen epicures.

If Linda and Irwin had nothing else (as far as I could tell, they had everything else), they had an innate sense of the spirit of a particular occasion. Monied beyond my wildest dreams, they occupied an apartment on upper Park Avenue that was roughly the size of Mount Vernon or Monticello and furnished with museum-quality pieces, which were brusquely shoved aside on the evening in question and temporarily replaced by a couple of rented trestle tables covered with butcher's paper and tastefully adorned with a can of beer at each place setting. The effect was dulled somewhat by the attire of the guests, which was far too formal for the business at hand, but I assumed that coats would be shed, ties loosened, and sleeves rolled up once the action got under way.

The donor of the crawfish* was an expatriate Brit who bore an uncanny resemblance to Pete Rose. "And who might Pete Rose be?" the good doctor asked when so informed. I explained that his doppelgänger was an eminent baseball player who had recently been voted the second-handsomest member of the Cincinnati Reds, his twenty-four teammates having tied for first place. The doctor was not amused. Nor was Curtis, who shot me a stiff under-the-table kick.

In the traditional fashion favored by both blue crab and crawdad fanciers, the delicacies were dumped directly onto the tables, where they were regarded with manifest alarm by the assembled three-piece-suiters and their designer-draped consorts. Curtis, Linda, Irwin, and I had smeared our faces pretty good with a blend of mudbug essence and down-home crab-boil spices by the time I looked around and realized that we four were the only active participants. Our fellow diners had dropped out of the competition after timidly picking at a few beasts apiece, and they were petitioning for small glasses of white wine while we knocked back can after can of beer, single-mindedly munched, and noisily sucked, strewing debris all over the place. Sotto voce, Curtis remarked that our tablemates were looking somewhat askance at our sustained glut-

---

*Variant spelling in respect of their Louisiana provenance.

tony. "Fuck 'em, the dumb bastards," I muttered, helping myself to another pound or so of crustaceous manna.

Clearly devastated, Linda was on the verge of tears. Couple by couple, her guests were departing prematurely, in all likelihood on the off chance of securing a table on short notice at Le Cirque. A good ten pounds of uneaten crawdads remained on the tables. If we liked, Linda said, she'd bag them for us to take home. Well, sure, we'd be delighted to take whatever she wasn't planning to . . .

"Oh, no, y'all take 'em all, the whole damn lot."

"But, Linda, you love them as much as we do."

"Not any more, I don't. Not after the way those people behaved with 'em." ("Those people" sounded unmistakably like a euphemism for the "no-account Yankee trash" she might have used had her husband, Curtis, and I not been born north of the Mason-Dixon line.) "You take 'em home. At least I'll know they're appreciated there."

We lugged them home in a shopping bag. At last, I gloated, there were crawfish enough to do them justice. The more we ate, the better they tasted. We feasted all that night and had gumbo the next.

Of my four sons, one has become an absolute vegetarian and another abstains from the flesh of quadrupeds. Mathieu, the absolutist, occasionally backslides by eating a butter cookie but otherwise shuns all animal foods. His vegetarianism, he tells me, is unconcerned with matters of conscience; he just feels better physically on a diet of nuts, grains, beanstuffs, and the like. His brother Sumner, on the other hand, discriminates between what he considers the more and less intelligent of the various species of fauna, restricting his animal nutrients to the presumably dumber species and having no gustatory traffic with anything brainier than a chicken, except for dairy products that entail no slaughter. In his view, to paraphrase the advertising slogan of the United Negro College Fund, a mind is a terrible thing to eat.

Leaving aside William Warner's well-documented contention

that the Atlantic blue crab—a creature Sumner devours with unstinting relish—is one of the most keenly intelligent creatures on
the planet, I've often pondered the quantitative-versus-qualitative
question the kid's position poses: Is a single beef steer, which may
provide hundreds of meals for as many humans, and which, whatever the degree of its sapience, is unlikely to make any original
contributions to the arts and sciences, less expendable than certain
species of seafoods, scores or hundreds of whose individual members must be sacrificed in order to provide a single dinner for a
single human of moderate appetency?

As a member of a species equipped with teeth specifically designed by nature for the rending of flesh and provided with digestive juices designed to facilitate its bodily absorption, and as an
inhabitant of a world in which the overwhelming majority of my
fellow beasts survive by preying on species more vulnerable than
their own, I simply can't buy the arguments of the animal-rights
advocates. Carried to their logical extremes, those arguments
would legislate the extinction of most nonvegetative forms of life
on earth. I can live with the notion, considered as an abstract
proposition, of a planet presided over by carrots, with myself and
my carnivorous brethren nowhere in evidence. The absence of
Leona Helmsley, Vanna White, both houses of Congress, Dr. Ruth
Westheimer, Roseanne Barr, the editors of *People,* Andy Rooney,
Bill Cosby, the geriatric rulers of the People's Republic of China,
and George Steinbrenner would be an enticing prospect indeed
were it not offset by a concomitant loss of the optimally flavorsome
roast rack of lamb served at La Côte Basque, the world-class rustic-
style veal and the meltingly tender and supremely sapid *ossobuco*
prepared at Felidia, or *tête de veau vinaigrette* with egg sauce in the
infinitely soothing Tout Va Bien treatment. To be sure, I side with
the animal sympathizers in their abhorrence of fur coats, never
having seen any creatures but humans garbed in pelts other than
those with which nature clothed them. On the other hand, our
world would be infinitely diminished were the self-styled animal-

rights advocates to realize their chimerical vision of a peaceable kingdom where no animals are eaten. The osprey and the tiger, the robin on your front lawn, the Atlantic blue crab, the whale that feeds on tons of krill, and the house cat on your lap clearly couldn't survive more than a few days on my son Mathieu's diet of tofu and bean sprouts. I'm not sure I could, either, or that vegetable-rights advocates wouldn't be heard from next.

When I poke along the beaches or wade into the bays and ponds of the South Fork in quest of whitebait, mussels, clams, oysters, crabs, periwinkles, whelks, or limpets (yes, limpets: try them some time in a pasta sauce, but get the sand out first), I commit myself to mass murder. When the whitebait, in particular, are running well, they run in uncountable numbers, and each closing of the seine condemns hundreds, if not thousands, to the deep fryer. Similarly (although professional hit men do the dirty for me), populous communities are sacrificed to my appetite when I sit down to a mess of 'dads at Ragtime, a scruffy beachfront joint in Jacksonville, or dine at Sandro's in New York, where a platterful of infant squid the size of lima beans is a house specialty, or when I belly up to a tapas bar in Madrid or Barcelona or Seville, to spend a couple of hours casually destroying a few hundred assorted *mariscos.* Have I more on my conscience than my son Sumner has on his on the occasions when I spare the lamb but wreak near-genocidal havoc on all manner of presumably less sentient sea creatures? I don't know. Until I find out, señor, just keep them *tallinas* coming!

In retrospect, relatively few of the really memorable dishes and meals of my years with the magazine were served where one most might expect to find them: the more highly acclaimed of the big-ticket restaurants. To be sure, I had hundreds—perhaps thousands—of excellent meals, and a few that verged on sublimity, in various full-service, white-tablecloth establishments with world-renowned chefs in residence. With few exceptions, however, they weren't truly *stirring* meals, and my most unforgettable eating experiences—those of which I retain the most indelibly vivid taste memories and recall with the utmost relish—took place in far less imposing surroundings.

Le Bernardin, a prohibitively posh French seafood restaurant on the West Side of town, opened in the mid-1980s to a deafening chorus of hosannas. With one exception that I know of, the nation's hired bellies fell all over themselves in their rush to hymn its praises. I was the exception, in part because of *Gourmet*'s wait-and-see editorial policy, but also because I harbored certain reservations about the chef's conceptual approach to his métier. I had two or three meals there, and I probably would have given the place some mildly enthusiastic ink had I remained with the magazine long enough to sort out my impressions, but whatever those meals may have consisted of has been long since disremembered. I'm fairly sure I had urchins as a starter one night (and had had better in certain Japanese restaurants), and I have dim memories of a chowder (not so termed on the menu) of some sort and a flatfish of forgotten species, in all likelihood Dover sole suffering from jet lag, mantled in a sauce I thought belonged on something else. The only real impressions I've retained are of the soothing décor, excellent service, and superb renditions of what seemed to me somewhat misconceived dishes.

Dissolve to Madrid, some years earlier. A nondescript little sidestreet *tasca,* La Oficina, somewhere off the Puerta del Sol, where Curtis and I have been hanging out late mornings for the better part of a week. The tapas bar is presided over by a youth of sixteen or seventeen, who has dedicated several hours over the last few days to the initiation of the *norteamericano* and his lady into the arcana of the comprehensive selection of *mariscos* in which the place specializes. The kid is vastly amused by the behavior of these *extranjeros,* who sample the tapas so purposefully and relentlessly, munching through *ración* after *ración,* long after the regular customers have contented themselves with small portions of this or that before moving on along their regular rounds; these unseemly, enthusiastic foreigners who tip like crazy.

Until this night, our last in town, the kid has seen us only at midday. He seems genuinely delighted when we show up after dark and manage to convey the unorthodox proposition that he compile a definitive anthology of the house specialties—indeed, everything the house has to offer—and serve it in lieu of the formal sit-down dinner we'd otherwise have taken in a proper restaurant. *Solamente tapas? Si, si,* just what you have, but lots of *everything* you have. An ear-to-ear grin splits his face. Conspiratorially, he tells us to stay put for a few moments while he performs some essential but unspecified errand, adding that we are to inform any droppers-in that he'll return *inmediatamente* to serve them. True to his word, he is back two minutes later, bearing in triumph, like the ears of a cleanly dispatched *toro bravo,* a yard-wide, heavily embossed silver salver, begged, borrowed, or stolen God alone knows where.

In view of the grandness of the occasion, we are instructed to seat ourselves at one of the establishment's two or three seldom-used tables, while our collation is assembled. We do so, wading through the traditional *tasca* carpet of discarded shrimp shells and paper napkins. Twenty minutes later, the kid sets between us an astonishing profusion of assorted shellfish: the infinitely varied crustaceans and molluscous delicacies in which Iberian waters abound. Our eyes goggle at the splendor of it all. The platter has been heaped mountainously high in an extravagantly florid composition that would have given pause to the painter Jan de Heem at the zenith of his Flemish baroque phase. This is at least a dozen pounds of seafood, including, of course, inedible shell.

Everything—*mejillones, percebes, almejas, ostras,* a half-dozen other varieties of mollusks I can't put names to, and a comprehensive selection of incredibly succulent decapods—tasted as good as or better than it looked. By the halfway point, Curtis's rapturous sighs had me feeling as though I'd been cuckolded by her dinner.

It was and remains a singularly unforgettable experience about which we still reminisce happily years after the fact and the dissolution of our life together. It cost a relative pittance.

The dinner at La Oficina had been a full-fledged, if somewhat unconventional, meal. What may have been the single most memorable dish of my life was served some years later at a nameless, open-faced eating house on the main drag of Thonburi, across the Chao Phraya from downtown Bangkok. Thonburi is seldom visited by tourists or outlanders of any stripe. There is nothing about it to attract them. No great temples. No shopping of any interest. No topless go-go dancers or prostitutes of whatever persuasion. No floating markets for vacationing Japanese to photograph. Nothing a round-eye might want to drink and no ice to put in it. No restaurants worth the name. It's a heat-prostrated torpor whose only major thoroughfare leads, via an alley cat's itinerary, to a rural nowheresville made up mostly of soaring coconut and banana groves traversed here and there by ill-defined footpaths.

I had taken the ferry from its landing near the Oriental Hotel. After cruising the main street, a grimy concatenation of machine shops and similar enterprises that bears a distinct resemblance to that part of Chicago that dribbles away into Cicero, I headed at random down a side alley, as is my wont on unfamiliar turf. A neighborhood of middle-class family dwellings—populated at that late-morning hour by a few gossiping housewives who glanced from their front yards with mild interest but no overt show of surprise at a passing stranger hung with photographic gear—abruptly gave way to a parajungle in which I was thoroughly lost after forty minutes or so of peripatetic communion with wild orchids and sunbathing lizards. After any number of false starts and excursions down blind alleys, one of which resulted in an alarming encounter with a Thai counterpart of a Hell's Angel who for one reason or another was pushing his cycle through the forest primeval, I found myself back on pavement.

Retracing my original route from the opposite direction and on the opposite side of the street, I was stopped in my tracks by a sidewalk display of tawny-shelled bivalve mollusks that looked delectably similar to some I'd eaten in various locations along the Mediterranean littoral: the small, delicate clams of the authentic *spaghetti con le vongole,* in lieu of which the littleneck quahogs pressed into service by Italian restaurateurs in the United States just don't measure up, tasty as the substitution may be on its own terms.

A frontless room. Six or eight tables. Two women of successive generations—the elder plump and jolly, the younger slim and lovely—presiding over a couple of woks and an open grill. The aforementioned stranger, still dripping cameras and carrying cases, pantomimes his desire to partake of the shellfish in whatever culinary treatment the women choose to apply to them. Total cracked-up hilarity on the part of the women (the Thai make something like a second religion of *sanuk,* or "good fun"). The stranger is seated and eventually served. The dish exceeds his wildest expectations. A plethora of the mollusks have been briefly sautéed in their shells (now, of course, opened) with significant quantities of minced garlic, a generous spangling of fresh coriander, a judicious admixture of finely chopped, hellaciously incendiary chili peppers, and just enough oil to facilitate the bivalves' passage to the afterlife. Sweet Jesus, what a dish! Better than sex. Better than dying in midorgasm.

Other gustatory memories surface like bits of egg white in a clarifying stock, to be savored as keenly in retrospect as they once were in actuality. There was a cabin in the woods near Phoenicia, New York, long before I became a professional eater, where cold pieces of local free-range chicken were suffused the day after they were broiled with the heightened smoke and sweetness of the burning hickory of the night before. There was a town house on Manhattan's Upper East Side, where the Italian-born painter Giorgio Cavallon (an undersung master of reductive abstract expressionism, master mechanic, metalsmith, and cook, whose entire kitchen—from its superbly wrought copper pots and pans and motorized pasta machine to its open-chimney rotisserie and even its immense freezer—were artifacts of his own fabrication) served a sumptuous *risotto nero,* dead-black with cooked-down cuttlefish ink, and followed it with the finest roast leg of lamb, redolent of rosemary, garlic, and parsley, I've ever eaten. There was a discouragingly glitzy, overlarge *tasca,* populated by half-naked Teutonic and Nordic types in tourist-blighted, once hauntingly spare Torremolinos, where Curtis and I swooned over briefly marinated raw fillets of anchovies only an hour or so removed from their natural habitat and offered as tapas. There was a drugstore lunch counter in Houston and the most sublime shrimp gumbo on the planet. There was my own kitchen in Manhattan, and the serendipitous discovery (when I neglected to turn off the gas) that the magenta syrup produced by reducing the water octopus had been cooked in added an unimaginable dimension to gumbo or bouillabaisse.

More or less in the line of duty, I was fairly active in the social life of the New York art world from the early 1960s through the mid-1970s, and found that most painters and sculptors, like Giorgio Cavallon, were no mean cooks. Resigned early in their careers to the prospect of years—in some cases, lifetimes—of financial hardship, but gifted with taste and discernment, many of them cultivate a sort of peasant genius for making the most of the least, which is what true cooking is all about. Many of the meals and dishes I recall most vividly were scraped together in Soho lofts, ratty little tenement pads in what is euphemistically styled the East Village (né Lower East Side), and, less often, in other, less bohemian purlieus.

I was *not* present, unfortunately, at what might have been the most memorable meal of them all: a dinner served by a permanently spaced-out sculptor of my acquaintance, who had once barely survived multiple perforation at the hands of a Hassidic rabbi when the rabbi's wife and the sculptor were discovered flagrante delicto, bedclothes flying. The dinner in question, I learned a year or so after the fact, had been a repast of several courses, with each presented in hues that departed radically from its natural coloration. Mashed potatoes were dyed indigo, fish fillets were stained St. Patrick's Day green, and so on. Inexplicably, the food remained untouched by the guests, some of whose complexions underwent similar changes of pigmentation.

Ed Giobbi already has turned up in these pages. The best-known cook among this country's working visual artists, he is treated as a respected peer by various food professionals, including a good many of the foremost chefs on two continents. Some years ago, around the time I first met him, he wrote a well-received cookbook, *Italian Family Cooking,* in which he explained the whys and wherefores of his culinary development. Other artists have told me substantially the same story, but this is how Ed tells it in his book:

> [While an art student] I was very, very poor. I *had* to live on one dollar a day and I soon realized that if I was going to eat meals nutritious enough to keep me alive and well, I would have to cook them myself. If I were to survive as an artist, I would have to learn to live the rest of my life on very little and that meant cooking nourishing food so that I would have the enormous energy it takes to paint.
>
> I was confident that I would not reach my peak as an artist before I was fifty . . . Thus, my original involvement with food was the wish to survive, to nourish my health in order to develop my art.

Ed, it should be noted, had the natural advantage of a well-developed culinary and gastronomic heritage: both his immigrant parents were superb cooks and serious eaters, and he had a fairly good idea of where he was going and how to get there when he embarked on his kitchen odyssey. (One painter of my acquaintance had no such head start and eats more bizarrely than any other artist I know. I have seen him concoct one-dish meals by mucking together such disparities as boiled spinach, steeped tea leaves, yogurt, honey, and chocolate pudding. As it happens, he's my mother's other son.)

Ed raises most of what he cooks and eats, animal and vegetable, at his place in Katonah, New York, about an hour's drive north of Manhattan. He keeps chickens, geese, and rabbits, and at one time kept a goat, which may or may not have found its way into the oven: when I last noticed it, Ed's then half-grown daughters were treating it as a member of the family. He forages the morels and other edible mushrooms that grow in some abundance on his property, and he and his family probably eat as well, day in and day out, as anyone in the forty-eight contiguous states. He certainly eats better than any hired belly can hope to on a meal-for-meal basis, and the many meals I've shared *chez* Giobbi over the years, whether casual or elaborately festive, have been occasions I can retrieve from my memory bank at will and savor in retrospect with a particularity more acute than I can most others.

"Oh, gross," groaned Lisa, the younger of the Giobbi daughters, who was then in her midteens, to a visiting schoolmate. The contents of the immense earthenware casserole Ed had set on a trestle table as the main course of an alfresco lunch one late-spring day weren't particularly comely, but the aroma had a pheremonic effect on my appetency. The dish, constructed around a fresh-killed hen of an interesting age—a fowl that had scratched dirt *en plein air* that very morning—was phenomenally sapid, as even Lisa conceded after demolishing a generous second helping. Mopping up the remains with broken-off hunks of Ellie Giobbi's freshly baked rustic bread and inhaling the young fruitiness of the previous fall's home-made wine, I lamented what fate had in store for me the next evening: a suit-and-tie dinner at the hottest showcase for the newly emergent California *nouvelle* glitz then operative in Manhattan. (My fears were confirmed the next night, when a logjam of shoestring potatoes exercised its territorial imperative by crowding my steak off the plate. When Curtis stuck an exploratory fork into the small bird she'd been served, a geyser of pink fluid spurted a foot into the air.)

There were Christmases spent at Katonah, too, when La Vigilia, a ritual observed with some variations in many parts of Italy, inspired some of Ed's more frenzied culinary efforts. La Vigilia is not undertaken lightly by an unassisted cook with a houseful of guests to feed. It takes the form of a seven-course supper, composed entirely of seafood dishes in its purest manifestations and served on Christmas Eve. I had gone to Patsy's restaurant for the observance two or three years running and had enjoyed the establishment's Neapolitan version (which gets under way with a fishless overture of *scarola alla monachina,* or escarole nun's style, which is to say, sautéed with raisins, pine nuts, anchovies, Gaeta olives, garlic, and herbs), but I suspected that La Vigilia at Ed's would necessarily be somewhat abbreviated. It wasn't. It ran the whole gamut from *baccalà con broccoli di rape* for starters to whiting in *salsa bianca* and included separate appearances by cold stuffed mussels, linguini with lobster, a copious mixed fry, stuffed cuttlefish, and broiled mackerel. Somehow, everything got to the table in its proper sequence—the hot dishes piping hot—and Ed somehow managed to sit through each course with the assembled company before dashing back to his Garland range to bring the next to its peak of perfection. It was one of the most joyous meals I've ever eaten, and the resultant gout that hobbled me until New Year's Eve seemed a small price to pay.

The most unflappably capable dinner hosts I've known are Grace Borgenicht and her husband Warren Brandt: respectively, a prominent art dealer and a noted figurative painter in a style often likened to that of Henry Matisse during the latter's snare-'em-in-the-harem period. When Curtis and I met them, Grace and Warren maintained a vast, meticulously manicured seignory overlooking Mecox Bay in the village of Water Mill, Long Island. Their house, girdled by a broad veranda colonnaded with soaring Corinthian pillars, was made up of more rooms than anyone ever had bothered to count, one whole floor of what had originally been servants' quarters included. They are both first-rate cooks whose eclectic culinary repertory reflects their extensive travels, and their kitchen was roughly the size of a high-school gymnasium, complete with state-of-the-art heavy equipment and a *batterie de cuisine* fit for a major hotel restaurant. Between them, Grace and Warren (a good old boy from Greensboro, North Carolina) did all the cooking. And they did it on an institutional scale, although most of their dinners were planned as intimate, spontaneous get-togethers.

Typically, they'd call us early in the afternoon with an invitation to an impromptu dinner: "Just the four of us, nothing fancy, and maybe one other couple." Typically, they'd play a round of golf during the afternoon, catch the opening of a show at some regional art gallery, and spend an hour or two at Bobby Van's saloon-cum-salon before going home to fix dinner, inviting thirty or forty people to their intimate little get-together during the course of their rounds. And somehow they always got dinner to the table on time and *au point.* Not some improvisatory collation cobbled together from packaged goods with the aid of a microwave, but a full-course blowout, complete with a massive roast of some sort and all the appropriate side dishes, sauces, and wines.

One somewhat improvisatory dish *was* served at their place one night. The evening's main course, a fragrant sauté of half a dozen or so cut-up chickens, was on the fire and almost ready by the time I showed up with a mess of hard clams I'd taken from their beds an hour earlier. The idea—my idea, unilaterally formed—had been cherrystones on the half shell for all hands during cocktails, but a late tide had delayed our arrival at the Brandts.

"Damn," said Warren, stirring his pans. "There's no time to shuck 'em all before we sit down. Look here, just dump 'em right in with the chicken and they'll be ready to eat with everything else." Fortunately, I'd given the clams a preliminary scrubbing at home. I started dumping them right in with the chicken. "Hold it!" Warren hollered. "Not *all* of 'em, goddamnit. You and I can eat a few dozen raw right here in the kitchen, while the rest of 'em are cooking."

The result of unanticipated exigency, the dish was the bastard offspring of a noble Iberian line, with antecedents in both Spanish and Portuguese cookery. Because it was riceless, Warren dubbed it "poor man's paella." It's one great dish I don't have to savor merely in retrospect. Separately or together, Warren and I have cooked it many times since. Each time I inhale its commingled aromas of onion, garlic, bell pepper, and saffron, of earth and sea, a whole party springs to life, with food shared joyously and noisily by the artists and writers of the South Fork.

The party has begun in earnest and centers in the living room, where, at Warren's urging, the action gets under way with Curtis singing "Your Cheatin' Heart" and "The Tennessee Waltz" to novelist Winston Groom's guitar accompaniments, then switching unaccompanied to the anguished bouzouki torch songs she picked up years earlier on a *Wanderjahr* spent mostly in the tavernas of the Greek Islands. James Jones talks dirty and Irwin Shaw talks Irwin Shaw, while Willie Morris launches into this night's installment of his never-ending dissertation on the supremacy of southern writers in general and his fellow-Mississippian Faulkner in particular, punctuating his remarks with an occasional rebel yell. By popular demand, Warren is persuaded to sing the one song he knows, "Lima Beans," which only *he* knows and which he renders off key in the voice of a rusty barn-door hinge. Enthroned in a corner of the room, gimpy Harold Rosenberg wields his cane like a scepter and pontificates for the edification of anyone who can hear him over the astonishing ululations of his loony daughter Patia, a student and vocalizer of tribal Arabic funeral dirges, whose unsolicited outpourings sound eerily like a whole pack of coyotes in full cry and threaten to shatter every window and eardrum for miles around. And after mass skinny-dipping in the pool at midnight, the party breaks up and I'm back in the present, wherever that may be, moiling a bit of bread around in the last vestiges of a half-congealed, chicken-mellowed, mollusk-saline sauce as hauntingly evocative as any I know.

Another painter treated me to another of the most memorable meals of my life, but in this case he happened to be a house painter, as was Señor Mestre of Wappingers Creek. Like Señor Mestre, Lindley Forsythe was Cuban-born. (I've known just two Cuban-born house painters, both of whom turned out to be redoubtable epicures and superlative cooks. Further intensive research is indicated.) Lindley had emigrated to Jamaica in early childhood and retained the sprung rhythms and Calypso accents of the island years after settling in Brooklyn. A wiry, handsome little guy gifted with the sunniest of dispositions and uncommonly keen practical intelligence, he was not only a painter but a general handyman of absolute genius: a master (albeit unlicensed) electrician and plumber, a first-rate machinist and carpenter.

Curtis and I had met him through Irwin Glusker, one of the co-instigators of this book, for whom Lindley had moonlighted in a variety of capacities (he was regularly employed by the photographer Carl Fisher). We had encountered him for the first time at a party given by Irwin and his wife, Lyl, where Lindley was tending bar with the smooth professionalism of any veteran mixologist. At the time, by dint of vigorous employment of sledgehammers, we were in the process of converting a five-room pad in the East Village—our first cohabitational venue—to unobstructed floor-through space.

Lindley agreed to install an immense freestanding walk-through closet between the living and sleeping areas and to accomplish a few other finishing touches beyond my limited, mostly reductive, talents. He would show up after his regular working day, put in two or three hours at our place, and often join us for dinner—served in situ or at a Szechuanese joint down the block—when he had knocked off for the evening.

The three of us were destroying a platter of ribs one night when Lindley proposed an alternative to our wonted revels. With a peripatetic aitch slipping in and out of his soft, pepper-cadenced prose rendition of Harry Belafonte's sung West Indian verses, he invited us to "come to my 'ouse to heat some real Jamaican food next week." Delighted by the prospect, we embarked for 'is 'ouse hearly on the appointed evening. Eventually we found ourselves somewhere in the farther reaches of untracked Brooklyn.

After several rounds of rye and ginger, an aperitif of which Curtis and I were normally disinclined to partake but which went down reasonably well in the context, an immense platter of spiced and steamed blue crabs was deposited on the living-room coffee table by Lindley's wife, Dorothy. The aroma was absolutely intoxicating, the flavor magnificent, and the quantity seemingly infinite during an hour or so of fervid crab dismantlement. Finally, foraging around in a mountain of emptied carapaces and sucked-out claws,

I realized we had done away with every last scrap of sweet, piquant flesh. "My God, what a dinner," I sighed. "Dinner? What dinner?" Lindley countered. *"Now* we'll 'ave dinner. Not 'ere, but in the dining room, proper-like. I 'ope you like your lobsters 'ot and spicy, 'ow we cook 'em howr way in the islands." Wow! did we ever like 'em 'ot and spicy, 'ow they were cooked in the islands. We gorged on three apiece, with our lips puffing as though stung by bees. I couldn't locomote for a month thereafter without acute pain, but the precipitating experience was worth every hour of gouty agony.

Looking back over my years of hired bellyhood, and beyond them to the years of gastronomic innocence, I find myself wondering why the meals that have lodged inextricably in my memory, that can be evoked more or less in their entirety at will and with vivid immediacy, so overwhelmingly outnumber restaurant meals, superior to them in every theoretical respect, that have faded from recall. Perhaps it's a matter of modest expectations grandly realized, as opposed to grand expectations that can't possibly be met as envisioned. Serendipity doubtless enters into the equation in some circumstances, as it never can when perfection is taken for granted. In any event, many of the meals I remember best are those of which I expected the least, and vice versa.

9

Feeding

Frenzy

My tenure as the magazine's hired belly fell just a bit short of a decade and a half, during which time gastronomy in this country underwent a revolution of sorts. At the commencement of my time at *Gourmet,* New York was the undisputed restaurant capital of the world. Individually, the multifarious cuisines the city had to offer hardly met the standards of their places of origin. There were infinitely better Chinese restaurants in Hong Kong and Taipei, far better Italian restaurants anywhere in Italy, better French restaurants in most French towns of any size. There were better fish and steak houses in some other American cities, better restaurants of almost any given ethnic orientation clustered in various cities from coast to coast, but nowhere else on the planet was there eating as diversified as there was in the Big Apple during my early years on the beat.

To be sure, the eating wasn't as sophisticated as it would become during the 1980s, and most restaurant patrons were no more capable of making sense of any menu more esoteric than the bill of fare at a diner in Boise, Idaho, than of the untranslated Dead Sea Scrolls. To order what almost always was pronounced "vichyswah" (originally concocted in Manhattan and unheard of in France until Americans created a demand for it in the tourist traps of Paris) was considered the height of gastronomic savoir-faire. Beef Wellington still wowed the clientele at most big-ticket restaurants, the *plato combinado* was considered Mexico's national dish, and not a few benighted souls resented the omission of grated cheese from their *spaghetti con le vongole.*

The assumption in most restaurants was that any diner not known to be otherwise was altogether devoid of table savvy. Accordingly, waiters would explain in numbing detail the composition of every jaded warhorse in the chef's culinary stable. Even in a magazine specifically targeted to food buffs, it was taken for granted that a good many readers weren't so knowledgeable about the standard dishes and nomenclature of a particular cuisine that all explanation could safely be dispensed with; that for every three or four who had at least a general idea of what went into a *cassoulet* or a *bollito misto* there might be one who hadn't the vaguest idea. This usually entailed some tightrope dancing on the part of the restaurant reviewer, who had to edify the ignorant without patronizing the better informed. Instruction that might be considered insultingly gratuitous by readers with well-developed food smarts had to be swaddled in mollifying locutions that implied acknowledgment of the reader's familiarity with the subject at hand and begged forbearance while the less experienced were introduced to it. "Of course" was always a dependable, as-you-and-I-both-well-know way out of these jams, but it had to be used sparingly, as did "prepared in the classical manner with" and various other arrangements of weasel words.

As the 1970s rolled into high gear, clearly detectable changes in American culinary and gastronomic attitudes were in the air. A new generation of professional chefs and avocational cooks, Julia's Children by James Beard, came of age at a time when air travel was becoming increasingly accessible and thitherto parochial American taste was exposed to whole new worlds of cooking and eating. Like any converts to a new faith, the nascent food cultists embraced theirs with zeal that would have been deemed unseemly not long earlier, when real men not only didn't eat quiche but didn't eat much of anything that hadn't been hacked from a bovine quadruped and served in its simplest form, along with fried, baked, or mashed potatoes. Serious gastronomy, which had languished since the onset of the First World War, underwent a renaissance that before the decade's end impelled *Time* to devote a cover story to "The Cooking Craze" and *New York* magazine to headline the efflorescence of "Restaurant Madness."

For all its preciosity and conceptual anomalies, French *nouvelle cuisine* had begun to revitalize cooking and eating in America by mid-decade and, unlike most previous importations, made its immediate influence felt not just in New York but across the nation. What later would be termed DINK couples had plenty of disposable income and were disposing of it with wild abandon in the chic restaurants and belly boutiques that proliferated from coast to coast. Erstwhile beer swillers and burger munchers could suddenly be heard hymning the praises of some obscure California Zin while savoring splodges of some newly discovered cottage industrialist's chèvre. Food, wine, and restaurant knowledgeability were flaunted with in-your-face one-upmanship, mother of vinegar and sourdough starter were treasured like an earlier generation's inherited pearls, and the Smiths stuck it to the Joneses, who had just graduated from radicchio to mâche, by being the first on their block to serve *mesclun.*

For me, the cooking craze of the 1970s (which wasn't to tail off appreciably until the late 1980s) and its concomitant feeding frenzy (apparently more durable, though its rituals are changing) came as a mixed blessing. I no longer saw any compelling reasons for cluttering my reviews with detailed anatomizations of standard dishes that had attained common currency. Anyone who still didn't know the difference between, say, tournedos Rossini and beef Stroganov had either been safely deceased for some time past or wouldn't be eligible for parole for some time to come. In either case, they weren't reading much of my prose, and for those who were, a lot of the pedantry with which it had been larded could now be dispensed with.

On the other hand, I had the distinct impression that the pack was gaining on me; that there wasn't much I could tell anyone that wasn't already common knowledge; that a good many of my readers were getting to the hottest new restaurants before I was and would in any case be little interested in evaluative ink wasted on anything as irrelevant as culinary quality or talent. The whole point of getting to the hottest new restaurants was getting to them as soon as they opened, making damned good and sure everyone who mattered knew it, and clearing off for the *next* hottest new restaurant. To facilitate matters, at least one of the town's hired bellies, a feverish rhetorician with a notoriously obedient readership, began jumping the gun on occasion, predicting torridity for places still under construction: a form of self-fulfilling prophecy that in no way advanced the shaky claims to legitimacy of restaurant coverage in general.

Paradoxically, at a time when the quality of home cooking was higher than it had been for about three generations, the quality of restaurant cooking didn't really seem to matter much, the lip service paid it notwithstanding. Whatever some chefly prodigy was garnishing with kiwifruit or puddling in raspberry *coulis* was of far less concern to a new breed of restaurant freaks than the identity and plumage of the clientele, the decibel output (optimum when unbearable), or the volume of coke snorted in the johns. Although some did manage to serve creditable food, a good many of the trendy new venues seemed mere adjuncts of the fashion industry, with culinary modistes fussing over the season's line of designer pizzas and color-coordinated grilled veggies.

Although I had been convinced from the start that restaurant writing properly entailed more than just assessment of what was placed under my nose on a plate, the manner in which it was placed there, and the physical surroundings in which that placement occurred—that any establishment's gestalt had to be considered in its entirety in order to convey any sort of meaningful idea of the sort of experience the place might offer—the New York restaurant scene of the 1970s and 1980s seemed almost to demand coverage of a sort *Gourmet* would never have countenanced, even had I been inclined to do a *People* magazine number on my readers.

My singular inability to recognize any celebrity who didn't happen to be named Sophia Loren or Katharine Hepburn had nothing to do with my early decision to drop no names in my reviews. As I saw it, who turned up where on my rounds was of no legitimate concern to anyone but those people and their tablemates, and while I occasionally might make generic reference to one place or another as a hangout of known personalities, no one was ever specified by name. If the magazine had ever considered the question and formed a coherent policy regarding it, I wasn't so informed, but I never knew about house guidelines of any sort and just flew by the seat of my pants, trusting my own instincts. They told me I wasn't cut out to be a gossip columnist, but other hired bellies began to sound increasingly like Walter Winchell or Earl Wilson as the madness accelerated.

My first real inkling of the extent of the culinary and gastronomic revolution of the 1970s came when word filtered north that it was now possible to eat a civilized meal at a civilized hour in Washington, D.C. Thanks to a heavy concentration of foreign diplomats and their entourages, the capital had long been a prime showcase for relatively obscure ethnic cuisines. There were at least three or four Ethiopian restaurants in Washington, for example, long before the first opened in New York, and Vietnam was well represented on the banks of the Potomac long before it was on the lower Hudson. As far as mainstream dining was concerned, however, Washington had been a perennial grim joke. In a city populated largely by transplanted farm-belt rubes and small-town hustlers, from the nation's chief executive of the moment on down through both houses of Congress and the entire swollen bureaucracy, eating was typified by Gerald Ford, who termed it "a waste of time," and Richard Nixon, who committed unspeakable acts with cottage cheese. Given more time, the Kennedy White House might have had a salutary influence on Washington dining, but not since Thomas Jefferson had any American president taken a direct personal interest in the maintenance of his table, assiduously cultivated his palate, and made a serious study of foodstuffs.

With few exceptions—notably the edacious William Howard

Taft—Jefferson's successors hadn't been renowned for their concern with comestibles, and most made deliberate pitches for populist support by publicly eatin' jes' like the plain folks. The image they cultivated was that of the meat-and-potatoes guy; Lyndon Johnson would nominally preside over a steer barbecue but leave the fancier stuff to the little woman.

Washington, a town that takes its social cues from the incumbent Big Enchilada, whatever his advertised tastes may be, consequently wasn't much concerned with the sorry state of its restaurants, and it's doubtful whether the awfulness of most of them could possibly have impinged on the consciousness of any career politician. After spending their adult lives on the rubber-chicken circuit, Washingtonians of any consequence might easily have mistaken Sans Souci for Lutèce South or Duke Zeibert's for The Four Seasons transplanted. The overriding criteria for the town's eating establishments were the clout of the patrons they attracted and their willingness to underbook on the off chance that some major honcho might demand a favored table on short notice.

Some observations along the foregoing lines had predictably been deleted from a Washington restaurant piece I'd written for *Gourmet* during the city's gastronomic dark ages, as had some curmudgeonly remarks about the city in general. The plain truth is that the place always has turned me off. I resent its manicured splendor, maintained at the expense of better, more deserving American cities in advancing states of decay. I find most of its official architecture brutally oppressive, its male population psychotically driven, its gossip-fixated women pathetically dowdy. To me, it's a city without a soul or, after the evening commuter exodus, even a pulse. To wake up alone in a Washington hotel room in the middle of the night is to experience exile to the dark side of the moon. There is no place on earth as devoid of signs of life after midnight. In view of my unbiased attitude toward the city, it seemed only natural that the magazine would choose me to return to Washington soon after it was widely reported that life had been discovered there, in the form of a spate of vital new restaurants.

To my surprise, the reports turned out to be founded on more than pure wishful thinking. Somewhat hesitantly, even Washington had allowed itself to be caught up in its own tepid version of the restaurant madness that by then had swept across the country. Three or four places of the *nouvelle cuisine* persuasion had sprung up there, and two or three of them compared favorably in some respects with the best of their counterparts in New York. Some Washingtonians had even abandoned the traditional notion, rooted in the customs of their rural constituencies, that the evening meal was properly eaten as soon as possible after sundown and were turning up for dinner when God-fearing souls back home were sleeping the sleep of the just. During the week or so I spent in the city, I had several excellent meals, but it was hard to avoid the conclusion that, beneath a new veneer of sophistication, Washingtonians still harbored some benighted notions of what state-of-the-art dining and world-class restaurants were all about. At Lion d'Or, for example, vaunted as one of the city's three finest *nouvelle cuisine* showcases, the cooking was unarguably representative of the best the mid-1970s had to offer, but everything else about the place was still mired in the late 1950s.

Our table captain not only spoke, but seemed to peer at us with distaste through his elevated nose. The quintessential broadloom-prowling popinjay, he scornfully suggested that he might condescend to enlighten a pair of indubitable rubes should the menu prove to be too abstruse for our comprehension. The chef, he intoned through a snot-clogged proboscis, was one of the world's most celebrated practitioners of an advanced cuisine of which we might have heard but doubtless had not yet partaken.

Having absorbed this twit's sermon, we studied the menu. We were ensconced in the sacrosanct precincts of the most lugubrious place I've ever entered in the expectation of having a good time. A suffocating hush hung over the place in an aura of unrelieved gloom. In the main dining room, furnished with what appeared to be the reliquary and high altar of the cathedral of Santiago de Compostela, the solemnity of a requiem Mass prevailed. Not a flicker of a smile was to be seen anywhere. Although it may have carried the city's prevailing style to its reductio ad absurdum, the restaurant exemplified Washington's benighted notions of what constituted a night on the town.

His Eminence deigned to revisit our table, once again seeming to regard us through his nasal passages. Overexposure during the previous few days to *nouvelle cuisine* and the fey arrangements of infant veggies emblematic of the style had left me craving real food. I ordered a chop of some sort. Determined to forestall its garnishment with the usual wee carrots, yellow squash, and zucchini, I conceded to the resident jackanapes that the request I was about to make would, of course, flout orthodoxy, but wondered if it might be possible to have potatoes in any form with my entrée.

The man's face underwent meltdown. *"Potatoes,* sir?"

"Yes, potatoes. Surely you've heard of them? Edible starchy tubers of the plant *Solanum tuberosum?* Any way the chef chooses to prepare them will do, but preferably in appreciable quantity and cooked through."

Our man very much doubted that the lowly potato had ever found its way into the restaurant's pantry, but my deviant request would of course be conveyed to the chef.

My dinner companion, a blind date arranged by a common friend in New York, had cringed during the exchange and now regarded me with the bruised expression of a trusting soul betrayed. Reading her compressed lips, I got the message: only a smart-ass New Yorker would presume to know more than an appointed official about what he wanted to eat and demand a breach of protocol in order to get it. She picked at her first course in gelid silence, fouling off my conversational pitches as though she had an obscene caller on the phone. I almost welcomed the reappearance of Nostrils, who arrived gesturing grandly over the plate a waiter had set before me. "Potatoes, sir," he purred.

A glance at the dish turned up no evidence in support of his claim; only the inevitable *nouvelle* garniture of stunted, half-raw roots and squashes. Closer inspection produced what appeared to be three chickpeas. As I donned my reading glasses, the chickpeas revealed themselves to be the advertised potatoes, scooped from some larger entity with the small end of a melon baller and further trimmed down to a size consonant with the chef's aesthetic.

"Sorbet, sir" my self-appointed tutor announced between courses, in the nasal drawl he fancied was an Oxbridge accent. What had been placed before us was manifestly, indubitably sorbet, but Nostrils was taking no chances in his dealings with the likes of me. "To clear the palate," he added.

"Hey, thanks, good buddy," I replied. " 'Preciate that. If you hadna warned me, I was fixin' to strip down and clean my armpits with it." My tablemate went into shock.

While cooking worth the name could at last be found in some Washington restaurants during the 1970s, the *status quo ante culinarius* obtained as far as all other aspects of the restaurant scene were concerned. Dining-room personnel still condescended to a presumably unpolished public. Diners were still sufficiently intimidated by unfamiliar cuisines, and by an aura of religiosity deliberately cultivated by most of the emergent restaurateurs, to regard the consumption of a meal in public as a solemn rite conducted by a new clergy who brooked no merriment on the part of the laity. As in the past, the chances of securing a preferred table in one of the better restaurants were virtually nil without clout or connections.

Having made reservations well in advance, Curtis and I entered one celebrated haunt of movers and shakers in the confident expectation of being seated somewhere within hailing distance of the action. As it happened, there was very little action that evening, and we surveyed a sea of unoccupied tables as we were herded off to an undersized deuce crammed into a remote corner of the dining room, alarmingly proximate to a swinging door. Was *this* the best the maître d' could do? Regrettably, yes sir, it was. But what about all those unpopulated tables a half-mile or so closer to habitable territory? All previously reserved, sir. I found this assertion hard to credit: Washington diners might no longer be observing the farmers' hours they had in the not-too-distant past, but it was now approaching nine o'clock and there were only a few couples in sight. Nor did anyone show up to claim their phantom reservations during the next half-hour or so.

We grumbled through our drinks and the first course in Siberian isolation, with the swinging door making violent contact with the back of my chair at regular intervals. Then, just as the entrées were being served, we were joined by a friend of Curtis's, a former senator and two-time presidential candidate who had promised to join us for a postprandial drink after a previous dinner engagement. "Senator!" the maître d' cried, homing in on us like an Exocet missile. "*You* can't sit *there.*" Our party was ushered, with all appropriate grovelings, to one of the ostensibly reserved tables—the best in the house and the only one occupied during the rest of the evening.

The effects on the New York restaurant scene of the burgeoning feeding frenzy were mixed. As food knowledgeability spread like wildfire during the last half of the decade, a brief interregnum obtained, during which dining-room flunkies, recognizing that a great many of the paying customers were now as familiar as themselves with standard menu terminology, abstained from the intrusive explanatory spiels that for years had driven experienced diners to distraction. This blessed state of affairs lasted only until *nouvelle cuisine* rolled into high gear, however. As the new French style and its various spin-offs spawned a pandemic infestation of culinary inventors, even the most savvy restaurant patrons found themselves grappling with an unknown language in which previously unequivocal terms were capriciously applied to all manner of unprecedented chefly creations. No matter that the then current edition of *Larousse Gastronomique* insisted that the term *navarin* was "used expressly for a ragout of mutton [and] should only be used of mutton dishes, or, in exceptional cases, lamb"; if some new-wave child prodigy chose to call Tuesday morning's culinary brainstorm—which combined cubed monkfish, pink grapefruit, and *poblano* chilies in a vanilla-flavored beurre blanc garnished with slices of carambola—*"navarin de lotte,"* so it appeared on his menu. And so, for the edification of his bemused clientele, the waitpersons perforce reverted to their former roles as motor-mouthed monologists.

What bugged me most about the new-wave restaurant fare of the late 1970s and early 1980s was neither its outré combinations of ingredients nor the stupefying quantities of explication on the part of servers who necessarily felt obliged to introduce themselves ("Hi, I'm Randy, and I'll be your waiter this evening") before turning a tête-à-tête into a ménage à trois. What really stuck in my craw was the arrogant inflexibility of a gang of self-proclaimed genius-chefs who seemed constitutionally incapable of adapting to the wants and needs of their patrons, lest some exquisitely nuanced and perfectly composed work of art be thrown an nth degree out of kilter.

Chanterelle, a SoHo *nouvelle cuisine* showcase that bore an eerie resemblance to a storefront shelter for the homeless, had received more favorable ink than Mother Teresa by the time Curtis and I got around to trying it. Seated at a table overlooking a curbside palisade of black plastic garbage bags, we studied the menu. One of the evening's featured dishes was lamb chops with (if memory serves) thirty-six cloves of garlic. Perhaps it was as few as twenty-four or as many as forty-eight cloves of garlic. In any event, it was at least two dozen more cloves of garlic than Curtis, who adores lamb but who usually can't physically tolerate the merest trace of garlic, could ingest with impunity. The waitperson was asked whether the garlic could be omitted, thereby obviating the need for an appearance by a squad of paramedics.

The waitperson stared in disbelief; the ninety-six cloves of garlic, she protested, were the heart, soul, essence, and raison d'être of the dish, the chef's signal contribution to Western civilization. We realized that of course, I explained, but a human life was at stake here, and surely the chef . . . The young woman promised to see what could be done. She approached the kitchen door with all the assurance of a minor imam dispatched to inform the Ayatollah Khomeini that the plat du jour was roast suckling pig. She returned a few minutes later to suggest that Curtis order something else; the chef wasn't prepared to sacrifice the integrity of his creation merely to spare the life of some unappreciative philistine. After a further half-hour of debate by proxy, we seemed to have made our point: the chops would be served *sans Allium sativum* and the blood would be on our heads. The chops were served with approximately one hundred and ninety-two cloves of garlic, whereupon Curtis lapsed into a deep swoon and I paid the check and carried her out, leaving our food untouched.

The Chanterelle incident was hardly unique during the *nouvelle* heyday and its immediate aftermath. (Indeed, we were subjected to the same treatment a few weeks later by an intransigent Greenwich Village chef.) Suddenly, every *gros bonnet* in town had rejected the role of mere performing artist in which all but a relative handful of truly creative talents had been cast for generations. Now, every unfinished kid fresh out of cooking school considered himself a certified genius, a composer with a repertory of signature dishes that he was no more inclined to modify to suit a customer's taste than Picasso would have been inclined to modify a masterpiece to match the sofa it would hang above.

In the not-too-distant past, when even really accomplished chefs had moiled in obscurity behind their kitchen doors, turning out textbook-precise readings of the established classics with true flair and style, a request from some free-spending cowboy in pinstripes to hold the gravy on that there *entrecôte béarnaise* might be received with eyes rolled into the back of the head and mutterings about ignorant Texas shit kickers, but the steak would be served as ordered, with no unwanted adhesives. The new breed of culinary originators was prepared to make no such accommodation. Let it be known that you didn't much fancy having your flatfish mantled in a banana *coulis* laced with Amaretto and dusted with bitter chocolate, and your flatfish would be served, as conceived in a flash of chefly inspiration, mantled in a banana *coulis* (the buzzword of the moment, divested of whatever meaning it once had) laced with Amaretto and dusted with bitter chocolate. Or, more likely, nothing about the menu designation or its gloss might have given you any reason to suspect that scaloppine of fluke Stanley (dedicated to its creator's current inamorato) might throw together culinary bedfellows as queer as the chef and the lover. In any event, with or without prior admonishment to the creator, what wound up on your plate would be a piece of flatfish mantled in a banana *coulis* laced with Amaretto and dusted with bitter chocolate. And if you didn't happen to deem the combination fit for human consumption, well, that was just tight pajamas.

Offal in any form is not a commodity at which I'm disposed to boggle. Whether it be a generous helping of my own prose or some deceased beast's insides, I can usually tackle it with equanimity, some risk of gout in the latter case notwithstanding. When the time comes to order my last meal in the shadow of the gallows, stay me with flagons, comfort me with innards: a light scramble of eggs and lamb's brains will do nicely for openers, thanks, to be followed perhaps by a mixed grill made up of the sweetbreads, kidneys, and butterflied heart of calf. Thus fortified, I'll be fit to face up to a generous platter of *fegato alla veneziana,* a double helping of *tripe à la mode de Caen,* and the grim postprandial observance. Once delivered from the childhood ordeal of having to ingest the weekly dose of my mother's dessicated calf's liver, I had almost never met a piece of organ meat I didn't like. Then I had my first dinner at the Quilted Giraffe.

When I got around to trying the restaurant for the first time in the fall of 1980, its praises had already been sung by a chorus of the town's hired bellies, augmented by a good many visiting soloists. I may not have ordered dinner altogether without hostility. The name of the place made my teeth ache, as did some interior designer's vision of a posh day-care center. Advance reports that the *chef-propriétaire* was a former lawyer and self-taught cook inspired little confidence. Nor did his prissy spouse, who in her capacity as maîtresse d'hôtel minced around the dining room as though her derriere were made of baked meringue, darting glances of disapproval at any paying customers boorish enough to crack a smile or otherwise mar the solemnity of the occasion. That patrons were not expected to enjoy themselves but merely derive from the evening whatever solace they might was explicitly spelled out on the menu, which informed them that the table represented their last, best hope of "reconciling body and spirit to the anguish of a life that is necessarily too short and too imperfect." Let the good times roll!

A number of intriguing selections were interspersed among the menu's more cautionary passages, which included an admonition to those who "don't speak French well" to "peruse" the French-language (rather than the translated) *carte,* "which provides a certain poetry, lyricism, and comedy" presumably unattainable in the native tongue of Shakespeare, Herrick, and Marvell. The listing that most tempted me was designated with Gallic lyricism as *"rognons rôti"* and in plain clumping English as "roasted kidneys."

The kidneys were served raw. Although their exteriors had clearly been exposed to dry heat for a moment or two, there was no evidence of thermal action beneath a tissue-thin surface. Cold and inviolate as sashimi, they leaked a lymphatic wetness when cut and tasted no better than they looked. Barely touched, the dish was removed without question or comment when it became obvious that I'd had as much of it as I could stomach.

The rest of the meal was first-rate, a succession of imaginative dishes executed with unerring precision and clarity, marred only by the chef's triumphal, intrusive tour of the dining room. He emerged from his kitchen with the sweat of honest toil on his brow, brandishing a daikon radish the size of a baseball bat, his tunic spangled with more grease than a transmission repairman's coveralls might absorb during a busy week. Having decided that the restaurant definitely merited further investigation, I returned a few nights later. Halfway through our martinis, Curtis and I were studying the menu when a table captain arrived and placed an unordered dish before me. "Compliments of the chef," I was told. "He thinks you'll find the roasted kidneys more to your taste this time than you did the other night." Well, one thing could certainly be said for the chef: he was a paragon of consistency. The kidneys were precisely as raw as they had been on the first go-round and would have been received with precisely the same lack of enthusiasm had the arrogant reprise not filled me with sheer rage.

I'd have been steamed enough had the twit in the kitchen not spotted me for a hired belly, but he had, and he still presumed to know more about my taste than I did. The guy had uncommon talent, no doubt about it, and I eventually gave the restaurant some enthusiastic ink. Like all his *nouvelle cuisine* confreres, though, he insisted on ramming his creations down his customers' throats, like them or not, with no regard for anything but his own conviction that they were the ultimate manifestations of culinary truth. Never mind that such redoubtable, vastly more experienced chefs as André Soltner of Lutèce, Jean-Jacques Rachou of La Côte Basque (a lapidary whose presentations made the labored *nouvelle* style look perfunctory by comparison), and Seppi Renggli of The Four Seasons were prepared to make adjustments and compromises at the whims or urgent dietary needs of *their* customers; the young Turks of the new wave adamantly refused to budge on any point of imagined principle, however specious it might be, supremely self-satisfied, supremely intransigent, supremely ignorant of the implicit obligations of their calling. In their obsessive drive for individual recognition, for the superstar status so negligently conferred on them by trend-fixated food writers concerned only with marketable novelty, they convinced themselves that any miscegenetic culinary marriage, previously unperpetrated by chefs too respectful of kitchen logic to sauce pompano with blueberries or oysters with maple syrup, was an original signature creation of immutable perfection.

It took some time for the public to realize that the emperor's new clothes were a pair of Adidas and a flasher's raincoat and to reject the more blatant absurdities of *nouvelle cuisine.* In the meantime, the savviest generation of eaters America has produced, confronted with wildly capricious menu nomenclature and bamboozled by culinary careerists whose brainstorms took the form of marginally palatable designer labels, had no better idea of what might turn up when a dish was ordered than the previous generation of gastronomic innocents had when it mispronounced the standard terminology of the Escoffier canon.

In the long run, the style's most notable contribution, not only to the fifteen-year-long feeding frenzy it helped to generate but to good eating in the foreseeable future, was a more or less accidental by-product of all the chefly ego-tripping it produced. In their frenzied rush to put their personal stamps on their creations with ever more startling combinations of edibles, the new-wave chefs found themselves caught up in what I then termed the ingredients race, using the analogy of the cold-war arms race. When a chef pranced around a dining room flourishing a radish unknown until then in Western kitchens, he was serving notice that he had the drop, at least momentarily, on his competitors; that in that day's stage of an ongoing tour of one-upmanship, he'd sprinted ahead of the pack.

As the ingredients race heated up, the participants increasingly sought out and relied on obscure sources of esoteric provender: cottage-industry cheesemakers, freelance foragers, small-scale herbalists, gatherers and growers and producers of all manner of culinary arcana, from *enokidake* to bison, *nopales* to mâche. The competition was fierce, often bitter. When I tried, as tactfully as I could, to disabuse chef Shirley King, then of Wilkinson's Seafood Café, of the notion that she had introduced samphire, or glasswort, to the New York dining public by pointing out that chef Michel Fitoussi had served the same shore green at 24 Fifth Avenue several weeks earlier, her response was "Goddamn that bastard." Chef King happened to be plying a heavy cleaver at the moment, and I prudently refrained from mentioning that I had been eating samphire (a.k.a. sea bean, marsh samphire, *pousse-pierre,* etc.), first on the Maine coast and later on the South Fork of Long Island, for upward of twenty years.

Qualitative differences aside, there hadn't been much to be found on a restaurant plate before the 1970s that any home cook couldn't pick up at the supermarket. For the most part, expatriated professionals who espoused one foreign cuisine or another made do with rough approximations of the ingredients they would have used far more selectively on their native turf. Red snapper and striped bass, for example, became multipurpose substitutes for various southern European fishes, none of which would have been used interchangeably in the chef's countries of origin; any sort of domestic flatfish became a surrogate for "Dover sole," and the oxymoronic "shrimp scampi" was the standard menu designation for the wrong crustacean masquerading as a beast to which it bore little resemblance.

To be sure, a few big-ticket restaurants had featured offbeat specialty foods back when the new-wave chefs were still in rompers. The "21" Club, for one, had maintained a virtual monopoly on farmed game for years, and to the best of my knowledge was the single source in town of a mixed fry of whitebait and minuscule oyster crabs, a dish that its fanciers may rightly believe is as good as eating gets. (Nelson Rockefeller traditionally had first dibs when the ingredients were on hand.) With the consultation of James Beard, the reigning authority on the regional foodstuffs of his time (a very long time), The Four Seasons had not only regaled its clientele with such then-rare delicacies as fresh morels, fiddlehead ferns, periwinkles, broccoli blossoms, nasturtium leaves, and the like, but anticipated salient characteristics of the *nouvelle* and subsequent so-called New American styles by playing ingredients off one against another in innovative combinations and by playing novel variations on traditional themes. Years before anything like them became the commonplaces of other menus, the restaurant regularly featured dishes like a beet and lobster madrilène, grilled quail with chestnut gnocchi, iced oysters with hot sausages, bouillabaisse salad, and pomegranate sherbet.

Still, such restaurants were isolated harbingers of developments to come, and it remained for the new-wave chefs to zero in with laserlike intensity on the multifarious, previously untapped resources that came to light as the ingredients race (which still shows no signs of slowing down) accelerated and, largely in response to their demands, new avenues of exploration opened up. With the pack in full cry, entrepreneurial purveyors like the two brash young New Englanders who launched an outfit called Flying Foods on a wing, a prayer, and one-digit capitalization streamlined methods of distribution that enabled restaurateurs to offer all manner of exotica, some of which arrived in the Big Apple from as far away as Australia bearing no traces of jet lag.

By the mid 1980s, while rates of exchange were still favorable, Adriatic and Mediterranean seafoods could be served in midtown Manhattan only hours after being taken from their home waters by fishermen who left port before dawn, returned early in the afternoon, and rushed their iced-down hauls to nearby airports as soon as they docked. Conversely, the American East Coast fishing fleet, four thousand miles closer to its retail outlets, bumbled about at sea for several days, sometimes weeks, with the result that what was taken early from local waters but arrived in port at the bottom of the heap was considerably deader than any of the European stuff. For the first time, New Yorkers were exposed to significant numbers of such previously unfamiliar critters as San Pietro (John Dory), *triglia* (red mullet), *orata* (gilt-head bream), *spigola* (Adriatic sea bass), genuine *scampi* (*Nephrops norvegicus,* a.k.a. *langoustine,* Dublin Bay prawns), and even *scorfano* (scorpionfish, the rascasse essential to bouillabaisse, whose nearest American cousin is the generally despised sculpin*).

Concurrently, Southeast Asians were arriving on American

---

*It was the city's Italian chefs, more than any others, who exploited the influx of new arrivals most enthusiastically; hence the Italian menu nomenclature.

shores in force, creating a demand for all sorts of market produce and cooking techniques that the eclectic, mix-and-match new-wave chefs were quick to adopt in their frenetic efforts to keep a step or two ahead of their colleagues. And with home cooks increasingly taking their cues from the pros, retail foodsellers lost little time in falling into line, if only to salvage some share of a produce market in which Korean immigrants played an increasingly dominant role, not just in their own communities but the city's more affluent neighborhoods as well.

Supermarkets that had traditionally relied on rapid turnover of the commonest garden varieties of produce and regarded any salad leaf more esoteric than Boston lettuce, and any herb but curly parsley, as not worth stocking suddenly bloomed with Treviso radicchio, arugula, cilantro and various other fresh herbs, shallots, previously unknown wild and cultivated mushrooms, kiwifruit, gingerroot, chayotes—anything and everything that maybe one home cook in a hundred might take it into his head to fool around with. Capsicum peppers, until then available only in green or, more ripely, red, now traversed a spectrum of designer colors from pale waxy yellow and bright orange through deep purple and near black. Even the lowly potato began turning up in previously unheard-of hues and shapes and flavors and textures. I realized that the millennium had arrived when I dropped into my local supermarket to find a couple of bins filled with star fruit (carambolas) and rambutans, fruits I'd seen before only in Southeast Asia.

A short—perhaps mercifully short—period of dominance by the French *nouvelle cuisine* mafia gave way to a chauvinistic backlash as a new generation of native-born chefs looked to their own culinary roots and native foodstuffs for inspiration. Their style and technique derived directly from *nouvelle cuisine* and often was just as maddeningly precious, but their emphasis on indigenous New World ingredients opened up still another area of exploration and brought all sorts of foods—some long forgotten, others of generationally preserved narrow regional interest—into mainstream late-twentieth-century cookery.

Not all the "new" ingredients could be described with any precision as unfamiliar or generally neglected commodities. Corn, a grain once deemed too cumbersome in its most desirable and most popular form—on the cob, picked while the cooking water boiled—for service in restaurants, underwent a sanctified second coming as adherents of the New American cuisine adapted venerable regional recipes and dishes to their own notions of avant-garde cookery. Gussied up one way or another, the traditional corn-based specialties of New England, the Deep South, the Southwest, and the American heartland became instant new-wave clichés as they switched from faded house dresses to smart designer frocks. Catfish, long a generally despised protein resource of poor southern blacks, became a darling of the northern radical-chic establishment.

In the long run, though, it was the Italian chefs who dominated the years of the feeding frenzy in New York—the Italians, whose cookery had essentially anticipated the more valid tenets of *nouvelle cuisine* by half a millennium at the very least. After decades of misrepresentation by the debased offerings of first-wave immigrants and their direct descendants, authentic Italian cooking began to make its influence felt in the early 1970s with the rapid proliferation of the glibly mistermed "northern" Italian restaurants, with their deemphasis of the sludgy red sauces and miscegenetic dishes that for generations had given an undeservingly bad name to the honest cooking of southern Italy and Sicily. To New Yorkers first, and the rest of the country soon thereafter, venerable classics of various regional Italian cuisines—dishes that had been taken for granted in their particular areas of provenance as long as anyone could remember—suddenly became "new": chic properties that accorded almost perfectly with emergent concepts of healthful eating and the fitness craze that was just getting under way.

The brief rage for French *nouvelle cuisine* notwithstanding (does anyone remember Le Coup de Fusil, La Folie, Dodin Bouffant, Tucano, and their like, each for a Warholan fifteen minutes famous exemplars of the genre?), the French and French-oriented restaurants added practically nothing of significance to dining out in New

York during the period in question, except for the attention they focused on previously neglected ingredients and a few valid ways in which they could be combined to novel effect. What happened was that a lot of hidebound old-line fortresses of haute cuisine bit the dust (in part thanks to the limitless rapacity of the city's landlords, but mostly because of their own inertia), to be momentarily replaced by upstart successors with no staying power, while scores upon scores of bright-eyed and bushy-tailed new Italian ventures, founded on proven culinary bedrock, assumed citywide dominance.

For at least one hired belly, these developments added up to rather heady stuff. The ingredients race provided a forum (if not many world-shaking ideas or a coherent philosophy) for new avenues of smart-ass pedagogy. Everything of any conceivable interest to anybody had already been written about chickens, steaks, or the more familiar seafoods and veggies, but as long as I could keep a step ahead of my readers, a whole new universe of comestibles lay before me, uncharted and infinitely explicable. I played it for all it was worth.

10

The

Muddle

Kingdom

A n obligation to cover thirty-six restaurants a year in print beats mining coal. With reasonable luck augmented by a gradually acquired feel for what may be reviewable and what positively isn't, a hired belly hardly puts in an eight-hour day or even has to devote every eating hour of his life to prospective review subjects. If neither his luck nor his instincts betray him, he stands a fair chance of leading a more or less normal life, spending little more time working at eating than many professionals in other fields do. Most of the people I worked and played with during my years with *Gourmet* were in the publishing game in one capacity or another. "Having lunch"—often dinner as well—came with the territory for them, and many spent at least as much of their working time in restaurants as I did. Notwithstanding the notion, apparently prevalent among my readers, that I was some sort of nonstop eating machine, I probably consumed less food and sat down to fewer meals than most adult Americans, and I often ingested nothing solid until after dark. When I *did* eat, I brought a hearty appetite to the table. Anything less, in my view, would have amounted to dereliction.

The light work load left plenty of time for pleasure and profit, which have been largely synonymous throughout my earning years. Except for a few months as a part-time furniture mover during my mid-twenties, I've never worked at anything I didn't enjoy immensely. Aside from the obvious exception (for which, alas, nobody ever has sought my professional services), the two activities I enjoy most are writing and eating, and I've been lucky enough to make a living at both, without making a full-time job of either.

As a hired belly, I was left plenty of time for other freelance assignments, many of which had nothing to do with food or eating, and I was able to turn out a book every other year or so, some related to food, some not. During the first couple of years on the restaurant beat, I also held down a full-time job as editor of one art magazine while reviewing books for another on a monthly basis. Most of my vacations were in effect paid, for they usually resulted in salable magazine pieces, and all of my travel assignments were lucrative vacations. I wasn't getting rich, but I was living as though I were.

Curtis and I had bought a small house in East Hampton, on the East End of Long Island, a year or so before I connected with *Gourmet,* and I soon found myself spending as much time there as possible. In retrospect, I don't know whether it was time well or ill spent. Unless a losing streak turned up one unreviewable place after another, I could usually get my restaurant reconnaissance done for the month in ten days or so of intensive eating and then clear out of town to write up my reports in more bucolic surroundings, in closer touch with foods at their primary source. For the first time in my life, I was able to cook and eat not only what I was able to forage in the wild, but food that I had raised myself. It was a heady, increasingly seductive state of affairs. More and more of my time was spent in the shellfish beds when the tide was out and in the garden or the kitchen when it wasn't. The lure of foods that weren't store-bought and (I naively believed) paid for was irresistible. Anything less than a bushel of clams and a peck of oysters in the fridge, a year's supply of put-up tomato sauce in the cellar, and forty gallons of stocks, soups, and chowders in the freezer seemed the verge of severe privation, and the prospect of getting through a winter without exhausting my stock of onions, leeks, and cabbages filled me with a sense of security.

There were a good many potato farms in the region, and by local custom anyone was free to glean any of the tubers left on the ground after the fall harvest. The machines invariably missed the very finest spuds of them all: diminutive specimens smaller than playing marbles, they were sensationally good sautéed in their jackets, but entailed hours of stoop labor over acres of loam before what I considered a respectable haul—say, two hundred pounds—could be dragged from some distant horizon to the car. My God, what eating those peewees were! And oh, God, what backaches they produced! Somehow, it never occurred to me to reckon the costs of all this "free" food, either in time that might have been spent more lucratively, the actual cash outlay that each tomato or melon or cabbage represented, the labor of picking bushels of beans over a summer, or the sweat expended in lopping the leaves from a couple of rows of brussels sprouts under an August sun in order to direct soil nutrients to the sprouts themselves.

Nor did I take into account the debilitating effects my prolonged absences from the city were having on my income until considerable damage had been done. Although just a phone call and a two-hour drive from midtown Manhattan, I might as well have been exiled to Baluchistan when some editors were handing out freelance assignments—assignments that, in my preoccupation with the largess of soil and sea, I wasn't pursuing quite as aggressively as I might have been.

If the intensity of my involvement with the gathering, growing, and preparation of food on the East End didn't do much for my fiscal stability, it did, I think, add a dimension to my work as a hired belly. It taught and constantly reminded me of the differences between truly pristine and merely market-fresh ingredients (differences unknown to most chefs and restaurateurs), and it left me somewhat less respectful than I once had been of many of the sauces the pros necessarily resorted to in their efforts to revive some of the highly perishable stuff they worked with. It reinforced whatever ability I may have had to distinguish between the superficial razzle-dazzle of wow-the-public restaurant cooking and restaurant cooking of genuine integrity.

At home, I put infinitely fresher fish and shellfish on the table than any restaurant in the city could. (A mess of squid and a couple of mako shark steaks, purchased on a Montauk dock minutes after they were landed and tossed on the grill within the hour, live on in my taste memory ten years or more later as one of the five or six unimprovable seafood meals of my life.) No restaurant's tomatoes or melons tasted remotely as good as ours, ripened on the vine to optimum sweetness and eaten while the warmth of the sun was still in them. Berries the finest restaurants in the Big Apple served with particular pride and priced accordingly didn't compare with those we ate out of hand as we picked them on the edge of our property, let alone those we picked at the edge of a seventeenth-century graveyard in nearby Amagansett, fertilized with the mortal remains of the region's settlers.

Access to all that culinary bounty imposed more stringent culinary responsibilities on me than I'd been used to: a guy thinks twice before messing up perfection, whether it takes the form of an oyster or a pod of okra, by subjecting it to some tarted-up treatment that divests it of or masks its essential character. From the outset, my restaurant writing had been as conscientious as I could make it within the limitations of my experience and knowledge, but I soon found that the eating I did *outside* the restaurants was the eating that taught me most about the cooking of the pros. It enabled me to make finer distinctions between those who genuinely respected their raw materials, whose work was marked by clarity, logic, and a coherent overview, and those who sacrificed all else to the advancement of their careers via the creation of signature dishes, no matter what contortions their primary ingredients had to be put through or whatever inappropriate substances they were bedded down with.

Travel, I found, was equally as seductive as husbanding our little patch of ground. Curtis and I had traveled abroad together for the first time a year or so before I landed the *Gourmet* gig, and someone destined to get into the food writing dodge couldn't have had a better traveling companion. As adventurous an eater as I've ever known, she shared my enthusiasm for raffish, boisterous blue-collar hangouts and boggled at absolutely nothing edible, however bizarre it might look. During my first several years as a hired belly, we traveled extensively around the Mediterranean, particularly in Spain, where her professional interests and mine coincided for a time and where we joyously pigged out on every conceivable sort of *marisco* in the *tascas* of every city, town, and village we hit. We invaded dark little kitchens in obscure back streets to lift the lids from grimy pots and inhale the porky redolence of lovingly simmered dishes and full-bodied soups.

Curtis was tied up in some lengthy transaction having to do with an exchange of airline tickets in an office on the Paseo del Prado, in Madrid, when I nipped out for a quick cognac. I could have dodged into the Ritz, which was right next door, but instead followed a stray cat up a narrow, sloping street named for Lope de Vega. An altogether nondescript little storefront café occupied a corner of the second block, and I went in. A bar barely long enough to accommodate the two burly street sweepers who had bellied up to it. Three rickety tables. Nothing on the walls but a thin coat of sickly green paint. The most marvelous cooking aromas I've ever inhaled.

I downed my drink and hurried to the airline office, where Curtis was just completing her errand. "Come on," I said. "I've found a great restaurant."

A woman in her late thirties was just emerging from her kitchen when we entered Casa Dolores. *"Un mesa para dos por favor,"* I said, using up all the Spanish I knew, menu nomenclature excepted, at one go. When I interrupted the woman's enthusiastic itemization of the day's lunch options with a rueful *"No habla español,"* she marched the two of us into the kitchen. She opened her oven and uncovered pots and pans for our inspection, then led us to a table when we'd made our selections: for openers, *pistou,* to be followed by the principal source of an olfactory symphony that had worked Curtis up to such a state of arousal that she began to moan.

The verdant soup was glorious. The stew was a flat-out wonderment, and an unlabeled bottle of the house plonk had a thick earthiness about it that was unlike anything I'd tasted since a passing motorist had literally changed water into wine when Gwynne and I were living at St.-Hippolyte. (In a typical Provençal gesture, the driver in question had expressed his gratitude for a bucketful of water from our kitchen pump by driving forty miles out of his way to fetch and present us with a demijohn of his homemade red. The container was the size of a fire hydrant, and its contents had kept us happily supplied for a month. Like the restaurant's, it was a wine almost silty enough to chew and complemented hearty rustic fare better than any pedigreed Burgundy possibly could. Almost as well, indeed, as the restaurant's wine paired with the stew.)

Dessert was an orange apiece. It's possible that we were hallucinating on the effects of the *pistou,* the main course, the wine, and even the brusque Spanish bread, but those oranges seemed, then and in vivid retrospect, altogether transcendent. As Curtis began to peel hers, ultimately producing an unbroken spiral of rind a yard long, our corner of the café was suffused with more fragrance than I would have thought anything less than a whole orchard in blossom could have generated. Less artistically, I tore the skin off mine in ragged swatches and bit deeply into sheer bliss as my mouth flooded with ineffably sweet juice. Of the thousands of desserts I've eaten before and since, many of them in some of the poshest restaurants on the planet, those straightforward oranges are what I remember most vividly and pleasurably. And of all the thousands of meals I can resavor to one degree or another in memory, I can recall only a relative handful in pinpoint detail, with a back-alley workingman's lunch that set us back the equivalent of sixty-five cents apiece salient among them.

A couple of years later, in the course of reviewing a Spanish restaurant in midtown Manhattan, I described our lunch at Casa Dolores. The account elicited uncommonly heavy reader response: everyone, it seemed, was headed for Madrid that summer and was determined to search out this diamond in the rough. For a few weeks after publication of the review (which did little for the fortunes of its ostensible subject), I spent a good deal of my time drawing street maps for the benefit of importunate would-be patrons of Casa Dolores, including a high-school Spanish teacher in Pennsylvania who planned to take her entire class on a tour of Madrid the next summer.

Toward the end of the summer in question, I received an invitation to a party at the home of the abstract expressionist painter Estéban Vicente, a native Madrileno, and his wife, who lived not far from our place on Long Island. As I entered his house, I experienced a sensation of *déjà senti:* an aroma of stewed meat and beans so compelling that I bypassed my usual frontal attack on the bar to see what was doing in the kitchen, which smelled eerily like a certain dive tucked away on a street corner on Calle Lope de Vega. I was met there by Estéban, who said, "How the hell do *you* know about Casa Dolores? I was taken there every Sunday for dinner from the time I was five years old until I left Spain." He had left Spain about a half-century earlier.

Three or four years ago, I found myself back in Madrid and immediately set out for lunch at Casa Dolores. It had been perhaps ten years since I last had set foot in the place, but I knew—or thought I knew—precisely where I'd find it, at the second corner up the hill from Paseo del Prado. It wasn't there. I dogged through the immediate neighborhood in bafflement, retracing my steps again and again, but couldn't find it. I must have passed a very chic-looking establishment, its facade paved with glossy ceramic tile, four or five times before I took a closer look at it and noticed the legend Casa Dolores discreetly inscribed beside the door. I entered to find Spanish yuppies jammed six-deep at a bar ten times longer than the one I remembered. The old café now occupied an abutting building in addition to the original premises, and a sea of tables, covered with white linen, was crowded with smart-looking thirtyish foursomes. The only aroma was of hairspray and underarm deodorant, the menu was *nouvelle cuisine* at its most outré, and the posted prices were shocking. I slunk out and had a few *cigalas,* a half-dozen oysters, and a glass of sour wine at a modest, un-populated place down the block.

Curtis and I didn't travel to China together. On the eve of our scheduled departure, she mumbled something crushing about a preemptive professional commitment.

The trip had been set up and was being underwritten by David Keh, a pioneering, somewhat flaky Chinese-born entrepreneur whom I'd known for years and was deeply fond of, despite his propensity for closing restaurants almost as soon as I'd reviewed them. David had invited me and a number of other hired bellies to accompany him to his homeland, simply because he needed some semblance of a legitimate delegation at a time before China's bor-ders were opened to casual tourism, when an ostensibly sanctioned mission of some sort still was a prerequisite for admission.

David only wanted to reestablish his own and his parents' ties to the obscure hamlet of his birth, in Hubei province, which he had left some forty years earlier. The ragtag group of professional food-ies and marginal hangers-on that he assembled for the trip was brazenly designated a "cultural and scientific" mission, although nobody in sight had the slightest pretensions to culture or the requisite familiarity with any branch of the sciences. As is often the case when food writers discover that one or more colleagues are slated to participate in the same junket, there were a number of last-minute dropouts, which suited me just fine. As things worked out, I was the only accredited mercenary eater on the team David ultimately fielded. Still, I took off for the Orient with some misgiv-ings. Not necessarily in order of importance, I was disturbed by the fact that the distinguished right arm attached to an aging native of Williamston, North Carolina, the pitcher Gaylord Perry, was seek-ing to prevail over major league opposition for the three hundredth time that very night (an effort not likely to attract the notice of the press in the People's Republic of China) and by Curtis's sudden defection, which had cast a pall on the prospects for my future happiness.

We were flying almost directly over Mount Fuji, which looked startlingly like Hiroshige's block-print depictions, when I rose from my seat and turned backward to prolong the view, only to find it blocked by an English-language newspaper being read in the seat behind mine. Look for a mountain, find a historical milestone: "Perry Wins No. 300." Sayonara, Fujiyama. Aside from what could be glimpsed from the plane, I'd seen nothing of Japan but Narita Airport, which might as well have been located in Cleveland, Ohio, for all the oriental exoticism it had to offer. I'd never been to the Far East before, and whatever mental images of the region I'd formed derived mostly from occasional explorations of New York's Chinatown and sedulous childhood reading of "Terry and the Pirates." As the plane began its descent toward Hong Kong, I noticed that the crown colony didn't look much different from Cleveland either.

David knew someone who knew someone who could facilitate our entry into the People's Republic. The first someone, Regina Lum, turned out to be the embodiment of my earliest comic strip–fueled erotic fantasies: the Dragon Lady in the flesh. She had been a leading Hong Kong film star, according to David, until her retirement. I expressed bafflement: whatever had impelled her to retire? She was absolutely gorgeous and in the prime of her staggering lushness. In Hong Kong, David explained, actresses are over the hill by their early twenties, too old to play glamor roles. Regina was now a successful businesswoman, the owner of an exclusive boutique and a posh beauty salon, among other things. She'd be joining us for dinner that evening, he added.

With the necessary paperwork completed, David herded his charges back to our hotel, the Regent, where I had every intention of drowning my sorrows in the lobby lounge until dinnertime. After several unanswered telephone calls to Curtis, placed at hours when she should have been at home and in bed, I knew for certain what I'd suspected the moment she announced that "something has come up" to prevent her from making the trip. I was changing clothes in my room when the phone rang. "Jay," a vaguely familiar voice purred, "it's Regina. Regina Lum. I'm downstairs in the lobby. May I come up?"

Sweet Jesus! Various articles of haberdashery, wet towels, and the like sailed through the air in the general direction of an open closet as I tried to set the scene for my first adulterous liaison since meeting Curtis. What's sauce for the goose, I reasoned, vaulting across the bed and closing the closet. There was a soft knock at the door, and Regina entered the room, dressed for the evening and more stunning than ever. "You don't mind, do you?" she asked. Of course I didn't mind, I was inexpressibly flattered, I babbled. "I have an urgent call to make, and all the phones downstairs are in use," she explained. She spent the next twenty minutes speaking in the language of Hong Kong's Chinese: numbers. A drink in the lobby was as far as I got with her, and that was cut short so that further urgent business could be accomplished before dinner.

The disparity between limitless affluence and the average standard of living in Hong Kong in 1982, between in-your-face conspicuous consumption and bare subsistence, was more pronounced than any I'd ever seen involving similar numbers of people at opposite ends of the divide. David was well connected in the colony, mostly with film producers and heavy hitters in the rag trade. With a single exception—a highly cultivated young garment-industry tycoon—the pack he ran with was made up of vulgarly ostentatious fat cats who flashed the equivalent or more of my annual income on their wrists, fingers, and shirt cuffs. They were massaged, manicured, and barbered daily to sea-lion sleekness, maintained chauffeured Rolls-Royces (of which there must be more in Hong Kong than anywhere else on earth), and talked almost exclusively in seven-, eight-, and nine-digit figures while their barely postadolescent bimbos, who flaunted impressive figures of another sort, made themselves seen but not heard. (To the best of my recollection, none of these doxies were ever introduced to dinner guests and none were addressed by any male present, their consorts included, during the course of otherwise convivial evenings. They were simply displayed, along with all the other status baubles.) Meanwhile, the sweatshop labor force on which all this opulence depended, as well as the street and boat people and the enormous number of workers who sustained one of the world's most pampered collective bellies, subsisted in abject squalor. Or so it seemed to me until we arrived in Beijing after a few days' layover.

Nothing about Hong Kong in any way prepared me for the cultural trauma I was to undergo in the People's Republic of China, for the shock of being thrust backward from a futuristic enclave rushing hell-for-leather into the next century to a nation mired in the technology, paranoia, and living standards of early medievalism. Its sociological inequities, cultural deficiencies, and preoccupation with crass materialism notwithstanding, Hong Kong was a vibrant, electrically animated, flamboyantly hedonistic organism, throbbing with life and hope, desire and greed. It was all about eating and hustling, gambling and sex. It was Fat City for those with balls enough to take it, relative misery for others, but for all a place where it was possible to hope and dream and scheme.

The People's Republic was ancient, immemorial Asia. It was dust and sweat and brutal stoop labor in involuntary servitude, its name a mockery of its ostensible ideals. It was human oppression in its most insidious forms. Government officials and rat-minded petty bureaucrats excepted, I loved the people, but I detested the state and everything it stood for. At the time, seven years before the fact, the mere idea of Tiananmen Square would have been dismissed as inconceivable, but its denouement, should the impossible actually occur, would be accepted as inevitable.

Beijing in 1982 was as grim a place as I ever hope to see. I hated the city and its asexuality, its tacit dress code that in effect castrated every male, kept every female in an arrested state of prepubescent development, and made it difficult to distinguish between one sex and the other. The farther from the capital and the watchful eye of Big Brother one traveled, the more relaxed the unstated strictures concerning attire became, although it was then still a rarity, even in relatively progressive cities like Shanghai and Canton, to see a woman clearly recognizable as such or to see anyone dressed in anything but what amounted to government-issue fatigue uniforms deliberately designed to obscure any and all evidence of gender. Foot binding had long since been done away with, to be replaced by de facto breast binding, implemented by constrictive little Band-Aid brassieres of inadequate capacity for most females past puberty. Hips, buttocks, and waists were lost somewhere inside pants that bagged like the behinds of elderly elephants. As David remarked of the distinctive accent of the city's young women, "They sing like birds—la-la-la-la." They did indeed, and there was an infantile charm about their twittering, but I found it depressingly symptomatic of a city where it wasn't at all unusual to find women in their mid-twenties carrying paper pinwheels through a public park while they and their male escorts rigorously avoided any semblance of physical contact, however wildly their hormones may have been raging.

I hated the city for the bleak, relentless Sovietism of its "modern" architecture, exemplified by lugubrious blocks of multiple-occupancy housing for the "privileged": misconceived half-finished warrens of worst-case barrio squalor hidden behind smugly cheerless facades designed to trumpet the magnanimity of the state. Through David's mysterious connections, we were granted the rare indulgence of an unchaperoned dinner party at home with a couple of tenants in one of these developments: a nationally renowned musician who had performed abroad and her husband, a noted composer. Their brutal flat, four flights up an unlighted stairwell, consisted of two rooms with no running water, a single electrical outlet, and floors of bare concrete. The one light socket dangled from the ceiling like something from a George Price or George Booth cartoon, dripping with extension cords that powered both a record player and the two-burner hot plate on which our hostess somehow contrived to cook an excellent, presumably bankruptive dinner.

In view of the state of "luxury" housing for favored intellectuals, an ordinary taxi driver's bitching, earlier that day, became somewhat more understandable. David had struck up a conversation with the guy and translated it for my benefit. "He says he makes the equivalent of about forty-five dollars a month and pays four dollars for rent." My observation that the ratio would be terrific in New York was relayed to the driver, who replied rather heatedly. Some of his vehemence may have been lost in translation, but the gist of his complaint was something like, "Yeah, sure, but *you* get a toilet and a bath and heat and enough space to breathe in. Okay, you're paying out a much larger proportion of your income, but *you* don't have to shit in a clay pot outdoors in winter. *You* don't have to go to a public bath, and *you* don't freeze your ass off half the year."

I hated Beijing for its unbreathable air, which had nothing in common with the relatively tolerable internal-combustion pollution of, say, downtown Bangkok or Mexico City or Los Angeles or the stifling Plaza Independencia in Gerona, near the Costa Brava. Instead, it was compounded of a chokingly dry mix, fine as baby powder, of windblown earth and dung, involuntarily ingested by anyone imprudent enough to abjure a plastic muzzle mask. At that transitional stage of its millennial development, the city was all raw soil, busted-up masonry, and pulverized plaster, its fractured lathing, beams, and stringers gasping disintegrated lime. All this respiratory crap was activated and pervasively airborne at the merest hint of a breeze.

To me, the most depressing aspect of an altogether depressing city was the virtually total absence of any other life forms in the midst of unimaginable human congestion. Since early childhood, I had known (mostly thanks to Ripley's "Believe It or Not" features) that China was somewhat heavily populated; that "Chinamen" marching six abreast around the globe would constitute an unending procession, that one of every four (or was it every three?) human births occurred in China, and so on. But until my arrival in Beijing these were abstract formulations that eluded concrete visualization. As putative VIPs, our first days in the city were spent in a compound, constructed by the dowager empress Tzlu Hsi in 1888, of one of two imperial palaces on Kunming Lake. The district in which it is situated (now a public park during daylight hours) is hauntingly poetic and disposed around an often mist-shrouded lake, but it's utterly devoid of ground-level vegetation, as is the rest of the city. Not a single blade of grass grows on soil trodden barren, generation after generation, by the hundreds of millions of pairs of human feet that have packed the ground hard as rock, leaving an almost metallic patina over much of its surface. Except for a single cat encountered one night hours after the park had been closed, no beasts prowled there, no birds sang, and no bugs buzzed. Nothing had survived the most effective pogrom since the passenger pigeon had been obliterated from the skies it once had darkened over much of the United States. During the daylight hours, the park was populated only by an infinite procession of humans, endlessly and aimlessly circling the lake and clotting its surface with rented row-boats rendered almost immovable by their density.

In comparison to the city's streets, the park and its lake were deserted. On any busy Beijing thoroughfare—and they were *all* busy—a leisurely solitary stroll was out of the question; any pedestrian (or bicyclist, for that matter) was simply swept along willy-nilly by a tidal wave of solidly packed humanity, a numberless horde that pushed and shoved and elbowed its way forward, hawking and spitting and discharging snot through its fingers. Despite the taboo against physical contact between well-acquainted males and females, there were no restrictions at all as far as total strangers were concerned, and sardine-can intimacy prevailed everywhere. Trapped in one such situation at the Imperial Palace, I felt as though I were being physically occupied from behind by a young woman who, forced by the sheer weight of numbers to forsake conventional Beijing modesty and oblivious of the simple fact that it's impossible for two objects of roughly equal volume to occupy space just large enough for one of them, came pretty close to insinuating herself inside my skin. Hospitable as I might have been to her advances had they been voluntary and less public, the involuntary invasion of my person by a total stranger and mere pawn of mass impetus wasn't entirely welcome. As it happens, I harbor a near-phobic aversion to physical mergers with people whose names I don't know and couldn't pronounce if I did.

What frustrated me most about Beijing in particular and China in general was the limpetlike tenacity of our appointed guides. According to that year's edition of *The China Guidebook,* "Contrary to some lingering preconceptions of China travel, there is no rule that visitors be led around or observed during every moment of their stay in China." Perhaps not for most groups engaged in simple tourism, but it was plain (indeed, it was candidly admitted) that David had ulterior motives in bringing us to the People's Republic and that his mission included the insinuation of a few (three, to be precise) round-eyes into regions off limits to them. Chinese officialdom in the guise of a "sponsoring agency" had no intention of allowing his Occidental companions to accompany David to his home village, and they quite possibly were taking more than ordinary precautions wherever we went. In any event, our principal cicerone stuck to us like glue. Quick to spot a potentially troublesome loose cannon, he spent most of his time chivvying me back into line every time some intriguingly fragrant side street, alleyway, or shop lured me off the beaten track.

Had he been born in the United States, the guide, Mr. Wu, would doubtless have had a splendid career with the FBI or some comparable agency of hugger-mugger. Trim, wiry, and well dressed, he was an uncommonly handsome dude in his late thirties, with clean-cut, rather tense features and prematurely gray hair. The quintessential company man, he spoke English fluently except when objections to his rote adherence to policy were raised or the logic of that policy was questioned. I found him almost likable but was put off by his stiff, guarded manner and his mendacious, temporizing acquiescence to requests and demands he had no intention of complying with.

Our principal activity in China was eating, and my impressions of what we ate were mixed. By and large, the quality of neither the food nor its preparation could compare with that of Hong Kong, Taipei, or even the better Chinese restaurants back in New York. We had a few superb meals in the People's Republic, a number of outstanding individual dishes in the course of otherwise undistinguished banquets, and a good many meals that were flat-out bummers from start to finish. Any chef worth his salt had long since decamped for greener pastures, and those who remained behind were forced by deficiencies of transportation and refrigeration to make do with whatever limited ingredients were in season locally. As a consequence, if cabbages or turnips or whatever were harvestable at the moment, cabbages or turnips or whatever would play salient roles, dish after dish, in even the most opulent banquet thrown by regional government honchos for presumed visiting dignitaries.

In some cases, even token recognition of seasonal availability was dispensed with. One of our lunches in Beijing, for example, took place in a six-story, two-thousand-seat restaurant. The menu consisted almost in its entirety of duck dishes in every imaginable form: duck webs, duck livers, sliced duck hearts, red-dyed duck wings in aspic, duck tongues, duck soup, duck guts, and, for all I knew, duck assholes. Everything was quite tasty and, after eating far more than I'd intended to, I slumped back, sated to the ears, remarking to David that it was quite a lunch. *"Was?"* he replied. "We haven't started yet." Out came pancakes, scallions, and hoisin sauce: unmistakable harbingers of the *pièce de résistance,* Peking duck.

Although my own table behavior at home or abroad was none too fastidious, I was appalled by Chinese standards of acceptable dining conduct, even at formal banquets, which resembled the food fights in *National Lampoon* movies. After one relatively staid occasion, presided over by an elderly provincial governor who was reputed to be a nationally respected poet, I found myself inscribing some verse of my own in a battered notebook:

In China, when the soup's served, slu-u-urp!
Slurp as loudly as you're able!
No one's offended if you burp,
Or if you pick your teeth at table.

When you've licked your chopsticks clean,
Use them in communal dishes
To snare some duckling or a bean
Or a mess of little fishes.

When beer is served, just pop the cap
And toss it anywhere you choose to;
You'll find no napkin on your lap,
But this is something you'll get used to.

Here's more soup, so slu-u-urp the broth;
Slurp as loudly as you're able!
Toss chicken bones upon the cloth
And dribble sauce upon the table.

The Chinese are a courteous race,
They'll welcome you with smiles and banners,
With sauce upon each smiling face,
But not, I fear, with table manners.

Increasingly and more succinctly, I fell under the spell of the muse during our sojourn in the People's Republic.

Of all of the countless Chinese,
The strangest is one Cantonese.
This fellow, called Wong,
Ties a knot in his schlong
And squirts figure eights when he pees.

To Mr. Wu's patent dismay, I managed to separate myself with some frequency from his strictly overseen tours of Beijing. By feigning illness as our group assembled in the hotel lobby each morning for its programmed itinerary of historic landmarks (usually rickety tables at which Chou En-lai had signed some document or other), I was able to skulk in my room until our assigned minibus was out of sight and then avail myself of the freedom of the city, poking around sections of town rarely if ever seen by outlanders and haunting the daily markets that Mr. Wu took infinite pains to skirt.

I bought gloriously greasy, intricately formed crullers from street vendors in godforsaken little alleyways, loaded up on dried mushrooms in out-of-the-way markets, and luxuriated in solitary meals of my own choosing while my traveling companions were served set menus at stiffly formal state banquets. Perhaps because of its slightly clandestine nature, a dinner on my own at the ultraposh Peking Hotel (a dinner that set me back the equivalent of six bucks and change) seems in retrospect one of the finest meals I had in China, or have had anywhere else. It got under way with preserved eggs in ginger sauce and progressed thence to bamboo shoots speckled with shrimp roe (a combination that produced curiously agreeable wheaty sensations); vermicelli spangled with tangy bits of pork; cabbage with what were billed as, and actually may have been, truffles; and sensationally good Yangzhou-style air-dried sausage, a sort of pepperoni in apotheosis. Chinese charcuterie, I discovered, rivaled or excelled the finest products of Italy, France, Spain, or Germany.

Other meals left something to be desired—namely, edible food. One evening, David managed to persuade the adhesive Mr. Wu to get lost for a few hours, and took us to a workers' restaurant. It was clear from the moment we entered the place that we weren't welcome. As nearly as I could gather from a rather heated exchange, David was told that the likes of him and his blue-eyed, big-nosed companions didn't belong in so humble an establishment and damned well ought to go back to whatever ritzy hotel they had come from. David protested that current appearances notwithstanding he had been born a peasant of hundreds of generations of peasants and had known poverty that no big-city restaurant worker could possibly visualize. (He wasn't exaggerating. A day or two earlier he had told me of his early childhood in his native village, when his mother would routinely walk fifteen miles to buy a pound of rice, reserve half of it for family use, and then walk fifteen miles in the opposite direction to sell the remainder at a minuscule profit.)

David's suasion was unavailing. At one point, the head chef joined the debate, declaring that he was a relative beginner and that if we insisted on eating at the restaurant we'd do better on the second floor, where slightly more expensive meals were served to the cognoscenti. No, David insisted, we had come to eat as anyone else ate. Finally and reluctantly, we were directed to a filthy table, apparently uncleared at any point during a busy evening, and David ordered dinner. Among other selections, he chose a squid dish reputed to be a specialty of the house and some prawns priced ten times higher than anything else on the menu.

While all this was going on, I surveyed a landscape of devastation made up in roughly equal parts of discarded animal bones, human phlegm, spittle, and snot, and the spatterings of various sauces. The dining-room floor was a slippery carpet of bodily evacuations of one sort or another, garnished with cigarette butts, bottle caps, and the detritus of countless earlier meals. Someone working from the ceiling down had run out of paint about six feet from the floor, leaving the walls half-covered with a sickly jade green that ended in a ragged smear of thin brushstrokes. Had the place not been run by the government, it would have been shut down by the government as a menace to public health.

David sniffed the squid dish as it was set before him, declared it absolutely rank, and pushed it away. Nobody had to sniff the prawns; from halfway across the room, they stank so loudly that we all grabbed our noses with our fingers. A tureen of notional hot and sour soup was a scummy gray sea of cornstarch. Framed in his kitchen window, the chef glared triumphantly as we beat an ignominious retreat.

We lunched one day at another state-operated restaurant, a two-room establishment in which tourists and other desirables were segregated from the common herd. The food—a pork-flecked cauliflower dish in particular—was inelegant but copious, dirt-cheap, and quite good. On our way out, we looked into the other dining room to see how the second-class members of the classless society were faring. At one large table, a young woman wore a lacy white cardigan over a light cotton blouse in lieu of the usual fatigue jacket worn by all other members of her party, male and female. "A wedding celebration," David explained. "She's the bride."

The majority of our meals in Beijing and elsewhere around the People's Republic were formal banquets presided over by various ranking government officials, as befitted a cultural and scientific mission, however spurious its accreditation may have been. In general, the food at these functions was considerably better than what we ate on our own, but our free lunches were paid for by having to endure endless speechifying by elderly party hacks, room-temperature beer, and countless glasses of maotai, a sorghum distillate that could easily convert me to teetotalism in a world where no spirituous alternatives were to be had. I've never imbibed paint remover, but my guess is that it would be considerably mellower than maotai, in comparison with the finest of which the harshest home-distilled Italian grappa or French *marc* would seem mother's milk. By reputation, maotai is lethally potent, but I found its flavor so disagreeable that it discouraged any empirical research. As far as I was concerned, the good news about the stuff was that it was drunk from glasses the size of thimbles and knocked back in a quick gulp, with minimal palatal contact. The bad news was that it was the quaff of choice when toasts were in order, and any formal banquet was the occasion for an unending succession of toasts.

David, a relatively abstemious soul who had long affected bemusement at my capacity for dry martinis, gleefully functioned as an advance man of sorts, informing local dignitaries wherever we traveled that his party included a legendary American drinker. As a result, each of the banquets thrown in our honor inevitably turned

into a *mano a mano,* with some bibulous local bigwig flinging down
the gauntlet at my feet. The most intense of these confrontations
took place in Chungking, where dinner was hosted by a certain
Professor King, the seventy-eight-year-old vice-president of
Chungking University and an alumnus of Purdue. Professor King
spoke excellent English, most of it devoted to Big Ten basketball
circa 1935, and drank like the proverbial fish. Apparently recognizing a kindred soul, he proposed a series of toasts in what he quite
obviously had determined would be a shoot-out between himself
and me. "To the greater glory of Indiana roundball and Chairman
Hu Yaobang," he crowed, tossing off his maotai at a gulp. Longev-
ity was proposed for assorted timeservers who had outlived their
usefulness two or three decades earlier, and the distinguished cultural and scientific delegation from across the seas was duly eulo-
gized. Innumerable toasts later, the good professor was so squiffed
he could barely rise from his chair at the evening's end. Somewhere
along the line, he had mentioned the possibility of his visiting New
York in the not-too-distant future. I'd told him that if he did I'd be
only too happy if he accompanied me on a pub-crawl of the city.
He responded with unfeigned enthusiasm. Alas, I've never heard
from him again and have never had the opportunity to see how he
might have handled *my* drink on *my* turf.

I spent most of our week or so in Beijing feigning illness. Blessed
with the digestive system of a billy goat, I'd hang back in my room
each morning, complaining of fictive stomach disruptions allegedly
incurred the night before, until the cultural and scientific mission
departed for the day's tour of factories and revolutionary landmarks
under the watchful eye of Mr. Wu. As the result of this malingering,
I missed a few genuine points of interest but was able to see something of real life in the city. While the other Occidentals in our
group (a photographer and his wife) shopped under strict supervi-
sion in the so-called Friendship Stores, loading up on shoddy kitsch
designed for and sold exclusively to tourists, I followed an alley
cat's itinerary, sniffing around in whatever food markets I ran
across, getting myself lost in semirural residential districts far from

the center of town, eating on the hoof wherever a street vendor had something interesting to offer. Once we left Beijing, however, Mr. Wu kept me on a much tighter rein, generally behaving as though he had a dangerous radical in custody.

As it turned out, Mr. Wu was uptight for good reason. The authorities were unanimous in their opposition to David's planned return to his birthplace, especially in the company of foreigners. David had struck it rich in New York and Hong Kong and made no secret of it in China. His pockets bulged with great thick rolls of greenbacks, which he dispensed with alarming prodigality. (In Hong Kong, he had gambled his nights away at mah-jongg with a group of similarly inclined high rollers, winning or losing thousands of dollars at a time with apparent unconcern.) As Chinese officialdom viewed the matter, this shining example of bootstrap success in the capitalistic West could only stir up discontent by returning to his native village and making his peasant kinfolk and childhood neighbors aware of what they were missing. Moreover, the state would lose face were a trio of Americans to see the real peasant China, with its grinding poverty, virtual slave labor, universal illiteracy, and total lack of civilized amenities, including the most elementary medical care.

As David had explained to me the morning after one formal banquet in Beijing—a function hosted by a trio of upper-echelon government officials—what I'd taken to be an evening of unconstrained bonhomie had actually involved an acrimonious debate with every conceivable argument arrayed against his proposal. He'd been told that there was nothing in his village of any interest to foreigners and certainly nothing to justify its inclusion in a cultural-cum-scientific tour; the place was inaccessible—four miles from the nearest road; the villagers would be ashamed to have visitors from the technologically advanced West see how simply they lived; the visitors would be mortally inconvenienced by the absence of plumbing; and so on and on and on.

Appeals were lodged with various functionaries and agencies, and, I strongly suspect, considerable quantities of pelf changed hands. After several days, it was decided that David would have his way after all. To facilitate matters for his traveling companions, the road would be extended to his village, to which no wheeled vehicle had penetrated since the beginning of time. A sizable unit of army engineers was dispatched to build the new road and put the village itself into some semblance of presentability. David was heartsick. " 'Why do you do this?' I asked the minister," he recounted in anguish. " 'I want to visit *my* village, not yours.' "

As it would turn out a few days later, David was more effective than I in circumventing government policy. Before leaving New York, I had wangled an assignment to write a piece for *Connoisseur* on the tomb of the Ch'in emperor Shih Huang Ti, which had been discovered accidentally in Xian some eight years earlier. The magazine had stipulated that I do the photography for the story, and so I had informed the New York representatives of the Cultural and Scientific Association, who seemed delighted to add a previously unscheduled visit to Xian to our group's itinerary.

The tomb is housed in a vast hangarlike shed that protects about three and a half acres of an archeological dig populated by a terra-cotta army of upward of six thousand life-size figures. I had seen a few of them a year or two earlier, during a temporary display at the Metropolitan Museum, and had been bowled over by them. In Xian at last, I approached the entrance to the protective hangar in a state of high excitement. A sign beside the door stated in several languages and no uncertain terms that photography was not permitted inside. Not for your ordinary tourist, I thought, but the taboo didn't apply to a journalist traveling on a professional assignment under the auspices of the Cultural and Scientific Association. Surely the ever-present, ever-capable Mr. Wu would fix things up with the appropriate resident officials so I could accomplish a mission for which we'd traveled an extra six hundred miles.

Mr. Wu looked doubtful. "The sign says no photography," he said. "If you desire photographs, there are color slides for sale in the souvenir shop." With as much patience as I could muster, I explained to Mr. Wu that we had journeyed to Xian for the express purpose of studying—and photographing—the tomb figures, that publication of my piece in one of America's most prestigious cultural periodicals was contingent on the delivery of original photographs taken for the magazine's exclusive use, and that everyone in any way connected with our trip, himself included, had been so apprised weeks in advance. "But the sign says no photography," Mr. Wu replied.

"I *know* what the bloody sign says. I'm asking you to intercede with whoever has the authority to make an exception for a professional on assignment."

Looking more doubtful than ever, Mr. Wu, who normally strode briskly, bearing himself in a military manner, let his shoulders droop and shambled off in the direction of some office or other. He returned some minutes later to say that no one in Xian had the authority to overrule a posted regulation, but that the problem would be referred to the proper officials in Beijing. Since no decision would be forthcoming for several days and we were leaving in a few hours, the local officials had respectfully suggested that I purchase a selection of the souvenir shop's color slides, which, he'd been assured, were of excellent quality. I exploded, launching into a tirade about these imbecilic bastards who were pissing away thousands of dollars' worth of prime press coverage in order to peddle a few cents' worth of stock color slides that were altogether useless for my purposes; these goddamn bureaucratic dingbats who . . . "Please explain," interrupted Mr. Wu. " 'Dingbats' is a term with which I am not familiar."

Although not particularly superstitious, I was a bit shaken to discover that I'd been assigned seat number thirteen on our flight from Wuhan to Nanjing. The scuttling of the Xian assignment had put me in a somewhat pessimistic frame of mind, as had a by-now settled conviction that, for all the sightseeing we'd done, all the natural and man-made wonders we'd seen, we were going to be allowed to see precious little of Chinese life. At the airport, I became convinced I was destined to see precious little more of my own life. I'd flown in some alarmingly dilapidated crates during my air force days but nothing as beat-up as the propeller-driven wreck scheduled to carry us some four hundred miles to the southeast.

In his usual overcautious fashion, Mr. Wu had hustled us to the airport an hour and a half before our scheduled departure, only to learn that our flight would be delayed by thirty minutes. Thirty minutes became sixty, with no explanation forthcoming and with Mr. Wu evincing nothing but infinite, unquestioning patience, apparently prepared to sit where he was until he shriveled up and died before taking any action on his own initiative. He was finally prevailed on to bestir his ass and find out the cause of the holdup. Ten minutes later, he returned to announce that the plane was ready for boarding and that the delay had been caused by a safety inspector's discovery that it needed new tires.

As we trooped out to the aircraft, I glanced at the "new" tires: two were literally threadbare; the others, treadless. The aircraft itself looked utterly exhausted—battered and dented, its engine housings black with scorched grease. Seat number thirteen had a lower-back problem of some sort that forced it and its occupant to lean forward at the same thirty-degree angle. The lap belt lacked a buckle, but no matter: its starboard end was no longer attached to anything. Engines smoking, we somehow got off the ground.

About halfway to Nanjing, I glanced down through the window to see what sort of terrain lay below and promptly went into shock: a westbound clone of our flying slum was passing directly beneath us, so close that every loose rivet was clearly visible. Once back on terra firma, a shaken David informed us that henceforth we'd travel by train, even at the cost of a thoroughly bollixed itinerary.

We were met at the airport by the usual committee of principal dignitaries and by an interpreter, a Mr. Li, who spoke fairly decent English and passed out copies of our timetable for the next day. Sweet suffering Jesus, this bunch of sadists had a twelve-stop tour planned, beginning at seven in the morning and ending at eight in the evening, with an hour's visit to the mausoleum of Sun Yat-sen salient among the scheduled merriments. Groans from the round-eyes. We'd already been forced to view the remains of Chairman Mao, laid out like a chicken in a butcher's showcase, and the burial sites and commemorative stelae of half of China's illustrious dead from the Hsia dynasty to the present. We'd already visited more temples and historical museums and revolutionary landmarks than we could sort out in retrospect. We'd had it to the ears with China's dead past, obligatory relics, rigidly structured daily programs, official receptions, formal banquets, leechlike escorts, and all the rest of it. In two weeks' time, we'd be leaving the country, having experienced nothing of its ordinary quotidian life.

As tactfully as possible in my state of barely suppressed rage, I explained to Mr. Li that we appreciated the infinite and well-thought-out pains his confreres had taken on our behalf, the importance of Dr. Sun Yat-sen's mausoleum to the triumphant history of the new China, the profound reverence in which the great Chinese people held it, blah, blah, blah, but if we saw one more bloody tomb, memorial, revolutionary landmark, or the like, not to mention day-care centers, factories, or agricultural communes, we'd go absolutely stark raving uncontrollably screaming bonkers. Had I made myself plain, Mr. Li? We'd be chewing the tapestries off the walls of the frigging museums, blowing the sacred icons of the People's Republic to kingdom-fucking-come.

"Just tell me what you wish to do," Mr. Li replied equably, "and I will arrange to have you do it."

Yeah, sure, we'd heard that crap before—from Mr. Wu and half a dozen local chain-gang bosses, from every provincial vice-governor and interpreter and college administrator we'd met. Still, I told Mr. Li that all we wished to do was roam at random around the city, set our own pace, mingle with the common people, take our photographs without any interference, and generally behave as travelers anywhere else in the civilized world were permitted to behave.

The invariable reply to past pleas of this sort had been a simple yes, which translated as something like "fat chance." Mr. Li's surprising answer wasn't "yes" but "I understand you completely and think the same way you do. You see, I traveled in *your* country earlier this year and was allowed to go wherever I wished, to do whatever I wished. I am canceling tomorrow's program. You are free to go where you wish and do as you wish. I will follow you only to see that you don't get lost or to supply any information you may need, but you'll be on your own." Mr. Wu, he added sotto voce, would be given a well-deserved day off.

Liberation!

Dusk was falling as we entered the city proper, but even with minimal visibility Nanjing had a different feel about it. The air smelled good and was free of the dust that hung over every other city we'd visited. The silhouettes of the graceful white pines that lined the streets could be made out against the darkening sky. The streets were mostly paved, there was far less rubble in evidence than elsewhere, and for once we were free of the stale, ratty, sewery stench of raw urban excavation. Our hotel accommodations were good even by Western standards, palatial by Chinese, and there were even ice cubes available in limited supply. For the first time in the People's Republic, I was able to luxuriate in reasonably cold gin.

By day, Nanjing turned out to be all it promised in whispers the evening before. With a few relatively minor adjustments, it could be Paris: a warmer, more forthcoming, more tolerant Paris. After a smashing breakfast in a handsome light-flooded restaurant, Mr. Li was as good as his word, and we spent the morning roaming about at will, as he followed at a distance discreet enough to allow me to dog down and temporarily lose myself in any interesting alleyways that turned up along our route. The city is one of "the four furnaces" of southeast China, and the temperature was well up in the eighties before nine o'clock, but it was far less oppressive than in, say, Wuhan. Moreover, the heat here had the redeeming feature of impelling most residents to wear light-textured colorful garb that made it possible to distinguish between the sexes. In one residential side street, a devastatingly pretty young woman was doing her laundry on the sidewalk. Unlike the inadequate brassieres offered for sale in the people's department stores of Beijing, the one she was scrubbing was capacious enough to do justice to her opulent bosom.

David had been invited to lunch at the home of a physician in "the most exclusive residential district of the city" and in turn had invited his "family" (i.e., the cultural and scientific mission) along. I protested that the dozen members of our steadily expanding group might put an intolerable strain on the host's budget, but David waved the objection away.

The most exclusive residential district of the city turned out to bear a closer similarity to the Mexican quarter of San Antonio than to Grosse Pointe, Michigan, or the River Oaks section of Houston. A few scrawny chickens scratched in the middle of a rubble-strewn yard overhung with drying laundry. Our host, a tall, gaunt, donnish type, greeted us in Mandarin and English and led us into his book-lined domain, which was crowded with various kinfolk and neighbors of assorted ages, ranging from a three-year-old to people in their sixties and seventies. One relative (daughter? niece?) was introduced as "Miss Nanjing," reigning or emeritus unspecified. She was a pleasant-looking kid who brandished a lot of teeth but didn't compare with the morning's sidewalk laundress, a sort of Chinese Silvana Mangano in the Italian actress's prime. There was a touchingly familial warmth about the whole scene, graciously extended to embrace a dozen strangers.

The relatively few glimpses we'd had of ordinary home life in the People's Republic had invariably revolved around a display of what I've come to think of as the Major Possession. As in the Jacques Tati film *Mon Oncle,* the Major Possession is activated just as guests arrive anywhere. In the film, the Major Possession was a ridiculously kitschy ornamental fountain, turned on only as company approached. At the musician's pad in Beijing, it had been a fairly sophisticated stereo set, in full cry as we entered the premises. At a peasant hovel somewhere in Anhui province, it had been an enormous, hippopotamus-size sow, which had been raised from slumber in a stinking extension of a communal bedroom and displayed as though it were a late-model Cadillac. At the doctor's house in Nanjing, it was a television set, built from a kit by the doctor himself, switched on just as the first guests arrived and allowed to blare away at top volume, the flower of the new China's youth whacking ping-pong balls on the screen, ignored by the assembled company.

Liquor would be quicker, but candy is what's handy as the icebreaker at social gatherings in Chinese homes. Cellophane-wrapped taffies, sour balls, and the like were passed as a prelude to lunch, which was being prepared by the doctor's womenfolk in an outbuilding somewhere behind the house. I would have much rather been sucking a chilled martini than this ferociously citric sour ball, which I surreptitiously rewrapped and pocketed for future disposal. The candy dish was passed again, and courtesy dictated further indulgence. I was nauseated by a lump of taffy chosen as an alternative to another horrid sour ball. Lunch arrived, putting a merciful end to my sweet sorrows.

What a lunch! Served in the customary manner, all at once, it was a splendacious array of complex dishes—hardly what I'd expected of a meal knocked together on short notice for a dozen unexpected guests. Division of labor among the host's womenfolk and a few conscripted neighbors had produced a spread as elaborate as any of the professionally prepared banquets we'd attended, and to my taste the best meal we'd had in the People's Republic. Individually and collectively, the dishes epitomized Chinese cookery, with its alternatingly subtle and emphatic contrasts of flavor, texture, color, and aroma and its adherence to culinary principles formulated nearly two and a half thousand years ago, when it was determined that a proper menu deliberately took into account the roles to be played by the five basic palatal sensations: sweetness, sourness, brininess, hotness, and bitterness.

The promotion of tourism in the People's Republic during the early 1980s was mismanaged in every possible way and was further hampered by an acknowledged shortage of capable chefs. Because most travelers arrived via Hong Kong, the disparity between the superb

professional cookery of the crown colony and the generally lackluster restaurant fare on the mainland was all too apparent. For one
reason or another, the city of Yangzhou had been designated as the
prospective center of a culinary renaissance. (Soon after our arrival
there, we toured the city's nationally renowned cooking school,
where a prominently displayed artifact in the attached culinary
museum was a bottle of Heinz ketchup. Coals to Newcastle: the
noun derives, via the Malay *kechap,* from the Chinese *ke-tsiap* of
Amoy.) For no clearly discernible reason, the culinary style
whereby the rebirth was to be accomplished was a sort of Sinofied
nouvelle cuisine. Largely dependent on pricey esoteric ingredients
and elaborately contrived presentation, the banquet cookery of
Yangzhou was the most effete we'd encountered in China. David,
who hadn't set foot in the city before but had come in high hopes
of hiring a couple of chefs who could launch a previously unknown
regional cuisine in New York (where he had introduced Szechuanese cookery about a decade earlier), was bitterly disappointed, bitching loud and long about the impossibility of getting
what he, a good old Chinese country boy, deemed a square meal.
"What the hell kind of Chinese cooking is *this?"* he wailed,
morosely surveying a tableful of trompe l'oeil artifice made up in
large part of egg whites masquerading as solid food. "No black
beans, no chili peppers . . ." He went on to itemize several dozen
staples of the southern Chinese culinary repertory that were conspicuous by their absence.

While David heaped muttered imprecations on everything set
before us, I found myself engaged in another bibulous shoot-out
with a vaunted local drinker—the provincial vice-chairman in
charge of chamber pots or some such. Innumerable toasts were
proposed and drinks downed at a gulp, the potable of choice on this
occasion being not maotai but a horrifically cloying rice wine that
I found altogether unfit for human consumption. Once again the
adversary was rendered comatose. Later, during the bus ride back
to our hotel, Mr. Li observed that I seemed to have "a considerable

capacity for wine." If we'd used the weapon of my choice, gin, I told him, his compatriot would now be in rigor mortis.

David was so upset with the caliber of the food in Yangzhou that he proposed to cook our last meal in the city himself. He was turned loose in the kitchen of the town's best hotel and, kvetching incessantly about the shortcomings of the available raw materials, produced an excellent lunch. As he chopped and sliced and diced his limited supply of ingredients, a young sous-chef consulted with Mr. Li, who translated a request that I cook "something Western." What to cook? There were eggs aplenty at hand, and all manner of prospective omelet fillings, but how the hell could I possibly get two dozen omelets to the table simultaneously when just two were about one more than I could manage with confidence at home? Inspecting a tub full of pork kidneys and an abundance of fresh mushrooms, I toyed briefly with the notion of attempting the largest single serving of *rognoncini trifolati* in recorded history. Then a bin of potatoes caught my eye.

Chinese food mavens in the West are oblivious of whatever role potatoes may play in their favored cuisine. To the best of my recollection, I've never encountered any evidence of the tubers in any Chinese restaurant or any Chinese cookbook. In my clandestine explorations of the free-enterprise markets of the People's Republic, however, I'd seen significant quantities of potatoes on display, just as I'd witnessed a lively early morning traffic in toasted presliced white bread, a commodity I'd have been no more inclined to associate with Chinese gastronomy than Liederkranz cheese, Key lime pie, or New England clam chowder.

In the hotel kitchen at Yangzhou, I selected five pounds or so of the firmest spuds I could find, reduced them to shoestrings with a wicked-looking cleaver, and stirred them into a wok filled with hot oil. Elementary as the procedure might have been anywhere else on the planet, it was regarded by the assembled culinary cadets as an unprecedented feat. Whether or not I was the first cook in some forty years to produce a batch of French fries on Communist Chi-

nese soil, I was treated to a heartfelt round of applause, and the
spuds were snaffled up as though they were so much caviar.

Inexorably, our expanding party (which by then included a delightful Chinese-born New Yorker named Mrs. Sobelman and a sister
of hers) approached David's holy grail, the obscure hamlet of his
birth in Hubei province. Along the way by train to Hefei, the last
city of any size on our itinerary, we traveled for five hours through
flatland monotonously given over to endless expanses of winter
wheat, transitionally replaced at that season by newly transplanted
rice. Except for the inescapable presence everywhere, in whatever
sweep of terrain the eye could encompass, of humans, this could
have been the great American prairie. It was the breadbasket of
China, virtually unchanged since the Han dynasty, its occupants'
backs stooped under an endless sweep of sky from dawn to dusk,
their prematurely gnarled hands groping in immemorial muck.

My habitual, partially affected cynicism notwithstanding, this was
to be the most emotional day of my life; the most rousing and most
poignant experience I've ever undergone. As it turned out when
we reached the end of it, the new road to David's birthplace had
fallen short by a couple of miles of its proposed destination; even
working around the clock, the army engineers hadn't been able to
complete the project. The road petered out at a nameless village a
half-hour's trek from David's ancestral hamlet.

We arrived by bus, to a tumultuous welcome. The peasantry had
obviously been apprised by the road builders of the imminent
arrival in their midst of a local boy who had made it big abroad.
Lined up beside their splendid new road, the villagers greeted us
with a hearty round of reciprocated applause. The first foreigners
these people had ever seen were stared at and exclaimed over as
though we'd come from another planet. David was clearly impa-
tient to get home at last, but one of the elders of this penultimate
village detained us with a flowery oration of near-filibuster length.
Finally we set off, David and I in the lead, along a footpath sur-
mounting an eight-foot-high dike. A few small children broke away

from the welcoming party and trotted along at the base of the dike, keeping pace with us. Then a few more joined them, then older siblings, and finally the entire ambulatory population of the village and its environs were marching along. Roused from torpor by the hullabaloo, a water buffalo struggled up from its wallow to join the parade. Other buffalo followed suit, along with pigs, geese, ducks, and chickens. Preoccupied with getting this startling procession on film, I paid no attention to the surrounding countryside during the first mile or so of the trek. When I finally glanced across the paddies and fields while reloading a camera, the entire landscape was in motion, swarming from horizon to horizon with figures slogging through the muck to converge on our line of march. Here—in the dead center of nowhere—a mob of thousands wildly cheered us on.

Several hundred yards from our destination, the crowds fell silent as a toothless ancient hobbled out alone from David's village to intercept us. Stooped, tattered, almost inconceivably wrinkled, he stood before us, beaming at the returned prodigal. David registered momentary confusion, although a flicker of recognition played across his face. He had, after all, left this place as a small child forty years earlier, when this wizened gaffer must have been about David's present age. Hesitantly, questioningly, he pronounced a name, then rushed forward to clamp the man in a joyous bear hug. Their embrace lasted a good two minutes and then our trek resumed, with David and the oldster walking arm in arm. "He was my best friend when I was six years old," David confided. "When we were the same age."

Sleek, well-fed, entrepreneurial David and his childhood coevals were generations apart now, separated by the vastly disparate rates of physical attrition imposed by medieval and modern life, by grinding hardship and Western ease. In this place, he was the youngest adult in evidence, parents of small children included, as he pushed fifty. Whatever their chronologic ages might be, his childhood contemporaries were nearly twice as old as he.

We gathered in a communal meeting room half an hour or so after our arrival, when a woman was ushered into David's presence.

She was as old as time—withered, fragile, hauntingly beautiful. She seated herself beside David on a crude wooden bench, and they talked quietly in a suddenly hushed room suffused with an almost palpable tenderness. Ten minutes went by, their hands touched lightly, and she was gone. I felt a great sorrow even before David explained that their marriage was arranged when they were both small children, that it was of course thwarted when his family fled the country, and that she had never married or had children of her own.

David has a lovely wife, two fine sons, and all the material trappings of success back in New York. Here, on his primitive hardscrabble native turf, he seemed at once exalted and humbled. Did I really detect a sense of self-betrayal on his part? A disturbing sense of loss? Did he feel, as I half-suspect he might, that his destiny had been abandoned and a chain broken that had been meant to link the beginning and end of time? (A few mornings later, when I happened to glance out of my hotel-room window, there was bluff, gregarious, high-rolling, Westernized David, alone in a distant field at dawn, seated in the lotus position, communing with his ancestral spirits. I thought then of his father, wanting for nothing in America; nothing but to be able to return to this mud-caked cluster of adobe hovels, to die where he was meant to die: where he and all his unnumbered generations had been born.)

It was as primitive a community as any I've seen, Indian jungle villages included, although there was minimal electrification in evidence. Of the several buildings I entered, one, the community house, had a single bare light bulb hanging from a rough-hewn rafter in the main room (through whose patchy thatched roof and unglazed windows rain would pour in torrents later in the afternoon; whether or not the bulb was functional, I would never learn). Although some exterior walls were plastered with buffalo chips, which I assumed were used as fuel, the cookstoves were stoked mostly with stubble, husks, and miscellaneous tinder, as has been the case throughout much of China since the prehistoric depletion of the timberlands, a direct consequence of which was the development of stir-frying as a means of subjecting maximum food surface to maximum heat in the shortest possible time. In the kitchens of David's native village, stoves were constructed of adobe: waist-high fireboxes surmounted by double chimneys that projected through thatched or tiled roofs. A pair of metal woks was set into circular surface holes and covered, when not in use, by crude wooden lids.

Furnishings were spartan homemade pieces, and decorative embellishments were virtually nonexistent, although the haphazard placement on the walls of simple utilitarian objects often resulted in arrangements aesthetically pleasing to my Western eyes. If there was reading matter of any kind—if there was *paper* of any kind aside from a few cigarette packets—in the hamlet, I missed it. Inside and out, the few buildings were the colors of the terrain they sprang from: the colors of mud and straw and charcoal-gray clay. At a glance, what tonal distinctions there were appeared to blend into general neutrality: a mostly buff ground against which any living greenery seemed to jump. The place looked almost preternaturally tidy, and my guess was that the authorities had seen to it that it was cleaned up for our benefit. It also seemed more than likely that one agency or another had provided the face-saving elements of the banquet to which we were treated, for the menu was replete with all manner of rarefied ingredients to which the locals had no ready access and included various fancy touches, such as labeled wines and state-packaged cigarettes, that smacked of bureaucratic intervention.

As it turned out, the cooking was flat-out marvelous: plain robust down-home fare full of bone and gelatinous viscosity; big flavorsome stick-to-the-ribs stuff that I chopsticked into my face with an enthusiasm that delighted the locals with whom I was communicating with precise intelligibility in an improvised vocabulary of heartfelt grunts, sighs, and lip smackings. Happy eating is China's lingua franca, and I was eating as happily as I ever had anywhere.

It was a meal, as I would learn later, that had cost David an arm and a leg. As had turned out to be the case with our lunch at the doctor's house in Nanjing, its cost had been reimbursed a hundred-fold by his unadvertised contributions to deserving local recipients. The Nanjing doctor had been all but buried under a pile of costly gifts ordinarily unobtainable in the People's Republic, generously augmented by cash. David's home village and its immediate environs, suddenly awash in previously unprecedented quantities of legal tender, had been pledged the endowment of a fully staffed elementary school.

A torrential cloudburst struck as the meal ended, making an instant quagmire of the hamlet. Rainwater sluiced down through gaps in the roof, and benches were moved to a relatively dry part of the room, where I sat smoking with four or five of the men. Their easy camaraderie seemed to include me, although all I could contribute by way of conversation was a much-reiterated "thank you," one of the few Chinese phrases I'd mastered. We were joined by a drenched goose that took refuge under our bench, to the amusement of its occupants. When the storm let up and Mr. Wu indicated that it was time to leave, I didn't want to go. Hard as it may have been, these people's lives seemed more meaningful, more fulfilling than my own. They were at peace, with themselves and with their world, such as it was.

The storm had turned the dike path to quicksand. As we slogged back along it, our feet were sucked deep into the mud. Every step had to be wrenched from fiercely possessive earth. I wondered what was going on in David's mind as I struggled along behind him.

Before leaving for the People's Republic, Taiwan, and Hong Kong, I'd asked about possible *Gourmet* assignments in that part of the world. No interest. A week after my return to New York, I received a call from the magazine. Would I be interested in doing a couple of pieces on the Hong Kong and Bangkok food markets? I repacked my gear and retraced the whole damned journey halfway around the planet before I had time to reacquaint myself with my cat, Pyewackett.

11

Over and Out

Although our relations remained superficially cordial over the years, an adversarial undercurrent ran through all my dealings with Jane Montant. There was nothing overtly confrontational about it. On Jane's part, there were only ambiguous signals, relayed through intermediaries and smacking vaguely of unspecified irritations or thinly veiled demands; on mine, a continuing refusal to review any restaurants of her choosing that I found unworthy. Even her compliments on my stuff (always received secondhand from one or another of her subordinates) seemed incomplete sentences hedged by tacit disclaimers. It was often reported to me that "Jane really likes the way you write," in doubtful tones suggestive of a lot of other, unspoken things Jane *didn't* like.

Whether or not a degree of paranoia may have colored my impressions, I still had the distinct feeling in 1980, when the magazine's founder and sole owner, Earle R. MacAusland, died, that I'd had since the onset of my tenure in 1972: Jane and I couldn't coexist indefinitely.

Mr. MacAusland, whom I'd never met, had operated the magazine mostly in absentia as long as I'd been associated with it, with Jane in unchallenged de facto control of its day-to-day and long-range operations. To the obvious surprise and consternation of almost all concerned, his widow, a feisty, blunt-spoken woman to whom I took an immediate, apparently reciprocated liking, assumed an active role—momentarily the preeminent role—in the magazine's affairs. One of the first things Jean MacAusland did was to call me into her office for a little chat that was to be nobody's business but ours. She thought, as I did, that the magazine was stagnating; it was sorely in need of some fresh ideas—ideas, in particular, that might make it appealing to a hitherto neglected potential male readership—and if I had any thoughts on the subject, she'd like to hear them. As it happened, I had a good many thoughts on the subject. I promised to sort them out and convey them to her in writing within the next few days.

Among other things, I thought the magazine could do with a transfusion of new blood: a few writers, preferably including some male writers, whose byline didn't regularly appear in *Gourmet*. Jean MacAusland's responses to my suggestions seemed generally enthusiastic. As it turned out, however, she was to dissociate herself from the magazine before implementing many of them, although she did add one previously unknown writer to the *Gourmet* stable: Hudson Bridges was assigned to revive and preside over a long-defunct feature titled Along the Avenues. The pieces appeared quarterly and, as readers of my restaurant reviews and travel articles were quick to recognize (so they informed me in their letters) Hudson Bridges was none other than the old hired belly, operating under an assumed name and writing in a slightly altered style. It had been decided, with my ready concurrence, that between the monthly restaurant pieces and occasional travel articles, my undisguised byline was appearing in the magazine too often to risk having it turn up three times in a single issue.

I had no objection to—indeed, rather relished—writing under a pseudonym. I'd once churned out, under a fake name, a handbook on a subject I had previously known nothing about, and I derived a certain Jekyll-and-Hyde sort of satisfaction from maintaining a dual persona in one skin. I submitted a list of what seemed to me acceptable pen names, including Madison Walker (because a good deal of my time was spent strolling on Madison Avenue) and Bayard Pell (two Chinatown street names, the first conferred by one of my former wife's ancestors). Thanks to one of the magazine's more brilliant editors, the first of the new pieces was ascribed to "Magnum Pomum."

After my brief masquerade as Big Apple and some heated remonstrances with Jean MacAusland, I became Hudson Bridges. The Bridges column was a catchall: a grab bag loosely modeled on *The New Yorker*'s Talk of the Town pieces and made up of whatever caught my notice or piqued my interest during my wanderings about the city. As it happened, my notice was caught and my interest piqued by everything from the town's surviving old-style saloon singers (Hugh Shannon, Blossom Dearie, Bobby Short) to both major and relatively little-known museums of one sort or another; from the Empire State Building, the Brooklyn Bridge, and the Statue of Liberty to arcane hole-in-the-wall enterprises specializing in everything from antique music boxes to custom-made parasols and pastas; from rookie ballplayers (Darryl Strawberry) to the food preferences and favored restaurants of the incumbent mayor, Ed Koch. It was a juicy gig that allowed me infinitely more scope than restaurant and travel writing did, and my only regrets about it stemmed from the necessity of turning in copy three months in advance of publication, which obviated the possibility of covering events of uncertain duration.

I'd felt a lot more secure about my future dealings with the magazine while Jean MacAusland ran the show than at any time before or thereafter. Soon, however, she was made an offer she couldn't refuse: *Gourmet* was added to the steadily expanding Condé Nast empire ruled by S. I. Newhouse, Jr., and her stewardship ended.

Until then, there had been something of a cottage-industry aura about the operation of the magazine. Roughly two dozen titles, aside from a few honorific contributing editorships, were carried on the masthead and accounted not only for the editorial, art, production, and circulation departments but the test-kitchen staff as well.

Neither subscribers nor potential advertisers were made privy to the identities of sales representatives or anyone involved with such crass concerns as business administration or promotional activity, if, indeed, any promotional activity went on.

The magazine's inner workings underwent dramatic and immediate change with the Condé Nast takeover. The atmosphere became charged with aggressiveness of a sort the patrician Earle MacAusland never would have countenanced. Killer sharks turned up in force to energize all manner of high-tech promotional pitches. The nominal circulation director, an affable old lush and longtime beneficiary of nepotism, was given his walking papers, as were other unproductive types who traditionally hadn't much concerned themselves with bottom-line practicality. The masthead expanded threefold, to include such titles as Editorial Director, Associate Editorial Director, Automotive Manager, Marketing Director, Fragrance and Beauty Manager, Administrative Director, Editorial Advisor, Promotion Art Director, Vice President–Corporate Resources, Corporate Marketing Director, Vice President–Manufacturing and Distribution, and Wine and Spirits Manager, to enumerate just a few.

I probably earned no brownie points the one and only time I met S. I. Newhouse, Jr. It was at a party aboard a chartered yacht, the purpose of which was to acquaint *Gourmet* staffers and regular contributors with their new corporate bedfellows. I was up on deck, talking baseball with a couple of guys from the magazine's revamped advertising department, when a somewhat prepossessing type insinuated himself into the group. As luck would have it, the boat's whistle emitted an ear-splitting blast just as he introduced himself, leaving me without a clue to his identity. When the din subsided, he was singing the praises of a restaurant I happened to detest. Cutting him off in midsentence, I mumbled something blatantly hypocritical about the pleasure of making his acquaintance, and fled. "Who the hell was that?" I asked the advertising guys a few minutes later. They informed me that I'd be happier not knowing, and it wasn't until several weeks later, when Newhouse's photograph turned up in a newspaper piece, that I learned it was he I'd brushed off so cavalierly.

I never had made any secret of my penchant for gin. My restaurant reviews were peppered with references to my fondness for a well-made dry martini, and I'd hymned the cocktail's praises with some fervor in a piece published by *Connoisseur* in the early eighties. My infrequent dinner dates with Jane Montant usually began with a juniper consommé at her apartment, followed by a couple more at a restaurant before the meal was ordered. It was a ritual she appeared to condone at the very least, and perhaps to encourage. Hence, I was somewhat taken aback one afternoon to be told, "Jane is concerned about your drinking," especially at a time when it was generally agreed that I was producing some of the best stuff I'd ever written while drinking neither more nor less than I had for years.

Since Jane's complaints were always phrased as cryptically as possible and relayed through intermediaries, I saw no point in asking what the specifics of this sudden concern might be and shrugged the matter off as just one more expression of groundless petulance, vented at a moment when my relations with Jane were more strained than they'd ever been.

A few months earlier, I'd been informed (through the usual intermediary) that I was to review a restaurant operated by a man who had managed to cozy up to Jane. I replied that I'd check the place out and review it if it was reviewable. I was told in no uncertain terms that I was expected to review it regardless of my opinion of its merit.

It was the first time I'd been handed an outright ultimatum, and if my response wasn't precisely shameful it did me no honor. My first impulse was to march into Jane's office and tell her to shove the whole gig. In view of subsequent developments, I might as well have done so and salvaged some self-respect, but I equivocated, repeating that I'd case the joint and review it only if I could do so without compromising my own, and the magazine's putative, standards of probity.

There's no way I can ever know with any moral certainty whether my judgment remained uncolored by Jane's intimidation. At the time, my hired bellyship was my major source of income, and its loss would have had drastic consequences for both my social life and my solvency. I've since done considerable soul-searching and convinced myself that there was nothing to be ashamed of in the review I finally turned in. I thought (or thought I thought) the restaurant was a borderline case worthy of the benefit of the doubt, and clearly implied as much in the least enthusiastic piece I ever wrote.

Even though the review appeared with a few of my more negative comments missing, the proprietor, who obviously had anticipated (and perhaps been promised) an unstinting dithyramb, was livid. Some years earlier, I'd interviewed him in the course of covering another of his ventures and had been told that before transforming himself into the Louis Sherry of his era he had been a fabric merchant who dealt in top-of-the-line goods. So I'd informed my readers at the time, with his apparent approval, and so I informed them on the next go-round, when he was described as "a former member of the class rag trade." Misreading (willfully, I suspect) as a noun what in the context could be only an adjective (as in "a class act") then in common currency, he bitched his head off in a letter to Jane Montant about my alleged discriminatory bias, which, he claimed, relegated him to a lower social order. He demanded an apology for the perceived affront, and Jane, with characteristic loyalty to her troops, in turn demanded that I express abject contrition in writing, with no time wasted.

Verne E. Westerberg, a Condé Nast honcho who then functioned as *Gourmet*'s publisher, beckoned me into his office and shut the door. "She's really hot about this one," he said.

"She's hot?" I bellowed. "What the hell is *she* hot about? If anyone has reason to be steamed, *I* have, goddamnit."

Verne explained that he was just doing his best to keep the peace; that Jane thought the characterization I'd applied to the restaurant owner was offensive, and my most prudent course of action would be to meet her demand. "If she thought it was offensive," I re-erupted, "why the hell did she let it get into print? She's the bloody editor-in-chief. Where the hell was she when she was supposed to be doing her job? What appears in the magazine—every goddamn word—is her responsibility, not mine or anyone else's, and she's supposed to stand behind it and her writers, not fold up like a shithouse in a tornado, if some outsider's lip quivers."

"Jay, write the letter," Verne sighed, showing me to the door.

I wrote the letter, but it was hardly a letter of apology. In so many words, it informed the aggrieved restaurateur that he was a cretin-ous, vindictive little shit who had reacted hysterically to a fancied slight. As directed, the letter was submitted for Jane's approval. A day or two later, I received a copy of a thoroughly bowdlerized version over a forgery of my signature of startling verisimilitude.

Somewhat sarcastically, I complimented Jane, the next time I ran into her, on her conciliatory emendations. "You didn't want to write that letter," she replied angrily, as though there had been no conceivable reason for my mulish recalcitrance.

A table for two at Scarlatti, an East Side tabernacle of *alta cucina*. For the third or fourth time in a month, I'm lunching with Verne Westerberg and wondering why. As the magazine's publisher, he functions outside the editorial sphere and certainly is under no obligation to regale a free-lance contributor with any frequency, if ever. He seems to be making a point of reordering dry martinis as soon as each round is drained. After three and halfway through the hors d'oeuvres, he clears his throat portentously and announces that I've been reinstated as numero uno on Jane's shit list. Why? "Some-one she and I had lunch with last week said you were 'out of it' at Felidia a few nights earlier."

Who was this someone, and what was 'out of it' supposed to mean? Verne can't reveal the someone's identity; the informant modestly had requested anonymity and dished the dirt on that condition. By "out of it," my unknown admirer had meant, in the Westerberg translation, "Out of it. Comatose at the bar. Totaled. Shit-faced." I respond with an appeal to reason: Both Verne and

Jane know Felidia, know it's a big-ticket operation that tolerates no manifest breaches of decorum, and know that I couldn't possibly have been in the condition imputed to me and not been eighty-sixed for life. Verne concedes the logic of my argument, but observes that logic doesn't count for diddly-squat once Jane has heard what she wants to hear.

"And of course she'll make damned good and sure she *won't* hear anything she *doesn't* want to hear, even though everyone connected with the restaurant will testify that I've been slandered," I reply.

Verne turns up his palms while I sputter. In a bungled attempt to mollify me, he says, "That's a good review of Petrossian you did for the current issue." (Petrossian, an ultraposh West Side café-cum-belly boutique, functions as a showcase for the delicacies marketed worldwide under its name. It was described in the review as "the world's sexiest corner deli.") "On your recommendation," Verne adds, "Jane and I had lunch there last week with Leo . . ."

"Lerman!" I bark, supplying the patronymic Verne has bitten off and swallowed. "Lerman's the son of a bitch who's been pouring his poison into Jane's all-too-receptive ear." Verne's hangdog non-denial is ample confirmation. "The old fart was pissed because I didn't recognize and fall all over him on the evening in question," I explain. "If I was 'out of it,' how come I can give you a minute-by-minute account of the whole night? How come I can describe his entrance, tell you precisely how he was dressed and what table he occupied for how long, give you the names and address of a married couple from Houston, both corporate lawyers, who were introduced to me as readers of my stuff and with whom I spent an hour chatting at the bar after he left? How was *I* able to walk fourteen blocks after *I* left, have a nightcap with Rusty Staub at *his* place, and walk seventeen blocks back home?"

Felidia, the site of my alleged insensibility, has been a favorite haunt of mine almost since the day it opened in 1981. I hang out there because it's a short walk from where I live, because the resident mixologist, Sime (Sam) Peroš, the protagonist of the aforementioned *Connoisseur* article, concocts a dry martini that is absolutely sui generis, because the food is extraordinary, because the owners, Lidia and her husband Felice, have imparted more of what I've learned of cooking and eating during the last ten years than the rest of the city's chefs and restaurateurs combined, and because their "family" (i.e, their staff) has become a sort of surrogate family of my own.

After I'd reviewed the place several months after its launching, I'd drop in most evenings, either for cocktails before or a nightcap after dinner somewhere else, often with Curtis, sometimes with stand-in table companions. As I'd feared—as I'd been certain— would be the case, Curtis had admitted that she was involved with another guy when I got back from China, but the involvement had broken up a year or so later, and things picked up where they'd left off. The revival didn't have a long run; after a couple of our best years together, Curtis was offered a revoltingly lucrative editorial post in Florida, and was gone.

By sheer coincidence, I received a similar offer to relocate in Florida not long thereafter. The job would have paid three times my aggregate yearly income and allowed me to spend weekends with Curtis but would have put an end to my hired bellyhood, my continuance as a regular contributor to *Gourmet,* and an intense love-hate relationship with my home town. After a weekend of indecision, I opted to stay put. *Quel idiot!*

At first, I continued to turn up at Felidia as before, with various dinner dates in tow, but my obvious despondency over Curtis's absence wasn't advancing my long-term prospects on other fronts, and I soon found myself coming in alone as often as not. In slack moments, Lidia or Felice would join me at the bar, usually to talk food with infectious animation. During the shank of the evening, of course, they were occupied in the dining room, and Sime, the bartender, was far too busy for casual conversation. At those times I usually withdrew into myself, passing the time occupied one way or another with the staples of my trade: words. Some nights, I'd work out the next morning's lead paragraph; others, I'd play with palindromes, anagrams, or the bawdy and/or scatological limericks in which I took particular delight. Because it wouldn't have been good form to make a writing desk of the bar, all this weighty creative activity went on in my head, and I suppose I wore a somewhat abstracted expression when the muse came calling.

Whatever may have occupied my thoughts at the moment, I happened to be gazing toward the restaurant's entrance when this bearded archeological artifact tottered in. I had resumed my quest for suitable rhymes for "Bangalore" (or whatever) when Lidia steered His Decrepitude over to where I was seated. "Jay, have you met Mr. Lerman?" she asked.

As it happened, I *had* met Mr. Lerman—just once, quite briefly, and from a decidedly disadvantageous position. I'd just been seated in the Bar Room of The Four Seasons one afternoon, when my lunchmate, *Gourmet*'s executive editor, looked across the table and past my left shoulder, to greet someone passing behind my chair. Twisting around awkwardly, I was introduced to Leo Lerman, who, from my worm's-eye perspective, appeared to be an ample paunch successively surmounted by a considerable quantity of mandibular hair, a brace of dilated nostrils, and a pristinely bald pate. Leo Lerman was then and remains at this writing the titular Editorial Advisor to the Condé Nast conglomerate.

Verona, Italy, a few weeks later. Along with several other food writers, I'm on a free ride organized by the Gruppo Ristoratori Italiani USA, and have fallen completely under the spell of what seems to me the loveliest city in the world. The Gruppo is holding its annual convention here, and most of our mornings are spent at windy symposiums, where an endless procession of pompous *dottori* speechify at paralyzing length and to no practicable purpose on the need (as perceived by them) to "codify" (the convention's buzz-word year after year) an exuberant cuisine whose lifeblood is drawn from its traditional contempt for codification. My fellow travelers sedulously attend these yawners, and spend the afternoons schlepping through Verona's annual food and wine fair, which I find the least by far of the city's manifold attractions. To my mild disappointment, one such fellow traveler—a food writer disguised as a petit four whom I've courted with less than resounding success since Curtis's defection and for whom I've wangled an invitation to this pilgrimage—has iced me out day after day since our arrival, happily communing with acres of bottled goods and groceries while I prowl this most celebrated city of star-cross'd lovers in solitude.

In love with the city itself, I soon forget my inamorata's rebuffs and the ominous turn my situation vis-à-vis *Gourmet* has taken. Dogging down obscure cul-de-sacs, I'm altogether knocked out by Renaissance frescoes so taken for granted that galvanized metal drainpipes bisect them and clothesline pulleys drip streaks of rust over pigmented surfaces still as luminously fresh as they were when the paints were applied upward of half a millennium ago. In the market, I notice a seed display at a florist's stall and pick up a few packets for the Houston couple mentioned earlier, who had complained of the unavailability of arugula seed in Texas.

Thus far, most of our meals in and around the city have been exceptional examples of what first-rate professionals can put out for visiting peers, but a bit too formal and elaborate for my taste. At Villa Arvedi, a ten-course dinner included Lake Garda whitebait, *sopressa veronese* (a spiced salami of beef and pork served with toasted *polenta*), and, as the pièce de résistance, *pastissada de caval,* a winy stew that requires three days of preparation and, according to legend, was served for the first time to Theodoric after a battle in which the most numerous casualties were Ostrogoth horses. At Villa Columbani, a converted fourteenth-century residence in Maleo, the highlights of an eight-course dinner were local air-dried beef, salmon trout with fennel sauce, and a combination of roast kid and lamb. A relatively restrained six courses at Il Cigno, in Mantua, produced an extraordinary rabbit salad garnished with pomegranate pips, for openers, followed in succession by pumpkin-filled *tortelli,* eel fillets in balsamic vinegar of great antiquity, duck in a liver sauce of killer richness, and a couple of desserts guaranteed to result in arterial gridlock. And so it has gone, meal after meal, until I've begun to long for a simple lunch on my own, preferably

consisting of five fewer than the average six courses, with no pre-
or postprandial oratory, no dress requirements more elaborate than
threadbare denims, and nothing more taxing to the digestive tract
than one or two plain seafood courses. I must have considered and
rejected sixty or seventy menus in promising little back streets
before I know with absolute conviction that I'm on the threshold
of a gastronomic epiphany.

The Trattoria Vecio Mulin perches on a bank of the twisting river
Adige in a quarter of Verona where nothing moves at midday. I've
seen no evidence of pedestrian or vehicular traffic for at least half
an hour when I haul up, footsore, thirsty, hungry, and discouraged,
before what may be the last restaurant in town that I haven't already
scoped and dismissed. The menu is posted beside a nondescript
entrance. I scan the top few entries, undergo the skin-bristling
sensations experienced by A. E. Housman when lines of poetry
strayed into his consciousness at unguarded moments, and enter the
place in the certain knowledge that I'm about to sit down to one
of the half-dozen most memorable meals of my life.

The *padrone* intercepts me in the vestibule. Dripping touristic
fatigue and photographic gear, I don't look as right to him as his
restaurant does to me. "Only feesh," he announces in an approximation of my language, with case-closed finality. *"Si, si, solamente
pesce, buono,"* I reply in an approximation of his language. Shrug-
ging, he leads me to a dining room overlooking the river. *Mirabile
dictu,* gin is available, although an unbroached dust-covered bottle
of Beefeater suggests that no customers have availed themselves of
it since Giotto was a pup. There isn't another soul in the dining
room, and I've begun to wonder whether my instincts have finally
failed me when a teenage kid places a plateful of *bruschetta* on the
table.

The bread is coarse-grained stuff, grilled and charred along the
edges of the crust. It's redolent of fresh young olive oil and rosemary, with a faint whiff of garlic making its presence felt almost
subliminally. This is peasant make-do in apotheosis: a kind of folk
poetry in which the Italians excel, the Spaniards bring off in rare

moments of inspiration, and the French never have got the hang of. Although the rudimentary elements (aside from the restaurant's somewhat idiosyncratic, startlingly elegant inclusion of *Rosmarinus officinalis*) are identical in theory, genuine *bruschetta* such as this bears about as much resemblance to the wretched "garlic bread" served with specious pride in cheap American spaghetti joints and by ingenuous suburban pseudosophisticates as Sophia Loren bears to the kid who bags your groceries at the checkout counter.

I haven't been given a menu. After a few minutes, I'm served an array of small *tapas*-like shellfish dishes: a quartet of *scampi*, a huddle of roseate *gamberoni*, a half-dozen corpulent oysters, and a like number of *vongole* on the half-shell, the clams still jittering in an alien environment. Also, a few fat mussels and their rock-boring cousins, *datteri*, or sea dates, and a single soft-shell crab, all presented with the utmost simplicity. Sweet Jesus, I've died and gone to heaven! This is a place where seafoods of pristine freshness are properly revered. No lemons. No sauces. What you get is what you taste, with no extrinsic distractions. This is as close as it's possible to come to gourmandizing with the gulls.

The table cleared, I'm served a brace of grilled *triglie:* red mullet—the barbel-mustachioed, half-trout-size, Day-Glo-pink critters that I just happen to consider the tastiest fish that swim. These have been cooked to perfection, over vine-cuttings and brushed with just enough olive oil to facilitate their intact removal from the grill. Like the shellfish, they're plated as is, unsauced and ungarnished, by a purist who refuses to mess with their inherent goodness. Only feesh. Who'd want more?

The Gruppo has no business scheduled for the rest of the day. That afternoon, Lidia Bastianich has rented a car, and she proposes that two other journalists and I accompany her on a drive up into the Dolomites, above Lake Garda. Asked whether I've eaten, I babble almost incoherently about my find beside the Adige.

"If it's that good," Lidia says, "maybe we should have dinner there tonight. Would you mind eating there twice in one day?"

"No more than I'd mind inheriting a few million bucks from a relative I didn't know existed."

"Should we make reservations?"

"No need. The place was deserted. The whole *neighborhood* was deserted."

It's the third week in April, and the weather in Verona has been delightfully mild, almost summery. As we ascend into the Alps, however, the temperature drops a couple of degrees every hundred feet or so, until, as we near the ridgeline, we are deep in mid-winter snow. Lidia, whose thoughts seldom stray far from food, asks whether anyone's hungry. We all can do with a light collation to tide us over until dinner at the Trattoria Vecio Mulin, but our prospects aren't bright. The ski season is effectively finished despite an unexpected late snowfall, and the few scattered lodges we pass are closed. As we drive past an isolated farm, a figure emerges from a barn and Lidia stops the car to inquire about possible eating places. A young woman approaches, somewhat skittishly, like a spooked foal. She's absolutely feral. Hair that appears never to have been touched by comb or soap is stuck with wisps of straw, bark, goat shit, God-knows-what. She's clad in clinging mud-smudged tatters that leave nothing of a sumptuous bod to the imagination and terminate raggedly at microskirt length to flaunt the most glorious set of stems I've ever seen. She's medieval peasantry incarnate and painfully erotic—the Anna Magnani of *Bitter Rice* intensified tenfold; the most haunting, intolerable female presence I've ever beheld, a consignment to oblivion of all other womanhood. She tells Lidia that there's just one place in the region where we may find sustenance: an inn about two miles away that remains open in the unlikely event that a few post-season skiers may turn up.

The *padrone* dolefully informs us that there is nothing to eat, unless we're prepared to make do with basic survival fare: some homemade prosciutto, a few other cold cuts and sausages cured in situ, rustic bread baked too early in the day for proper human consumption at this late-afternoon hour, perhaps a little plain polenta and some leftover cold white beans, a splodge or two of his wife's cheese. His disclaimers have the four of us practically jumping out of our pants.

As it turns out, our late lunch is marvelous: one shapely, clean-tasting offering after another, punctuated with all manner of crisp pickles and zesty condiments. The tab is negligible, and I'm beginning to wonder how we possibly can do justice to a bang-up fish dinner back in Verona while Lidia, an ethnic Italian whose surname and her future husband's were Slavicized by law when their native Istria was annexed by Yugoslavia in 1946, drives like an ethnic Italian, taking shoulderless hairpin mountain turns at full tilt.

Back in the city at about ten o'clock, my erratic sense of direction for once seems reliable. We reach the general vicinity of Via Sottoriva with minimal confusion, but the neighborhood has undergone a drastic change since midday. Streets deserted at noon are now clotted with parked cars, and the closer we get to the restaurant the greater the vehicular congestion turns out to be. After cruising the area for the better part of half an hour, we finally find a vacant slot four or five blocks from where we want to be. When we get there, Vecio Mulin is packed. Waiters rush relays of grilled fish to tables as though delivering life-support systems to trauma victims. Lidia dickers with the *padrone* for seating, only to be informed that there isn't and won't be any: last orders already have been taken. *Buona notte.* Lidia persists. These, *signor* should understand, are renowned authorities on gastronomy, whose merest mention in their respective journals will generate patronage beyond his wildest dreams.

Yeah, yeah, if the *signora* will trouble to look around, she'll see that we've already *got* patronage beyond our wildest dreams.

But the *signor* must understand that this gentleman (indicating me) is one of the foremost restaurant authorities in the entire . . .

Yeah, sure. The *signora*'s friend was in for lunch today. If he knows so much, why didn't he have sense enough to make a dinner reservation? Case closed. The chef has gone home. If the *signora* doesn't waste any more time, her party still can get a table at Il Malocchio (or some such name), a couple of blocks down the street.

The recommended alternative turns out, of course, to be a thoroughgoing stinker; an egregious tourist trap, done up in pisselegant furbelows, that would go belly-up in a month in midtown Manhattan. Murderously overboiled pasta suffocating beneath Vesuvian fallout; veal (or possibly cat) scaloppine in rigor mortis. A tab that would cover major surgery. The only member of our foursome who knows precisely what we're missing, I grieve inconsolably while pushing this crap around on my plate.

Worse is yet to come. For the last three or four years I've had a standing invitation to visit my brother Ted, the proud possessor of what he terms "virtually a chateau" in Anjou, a part of France of which I know nothing except that it's watered by the Loire, has given its name to a distinctively tasty pear, and produces a lot of rosé wine. On the strength of this encyclopedic knowledge, I've wangled an assignment to write a piece on the region for a Texas-based advertising flyer masquerading as a magazine, and I travel there from Verona via Paris.

Ted's fiefdom, acquired sight unseen a few years earlier for a sum in the low five figures, comprises an old stone house in a minuscule village, Les Cerqueux sous Passavant, and a weedy plot of ground at some distance from it. The previous winter—a pipe-burster—has been the coldest in living memory in this part of the world (back in Italy, thousand-year-old olive groves have been devastated), and it persists well into a mild spring within Ted's yard-thick stone walls. Except for an inadequate hearth that fills the dining hall with acrid clouds of smoke while producing no warmth, there's not even a putative source of heat. A strangulating stench of mildew clogs the lungs, pervasive dank infiltrates the marrow of one's bones, and mushrooms sprout between the flagstones of the john. Impervious to cold at home where, with a tankful of antifreeze under my belt, I run local errands in shirtsleeved comfort in the dead of winter, I jitter miserably and ceaselessly in this stone crypt, finding warmth only out of doors.

We drive to Saumur one afternoon, and because there are no restaurants of any kind within hailing distance of Ted's bailiwick I purchase a chicken for our dinner at a local *boucherie.* After years of summering in France, Ted still eats like a beast. Assured that his larder is well-stocked with staples ("flour, oil, butter, potatoes, wine—whatever you need"), I plan a simple comforting meal of roast fowl, plenty of starch for body warmth, fresh-baked bread. I pick up some yeast and a head of broccoli, down a couple of cognacs at a *bar-tabac* to ward off the impending chill *chez mon frère,* and we're off for home.

All the promised staples are in place when we get there—as they have been since the previous September, seven months ago. The oil and butter long since have gone rancid, the better part of a year of unforeseen natural refrigeration notwithstanding. The flour pullulates with maggots, the potatoes have sprouted poisonous-looking green tentacles, the salt is a petrified block, and what may or may not have once been a slab of cheese has undergone mineralization: to my inexpert eye, it could be lazurite, the source of the distinctive blue pigment favored by Vermeer, which to the best of my knowledge never has been ingested with impunity.

Still, the situation seems salvageable: the chicken can be basted with its own rendered fat, which also can serve as a lubricating medium for the broccoli: the bird goes into Ted's oven a bit more easily than the infamous Christmas turkey went into mine at St.-Hippolyte, and I check its condition every twenty minutes or so. Its condition remains unchanged; it's not a shade browner than when it left the *boucherie* in Saumur, its fat isn't rendering, it's cold to the touch. With the oven now turned up as high as it can be, the feeblest of blue flames hasn't raised the interior temperature of the appliance or the superficies of the bird by a single degree, Fahrenheit or centigrade. Another hour goes by before I concede that our dinner has a better chance of roasting in the fridge than in this blasted oven.

The situation fills me with a lugubrious sense of déjà vu, but not even those pathetic Christmas dinners beneath Les Baux and at St.-Hippolyte were travesties of *this* magnitude. I decide that some other cooking technique is indicated, but Ted's *batterie de cuisine* is deficient almost to the point of nonexistence; there isn't a pot or pan in which the chicken can be poached, sautéed, or steamed. Water for a single cup of tea might be boiled in the largest vessel in evidence. "Stir up that goddamn fire," I bawl into the next room, where Ted is dozing before the hearth.

The intention now is to quarter the bird and broil it over open flame, but once again Ted's kitchen equipment fails me; the single knife he owns is so dull that its theoretical cutting edge can't be distinguished from the heel of the blade. Swearing lustily, I tear the chicken apart with my bare hands. Needless to say, there are no andirons in the fireplace that might support a broiler rack borrowed from the wretched oven. Nor are there any skewers, but this rusted screwdriver, found in a kitchen drawer, may do the job. A ragged hunk of chicken is impaled thereon and borne to the' fireplace, where the envisioned roaring blaze turns out to be a puny sputter at the juncture of two sodden, pencil-size sticks—the last of the tinder that passes for firewood *chez mon frère*. *"Poulet cru,"* I announce, bouncing a plate off the dining room table. *"Bon appetit!"*

Hours later, sleepless and unfed, I lie fully clothed on a gelid, still-waterlogged mattress, my frozen bones jangling like a gamelan. I hear a voice, stuttering uncontrollably as facial muscles fibrillate: "You p-p-poor d-d-dumb b-b-b-bastard, you really are a g-g-glut-g-g-g-glutton for p-punishment."

Not long after my return from Europe, Jane Montant informed me that I'd had it as *Gourmet*'s New York restaurant pundit. Life as an unfrocked hired belly goes on much as it did during my years on the beat, with two differences: I'm dining out with fewer women these days, but I'm eating better.